Tony Wright

'*… is one of the wisest heads in Westminster*'
Polly Toynbee

'*… is always a voice of sanity*'
Ann Treneman

'*… always put the interests of the House above tribal politics*'
The Times

'*… is one of the most dedicated parliamentarians in Westminster:
acidic, pithy, sharp, delighted to give the pip to the powerful,
and utterly assured in his role*'
Ben Macintyre

'*… carved out a distinctive niche in the Commons as an MP
who looks at the broader political and constitutional picture*'
Peter Riddell

'*… is a mensch, one of the few mensches in modern politics …
impressive, strategic and free-thinking … Dr Wright has thought –
and thought hard – about how modern politics should be organised,
its ethics and the contract between the politician and the polity*'
David Aaronovitch

'*… had been warning of the expenses apocalypse for seven years*'
Martin Bell

Doing Politics

Tony Wright

Biteback Publishing

First published in Great Britain in 2012 by
Biteback Publishing Ltd
Westminster Tower
3 Albert Embankment
London SE1 7SP
Copyright © Tony Wright 2012

Tony Wright has asserted his right under the Copyright, Designs and Patents
Act 1988 to be identified as the author of this work.

Previously published material is reproduced with permission.

Every reasonable effort has been made to trace copyright holders of material
reproduced in this book, but if any have been inadvertently overlooked the
publishers would be glad to hear from them.

ISBN 978-1-84954-042-1

10 9 8 7 6 5 4 3 2 1

A CIP catalogue record for this book is available from the British Library.

Set in Adobe Garamond.
Cover design by Soapbox

Printed and bound in Great Britain by
CPI Group (UK) Ltd, Croydon CR0 4YY

In memory of Edmor Phillips (1923–2010)

Contents

Preface

'Good morning, sir. How is East Devon today?'

This cheery greeting, delivered by one of the policemen watching over the entrance to the House of Commons on my last day in the place, after nearly twenty years, reminded me why I should never write any kind of memoir. He had got the wrong person. And the wrong constituency.

Apart from musing on how cushy it must be to represent somewhere like East Devon (and how unfair it was that Labour MPs got all the tough places), I felt a sense of profound political insignificance. I was the sort of person who had sat at the Cabinet table but not, alas, when the Cabinet was meeting. Consulting Alastair Campbell's voluminous diary record of the New Labour years to see if I appeared on his radar, I found only this: 'Got a message to Tony Wright to shut up.'

So when it was suggested to me by my old friend Sean Magee, now at Biteback Publishing, that I might write a book, I knew it could not be a memoir. He agreed that I might instead bring together some of the political writing I had done over the years, supplemented by a more personal opening chapter. This is what I have done.

In the opening section I have tried to give a sense of what

life was like for someone born shortly after the end of the Second World War who became interested in politics from an early age and, in different ways over subsequent decades, took some small part in it. I hope it gives a flavour of the times, and what has changed. The rest of the book – a mixture of longer articles and shorter pieces – reflects some of the themes and issues I have been interested in over this long period, and which still seem to have some relevance today.

I am grateful to Sean for asking me to do this book and for making sure I did it, even when he would much rather have been at the races. It is dedicated to my father-in-law, Edmor Phillips, who died on general election day in 2010. He could rarely be prised away from his corner of west Wales, but was nevertheless a genuine citizen of the world. I hope he knew he was the audience for everything I said and wrote, and the person whose opinion and approval I most valued.

Tony Wright
January 2012

PART ONE

DOING POLITICS:
THEN AND NOW

It was different then. The first general election of my lifetime was in February 1950, when I was nearly two. The great reforming post-war Labour government, led by the unassuming Clement Attlee, scraped a win but without a working majority. Another election soon followed in 1951, narrowly won by the Conservatives with more seats but fewer votes than Labour. A commentator on the 1950 election, writing in the *Political Quarterly* (which I now edit) declared: 'It is good to record a record poll, and a hard, clean fight ... The record poll of 84 per cent is a reflection of the high level of political interest and concern throughout the country. Correspondents from other lands have applauded it as another tribute to the political maturity of the British electorate.'

It is not just the turnout that now seems remarkable. In 1950 no less than 90 per cent of the total vote went to the Labour and Conservative parties between them, and this rose to a staggering 97 per cent the following year. In

2010, by contrast, the figure was only 65 per cent. Behind the 1950/51 voting figures were party memberships that ran into the millions, although the exact numbers are uncertain. What is certain is that politics was rooted in rival political traditions, each embedded in its own political culture.

My family were Labour. That was our tribe. It was also the dominant political tribe in our little Northamptonshire town, where most men worked in the shoe factories (many had the top of a finger missing, caused by the 'clicking' machines), and in the strange-speaking place a few miles away called Corby (known as 'little Scotland') where my father worked as a clerk in the steelworks. The surrounding Northamptonshire countryside was inhabited, in our eyes, by a different tribe of squires and foxhunters, demanding deference from the villagers, blue to our red. In our town, as in similar working-class communities, being Labour really was part of a dense culture of chapel and Sunday school, Co-op shop and working men's club. These were the institutions, along with the football club, which framed my early life. Even today I have our 'divi' number at the Co-op (4735) engraved in my memory.

So I was Labour by cultural immersion, not intellectual conversion (which only came later, reading R. H. Tawney's *The Acquisitive Society* while working on a kibbutz in Israel in 1967, just after the war). There was Us and Them, and Labour was the party of Us just as the Tories were the party of Them. We lived in our own house, just across the road from the council estate, which made us 'upper' working class, but such distinctions – though important in other ways – did not detract from the general sense of political Us-ness. Evidence of the recent war was all around in the remains of old army huts, the concrete floors of which provided our football pitches. My father had emerged from the war as an officer in the RAF, meeting and marrying my mother when he was stationed at the local air base, and as a Conservative. In the early days my mother would put up a Labour election poster in the window when my father had gone to work and take it down before he came home. He too, though, soon succumbed to the Us-ness of the community he had joined, and to the political assaults of my mother, and before long he was secretary both of the local Labour Party and of his trade union branch.

There was one occasion, before his re-education was complete, when he made the mistake of referring to Churchill as 'the greatest living Englishman'. This set my mother off – did he not know that Churchill had set the troops on the striking miners at Tonypandy? – and my father was banished to the shed until he recanted such political heresy. It is not surprising, then, that I grew up thinking that politics was something that mattered in a rather profound way – that it defined who we were, where we had come from and what future we might have. It was not expressed like this, of course, but this is what I took it to mean. My understanding was not very sophisticated at this stage, but it was fundamental.

It meant that politics was part of my life from a very early age, in a way that seems odd now but was entirely natural then. Politics (Labour) and football (Wolverhampton Wanderers) became my twin enthusiasms. (I had no idea where Wolverhampton was, just that they were the team of the moment.) On one side, my heroes were our Labour leaders Bevan and Gaitskell; on the other, Peter Broadbent, the dazzling inside left of that great Wolves side of the 1950s (whose skills I tried to emulate). I was decked out, interchangeably, in Labour red and the old gold and black of Wolves. As soon as I was old enough, I got a job delivering newspapers before school, which allowed me both to scrutinise the opinion polls to see how the political battle was going and to examine the football forecasts so that I could fill in my fixed-odds pools coupon. The result of both activities was that I regularly missed the school bus.

On election days in the 1950s my job was to run from the polling station at my primary school to the Co-op Hall at the top of the road with the lists of polling numbers, which were then marked off by the party workers on the electoral registers pinned to large trestle tables. This showed who had voted and who had not, so that the latter could be 'knocked up'. Many Conservatives had cars, while most Labour voters didn't, so a good ruse was to get our elderly supporters to ask for lifts to the polling station from the Conservatives. I remember my grandfather, retired from managing the Co-op grocery shop, winking at me on one occasion as he alighted from a large Conservative car to cast his Labour vote. What puzzled me at the time about these general elections was that our town voted solidly Labour but the Conservatives always won. This seemed very unfair.

At the 1959 general election, a headline in the local news-paper reported that an open-air election meeting in our town addressed by the Conservative candidate had been inter-rupted by an eleven-year-old boy who had asked questions about the H-bomb and old-age pensions. What it did not report was that I then arranged with my friends to drive this Conservative candidate out of town on our bikes, planting fireworks in the back of his Land Rover that exploded as he furiously drove away with us in hot pursuit. We had expelled the class enemy from our territory. At least that was how I saw it; I suspect my friends thought it was just a bit of fun.

In 1958, during the run-up to the general election of the following year, the local Labour Party hired a coach to take members to a big rally in the De Montfort Hall in Leicester, some twenty miles away, where both Hugh Gaitskell and Nye Bevan were to speak. This was the period when the Labour Party was divided into Bevanites and Gaitskellites – the fundamentalists and the revisionists – but I did not know this at the time. We were just Labour, loyal to our leaders, untroubled by faraway schisms and united in our opposition to the Conservative enemy; though for some reason my mother was particularly taken with the fact that Hugh Gaitskell was an accomplished dancer. What we did not know, of course, was that within the next few years both Bevan and Gaitskell would be dead, our leaders taken from us before their victories could be won. For years afterwards I kept the copy of the *Daily Mirror* that announced Gaitskell's death in the cupboard beside my bed, along with my prized collection of football programmes (and, shamefully, birds' eggs).

Allowed to go, I had a chance to see my political heroes in the flesh. Coaches disgorged party members from all over the East Midlands and the hall was packed. In my memory there were thousands there, and I had a perch high up on the front row of the balcony. Since I was only ten, much of it went over my head, except for the exciting atmosphere and one line from Bevan which stayed with me. 'Those Tories,' he said, in that captivating Welsh lilt, 'they might be trusted to look after animals but they should not be trusted to look after the country.' I thought this was very good. What was even better was that afterwards – because my father was a party secretary – we were allowed to go backstage to meet the great men. I wish I could record a memorable exchange, but I was probably too star-struck to do anything but look gormless.

The only politician I had encountered in person until then was our own MP, G. R. (Dick) Mitchison, who would some-times come to social events or political meetings in the Co-op Hall. He was a kindly man with a disarming stutter, but also rather grand. Not only was he a QC but also the owner of a castle in Scotland, which I then assumed was entirely natural for a Member of Parliament, even a Labour one. Even more exotic, though, was his wife, Naomi, who combined being a famous writer with the honorary chieftainship of a tribe in Africa. To the ladies of the Co-operative Women's Guild she must have seemed like a visitor from another planet, but valiant efforts at communication were made on both sides. The Mitchisons were liked and respected, and when my parents were invited to their daughter's wedding in the crypt chapel at the House of Commons I was included too, my first step inside the place.

Our next MP, after Mitchison retired, was another grand figure, Sir Geoffrey de Freitas. A former Wing Commander, who had also been a High Commissioner, he sported a mag-nificent moustache and a dashing demeanour. By this time I was in the sixth form at grammar school and chairman of the Young Socialists in Kettering. In this capacity, one day in 1966 I received a letter from Sir Geoffrey at the House of Commons, enclosing a ticket for the forthcoming final of the World Cup. The letter invited me either to attend the final myself or to raffle the ticket for branch funds. A nanosecond of reflection persuaded me that the latter course of action would be far too complicated and divisive and that I had a clear duty to go myself. So, courtesy of our MP, I watched England win the World Cup from a seat not far from the Royal Box. Still a schoolboy, I sensed that the rest of life might be something of an anti-climax after this.

By now I really was a political obsessive. I filled the letters page of the Kettering *Evening Telegraph* with a running commentary on the political issues of the day, drawing responses from people who had no idea they were arguing with a mere schoolboy. My teachers at the grammar school, a mixture of the mad and the inspirational, must have found me very irritating. Certainly my English teacher did, who reported in my last term: 'When he sets his mind to it, he can produce most competent work; when he allows his political prejudices to influence his literary criticism, his work is usually irrelevant and tedious.' A great inspiration to me was our History teacher, Mr Cowell, known to us for some reason as Tarzan, who managed to weave irreverent references to contemporary politicians like Harold Macmillan and Selwyn Lloyd (whom he called 'Selluloid') into accounts of the Great Reform Act and changes to the Corn Laws. On my last day at school the deputy head, Mr Wood, who taught Latin and was normally a master to be feared, summoned me to his room. I expected the worst. He took down from his shelves the two volumes of *The History of British Socialism* by Max Beer and said that he would like me to have them. I cherish those books, along with the memory of the teacher who gave them to me.

The only other books in our house were on biblical prophecy. My father spent much of the Second World War in the Middle East and had immersed himself in the Bible and its prophecies. Even the Jehovah's Witnesses learned to avoid our house, as my father was always ready to break off from his gardening to instruct them in their prophetic errors. So I had to find reading material elsewhere, which I did first in our little local library and then in the cornucopia of Kettering Public Library. This magnificent civic building, with an art gallery attached, became an integral part of my life. It was where I went every afternoon after school before I caught the bus home, and also where I found a Saturday job. My preference for the library over the school rugby team incurred (not for the first time) headmasterly wrath: I was stripped of the prefect's stripes on the wrists of my blazer, leaving only the faded rings where they had been. But the library provided history, politics and literature in glorious abundance, whereas rugby only gave me cuts and bruises. Many years later when I wrote a book on R. H. Tawney, I dedicated it to Kettering Public Library. It would have seemed unthinkable to me then that libraries, a core part of the civic infrastructure, would one day be in peril.

Like all of my school friends, I was the first in my family to go to university. I wanted, inevitably, to study politics. The headmaster had decided that I should go to Oxford to study PPE (Politics, Philosophy and Economics). This I duly did, but I stayed only for one term, which caused distress for my proud parents and invoked yet more headmasterly wrath. I enjoyed the delights of Oxford (and went back later to do a doctorate), but at that time the first year of PPE had no politics in it and that was what I wanted to do. So I arranged a transfer to the London School of Economics for the following year, and spent the intervening months (after a winter as a daffodil inspector in Jersey, patrolling the fields and inspecting the hold of ships in search of the dreaded eelworm) wandering around Europe and North Africa with my thumb extended, as many of my generation did in the 1960s.

While living in a cave on the side of the rock of Gibraltar, I read in a newspaper that Spanish students were protesting against Franco's Fascism under the slogan '*Franco no, democracia si*'. I decided, as an act of solidarity, that I would attach a piece of cardboard with this slogan on it to my rucksack before travelling back up through Spain. When I presented myself at the Spanish border post, I soon realised that this had not been a good idea. I was taken by the guards into a side room, and they began to question me about where I had come from and what I was doing. Every time I said the word 'Gibraltar' they would spit on the floor in unison. When they asked where I was a student and I gave them the name of the LSE a book was consulted, producing much excitable chatter. I was then removed to a holding room in the town police station. After a while, realising that matters were now getting serious, I went up to the desk and demanded (just like in the films) that I should be allowed to see the British consul. In response a policeman hit me, sending me reeling back into my seat.

Eventually I was marched out to a bus, put on the front seat, with a row of policemen on the back row holding rifles, and driven to the Gibraltar border. There I was kicked off the bus and handed my passport, which had been stamped to say that I was henceforth prohibited from entering Spain. It was a forlorn ending to my anti-Fascist crusade. It also left me with the problem of how to get to France and home without going through Spain, which was only solved by signing up for the Swedish Merchant Navy. It was hardly *Homage to Catalonia*, but it was a sharp lesson for a youthful socialist that liberal democracy should not be taken for granted.

Arriving at the LSE in 1967 after a spell of portering at the old Middlesex Hospital, I soon found myself at the epicentre of the student revolution. The place was in constant turmoil. During one student occupation a porter died. Daily mass meetings brought student leaders from all over the world to the university in revolutionary solidarity. It was impossible not to feel in some way part of what was happening. I duly wrote a long (and now embarrassing) article for my local paper at home, explaining that it was all about participatory democracy and the breaking of oppressive bureaucratic structures. This was the spirit and meaning of 1968.

Yet in truth I had a far more ambivalent attitude to what I was witnessing, though this did not stop me getting involved in various kinds of mischief, helped by the convenient proximity of the LSE to inviting targets. I organised a group from our hall of residence to occupy Rhodesia House in the Strand every Thursday. We would walk in, sit down and wait for the police to carry us out into the street (where, on one occasion, I was interviewed by a young BBC television reporter called Martin Bell). There were endless demonstrations and at one of these, again in the Strand, I was arrested and carted off to the cells at Bow Street police station. I was charged with obstructing the police, which I knew I had not. Alarmed to discover that the charge (and sentence) was potentially very serious, I resolved to plead not guilty, and spent many hours in the Law Library at the LSE working on a defence. When the case was heard at Bow Street Magistrates' Court, I was shocked – in my innocence – when a police inspector gave a version of events that was entirely fictitious. He knew it was – and knew that I knew it was, as I put to him in questioning – but he also knew that a court would accept his version rather than mine. In the event, the wily stipendiary magistrate said that he had no alternative but to find me guilty, but had decided to fine me the princely sum of ten shillings. He inquired – with a twinkle in his eye – if I would like time to pay. It felt like a magnificent vindication.

I had no qualms about this kind of activity – occupying Rhodesia House to support the fight against minority rule, opposing the Vietnam War in Grosvenor Square, invading the pitch at Twickenham to disrupt the Springbok tour in the name of anti-apartheid – but I did have a growing feeling of unease about student militancy itself. I wanted to be part of a university, not to destroy it. The idea that university authorities were agents of oppression seemed to me to be ludicrous and self-indulgent. Besides, I was Labour, by background and identity, and I had nothing in common with those self-styled revolutionaries of assorted sectarian affiliations who thought that social democracy was an enemy that had to be attacked. They thought that its defeat would open the door for the triumph of the revolutionary left, whereas it seemed obvious to me that it would instead clear the path for the advance of the political right (as it did).

If I was troubled by such political illiteracy (and by actual illiteracy – throughout the 'troubles' at LSE the wall of the Old Theatre had 'Anarchism' sprayed on it, but misspelt), I was even more disturbed by the sheer intolerance and illiberalism of some of the student Trots. Opposing views were shouted down and their proponents intimidated. This was not my idea of how a university, or politics, should function. One occasion in particular sticks in my mind. Michael Oakeshott, the distinguished conservative philosopher, was delivering a lecture on Roman political thought when a group of Trotskyite thugs burst into the room, roughed him up and poured a jug of water over his head. It was all over in seconds. The elderly philosopher simply shook himself down, said nothing about the incident (which doubtless just confirmed his general view of the world) and calmly continued his description of the Roman understanding of *potestas* and *auctoritas* as forms of rule.

I was learning that there were different kinds of socialism (and politics) and that some I wanted nothing to do with. At this time Marxism was the dominant discourse of the social sciences, stripping away the liberal veneer of bourgeois societies to reveal the class power beneath. Politics was a function of economics. It seemed to me that, despite the analytical value of this approach, it carried with it a devaluation and misunderstanding of politics that was wrong and even dangerous. I was being taught at this time by Ralph Miliband (father of David and Ed), who was the leading political theorist of British Marxism. Handing back an essay I had done on Lenin's *State and Revolution*, he said: 'The trouble with you, Wright, is that you are basically a liberal.' I did not regard it as a 'trouble' to be associated with a kind of politics that wanted to combine liberty and equality, and refused to make politics only a derivative of something else. Nor did I regard it as accidental that Marxists managed to get so much analysis right, and so much politics wrong.

After the LSE I had a year in the United States, courtesy of a scholarship to Harvard. From the moment I arrived (on the new *QE2*, glimpsing the Manhattan skyline at dawn) it was exhilarating. All the academic giants were at Harvard – figures like Daniel Bell and John Rawls – and I was able to attend classes with all of them, while my personal tutor was Seymour Martin Lipset, the renowned political sociologist whose book, *Political Man*, was already a classic. In one lecture series, where there was always standing room only, the rival political theorists Robert Nozick (on the right) and Michael Walzer (on the left) conducted a running debate on the relationship between liberty and equality. This was heady stuff, and a kind of teaching I had never experienced before.

There was also the headiness of America itself. At Christmas some of us drove non-stop, three days and nights, from snowbound Boston to sun-drenched California. There were regular bus trips down to Washington for Vietnam demonstrations outside Congress. Greyhound buses provided a means of exploring every corner of this extraordinary country. Above all, there was the atmosphere of civic energy and democratic optimism of a kind that I had never encountered before and which I decided was a well from which I would periodically need to drink thereafter. Yet I came to feel something else too, a sense that here was a country that was simply too vast and various for the kind of political movement I was attracted to; and it was this that finally reconciled me to the prospect of returning to a Britain that might be less exciting, but was somehow more manageable.

At this stage I was not certain what I would do when I returned home. It would be something to do with politics, but whether this would be of an academic or more worldly kind I was not sure (a dilemma I never really resolved). I remember telling an American girlfriend, as we sat in a fish restaurant on Boston harbour, that I thought I would probably become a Labour MP, but this was a notion rather than a plan. I already had a place waiting for me at Oxford to do a doctorate; however, this was the default option rather than a settled intention. I tried to become a journalist, writing from America to the BBC, *The Guardian* and *The Times*, inviting them to take me on – an invitation which they lost no time in declining.

So it was Oxford, and the academy. More precisely, it was a thesis on the political thought of G. D. H. Cole, the scourge of Fabian centralism and an apostle of a creed of participatory democracy known as guild socialism. Happy days were spent poring over Cole's papers in Nuffield College, or interviewing remaining members of the Cole Group, which had been a central fixture of left-wing life in Oxford in the 1930s. The redoubtable Margaret Cole, widow and ferocious guardian of her husband's legacy, came to visit, gamely agreeing to be picked up from the station on the back of my motorbike. Even happier days were spent meeting, and marrying, Moira, my Welsh wife.

Yet I was still trying to break out of the academy. I applied to be one of the researchers for the Labour shadow Cabinet (posts which were funded by Rowntree and so known as 'chocolate soldiers') and was invited to interview at the House of Commons. Most of the shadow Cabinet appeared to be in the room, with Roy Jenkins presiding. The interview seemed to be going extremely well and my hopes were steadily rising. Then, Tony Crosland, whose 1956 book *The Future of Socialism* was the key text of post-war social democracy, slowly uncurled himself from his near-somnolent state on the chair next to mine and, through a fog of cheroot smoke, drawled out his single devastating question: 'So, tell us Mr Wright, how would *you* solve the problems of the British economy?' That was the moment I failed to get the job. A long and kindly letter from Douglas Houghton, the chairman of the Parliamentary Labour Party, informed me that it had been very close and that I was the runner-up, but that the job had gone to someone called Matthew Oakeshott (now Lord Oakeshott, the Liberal Democrat peer). It seemed that I was destined to remain in scholarly life, despite my periodic attempts at escape.

There followed a first lecturing job at the University College of North Wales in Bangor, where I encountered the troubling politics of nationalism (and tried valiantly to learn just enough Welsh to impress my wife's Welsh-speaking parents). On one occasion the college was closed by a student protest demanding that Hebrew should be taught through the medium of Welsh. This was a more complicated kind of politics than I had previously experienced, organised around different kinds of division. Then I spotted an opportunity to work in a more worldly version of a university and moved to the extramural department at the University of Birmingham, which was to become my academic home. I felt I was joining a great academic tradition that included the Workers' Educational Association and the university extension movement, bringing learning to the masses and nourishing an active democracy. In fact, this tradition was already in decline (and in universities now has, disgracefully, almost entirely disappeared), but I believed in it and felt proud to be part of it.

It was also great fun. The department was full of wonderful characters (like my roommate Harry, the son of Marie Stopes, the patron saint of modern birth control) and housed in a magnificent Edwardian mansion on the edge of the leafy

Edgbaston campus that had once been the family home of the screw-making Nettlefold family. Its majestic grounds were now the university's botanical garden. From this base we sallied forth, armed with boxes of books, to run courses on every subject under the sun in towns and villages from Birmingham to the Welsh border, aided by organising tutors who were resident in the different parts of our great educational empire. Looking back, it feels like a lost golden age.

I settled into a pattern of life that, typically, involved writing during the day and teaching in the evening and, often, also on Saturdays. Much inventiveness was needed, especially for someone teaching politics, in devising titles for courses for which people might be persuaded to sign up. One particularly unfortunate title that I remember in the departmental brochure was 'Child Abuse – A Practitioner's Guide'. Many of mine were called 'The Politics of …', with the missing word carefully crafted to sound more interesting than politics. Classes attracted a wide variety of people, which made teaching interesting, and some of the very best students were those who had brought up children and missed out on university but now wanted to do something else with their life.

There were special courses for the Armed Forces, and also for the growing army of school governors. (At one of the latter, in deepest Worcestershire, I first encountered a bolshy German parent who is now the admirably feisty Gisela Stuart MP.) A class at a Birmingham mosque was regularly interrupted by the call to prayer; and one for miners was held in a Staffordshire town that I did not know would one day be part of my constituency. I also ran regular day conferences, particularly aimed at schools, on the political issues of the day, with both politicians and academics as speakers.

16

For one of these conferences, on the issues raised by the Brandt report on international development, I had secured the former Prime Minister Edward Heath as a speaker. Thinking I needed a suitably impressive vehicle to transport him from New Street station to the university, I asked Harry, who drove one of those vast elongated Citröens, if he would oblige. He readily agreed. The only problem was that he was a notoriously dangerous driver – colleagues would routinely inquire if Harry was on the road before setting out for a class in the same vicinity. My first meeting with him had been interrupted by a call from his solicitor, with Harry enquiring 'how this relates to the last dangerous driving charge I had'. Perhaps it was his mother's fault: she had prevented him riding a bike in case it damaged his reproductive organs.

A message came from the Vice-Chancellor that under no circumstances would Harry be allowed to transport a former Prime Minister to the university. I therefore turned to another colleague, who had recently inherited an ancient Rover with all the trimmings and was happy to help, although he warned me that the car sometimes had difficulty engaging first gear. On the appointed day, Heath emerged from the station accompanied by his security officer, and we set off for the university. All went well, until we had to stop at the traffic lights near Edgbaston cricket ground. The lights changed, and changed again, and again, but the car resolutely refused to find first gear. The security man started looking around anxiously. Heath remained impassive and uncommunicative. Finally, the car lurched forward – and the rest of the day, including Heath's impressive speech (who by then had relaxed), went well.

I had not given up on practical politics, though. Soon

after arriving in Birmingham I had been selected as the Labour candidate for Kidderminster. The constituency was based in the carpet-making town but also covered a large chunk of lovely Worcestershire countryside. When our first child was born the local paper announced it as a 'Victory for Labour'; but it was to be the only one. There was no chance of winning – the seat was securely held for the Conservatives by the scion of the Bulmer cider family, and the 1978–9 'winter of discontent' was the final nail in the Labour government's coffin – but the whole campaign was thoroughly enjoyable. It was also my first experience of the Liberals, who ran the local council, and their particular style of campaigning, which seemed to involve making up fictitious 'facts' (including the fact that they were going to win) and shamelessly disseminating them. It was a style of campaigning – making promises in the sure knowledge that they would never have to be implemented – that eventually caught up with them when they formed part of a coalition government.

Among my party members were Edward (E. P.) and Dorothy Thompson, great historians and figures of the left, who lived in a manor house near Worcester. Edward's *The Making of the English Working Class* had become a key Labour movement text, but when I made the mistake at one party meeting of referring to it, and saying how much we valued having . them with us, they almost resigned on the spot. Campaigning around the villages in Edward's Land Rover one day we were greeted by an old man who declared that it was the first time he had seen a Labour candidate since 1945. This immediately persuaded Edward, an inveterate romantic, that the historical tide was moving in our direction. What was actually happening was that the Labour Party was in the process of putting itself out of power for a generation.

These were dismal political years, at least for social democrats, as Labour turned itself into a basket case after 1979. I recalled a remark by my old LSE tutor, Bob McKenzie (of election television 'swing-o-meter' fame), that he could not understand why the Trots spent all their time attacking the Labour Party when they could easily take it over instead. This they now did, to the despair of traditional party supporters and to the benefit of the Thatcherised Conservative Party. In this bleak political environment, I concentrated on producing books and, with my wife's help, babies.

I was now watching politics, and writing about it, much more than doing it. My civic energies went into school government and the local community health council rather than into the Labour Party. I did chair the Birmingham Fabian Society, though, where we regularly agonised over the state of the moderate left with visiting politicians. Our most memorable meeting was with Shirley Williams, her last as a member of the Labour Party, just as the Gang of Four was breaking away to set up the Social Democratic Party (SDP). I introduced her by quoting, mischievously, from a book by her father, George Catlin, on the importance of loyalty in politics. The room was packed, the atmosphere charged, and Shirley was magnificent. For many people present it was the evening when they decided whether to stay in or leave the Labour Party. I knew that I could never abandon the party that had always been part of my family's life; but I was deeply unhappy that it had got itself into such a state that Shirley Williams felt she had to give up on it.

Then a far more profound misery descended, which had

nothing to do with politics, and which changed everything. In 1985 our youngest son died, aged two years and eight months, after heart surgery that was supposed to put him right. Nothing can prepare a parent for this. Years later, I told a television interviewer how this experience created a particular bond between Gordon Brown and David Cameron, behind and beyond the antagonism. At the time I could not see how the rest of life would be possible. I even searched for solace, and solidarity, in churchyards among the graves of young children from a distant age when infant deaths were common. I tried to escape my grief by railing against the slum that was then Birmingham Children's Hospital, where children had to be wheeled outside on their way to the operating theatre, and the lack of paediatric intensive care beds meant that several times our son was prepared for surgery that was then postponed. This was – almost literally – the roof that needed fixing by a future Labour government. I became a public service reformer because of my frustration at the impossibility of getting information about surgical success rates at different hospitals. The lack of bereavement support at the hospital drove me to compile a research report on the whole issue. Yet I was really only trying to find ways to cope with what had happened.

There was something else, though, which I like to think changed everything afterwards. Partly it was a feeling that nothing worse could ever happen, and that this provided a kind of protection in the rest of life. Partly a sharp sense of perspective about what mattered and what did not. I like to think, whether true or not, that this fostered a spirit of independence, a feeling of detachment, of not being beholden to anyone or anything, and an impatience with stuff that did not really matter. Perhaps all this was a construct I had created for myself, a way of keeping my son as an active presence in my life, but I wanted it to be true.

‡

Becoming a Member of Parliament in 1992 was the result of several happy accidents. I was not scouring the country for a seat, but when I was encouraged by some local party members in the Staffordshire constituency of Cannock & Burntwood, a Tory-held marginal just north of Birmingham, to put my name forward, I readily did so. I nearly missed the selection meeting as my ancient Volvo broke down on the M6 and I only arrived just in time, accompanied by an AA escort. I had no expectation of winning, assuming that some union stitch-up had probably fixed the outcome, and almost decided there was no point in turning up for the meeting the following morning when the result would be announced.

In the event, I did turn up, and was taken aback to hear that I had won. My good fortune was in having found a constituency in which there was not only a genuinely open contest, but which had already adopted a one-member-one-vote selection system long before the party as a whole. Many years later an elderly party member, recalling this selection meeting, told me, 'Nobody had ever talked to us like you did.' When I asked her what she meant, hoping to hear about my compelling oratory, she said I was 'like a lecturer, walking about'.

Over the years the constituency changed its boundaries, and its name, but my happy relationship with it endured. When the local party disagreed with my stance on the hunting ban and I invited party members to instruct me how to vote, as they clearly had much stronger views on the issue than me, they adamantly refused to do so.

There was also the good fortune of a win in 1992, by a nail-biting 1,000 votes or so, one of only a couple of dozen Labour gains in that election. Despite its recovery from the nadir of the 1980s, it was still obvious on the ground that Labour had not yet done enough to win an election. The Tories had dumped Mrs Thatcher and installed John Major, and could still play the tax card against Labour with telling effect. Our own local contest had a sharp ideological edge to it (at least for our supporters) as the incumbent MP, Gerald Howarth, had been Mrs Thatcher's PPS and was a prominent member of the right-wing 'No Turning Back' group. For us, he represented the handbag over the water. Evicting him was therefore a particular pleasure, although (as I later pointed out to him) it enabled him to find a much safer seat elsewhere. He was not grateful for this favour at the time.

Cannock & Burntwood was a traditional coal-mining constituency, straddling the Cannock Chase coalfield, but in 1992 there was only one pit left. Taken down it for the first time, I was in the cage at the surface, preparing to plunge into the depths, when one of the men slammed the cage door shut with the reassuring words, 'We have the worst safety record of any pit in the country.' It is impossible not to feel a particular privilege in representing coal miners, and we waged a passionate but futile campaign to save the pit from the mass closure programme that the Conservative government had embarked upon. The issue dominated my Parliamentary apprenticeship. On a cold December dawn in 1993 some of us waited at the pit head for the final shift to come up. Then, led by a lone piper, and with banners flying, there was a march that snaked its way from the pit and through the town. It was extraordinarily moving, as people clapped and cried and shouted support, knowing that this was the end not just of a pit but of a way of life that had sustained the community for a century. The future was going to be a different country.

Having won a fourth successive election, despite everything, the Conservatives began to think that they might be in office for ever. Many on the Labour side had come to the same gloomy conclusion. Commentators who should have known better started announcing the arrival of one-party rule. That was the background against which a small group, all of us newly elected MPs, formed a New Agenda Forum to 'promote new thinking on key political issues to help the Labour Party regain the political initiative'. *The Guardian* promptly dubbed us the 'Cerebral Tendency'. In a pamphlet we announced: 'Our message is one of modernization and renewal'. We argued that it was time to ditch Clause IV as the statement of what the party stood for, and drafted our own replacement for it.

I was also part of a discussion group that had been convened at the Institute for Public Policy Research (IPPR), the Labour-leaning think tank, to talk through these same issues. At our first gathering someone pointed out that our meetings would clash with those of the party's National Executive Committee. David Miliband (then at IPPR) promptly suggested that we call ourselves the Not the NEC Group, to merry agreement. That evening we were going through the division lobby in the Commons when John Smith, who had replaced Neil Kinnock as Labour leader, said he wanted to see me ('laddie') in his room. This sounded very promising for my future career. It turned out he had heard about our little group and was furious about its name. ('If Peter Hain gets to hear about this he will make all kinds of trouble.') I tried to explain that it was just a joke, but he found it anything but funny. It had to be stopped, now. This was my first brush with a more muscular kind of politics.

Under John Smith's leadership, Labour strengthened its position; but there was underlying tension between those who believed in 'one more heave' and those who thought something more radical would be needed to restore Labour's fortunes. I was emphatically, and vociferously, in the latter camp. So was Tony Blair, then shadow Home Secretary. Sharing a table with him in the Commons cafeteria one evening, I said I hoped he was ready for the red boxes and the black cars that were on their way. He simply did not believe this, still insisting that we had 'not yet done enough' to convince people that we were a genuinely changed party and that something more fundamental was required.

On the morning of John Smith's sudden death I was sitting on a London bus behind two elderly women. Looking at the newspaper billboard announcing his death, one said, 'He was a good man,' and the other replied, 'Yes, he was.' That's all, nothing more, but they had said it all. In the constituency we held our own memorial service and put a bench in the churchyard in his memory. This meant that Labour needed a new leader, and I had no doubt that it should be Tony Blair – I was the first Labour MP to say so publicly (which probably also secured my first entry in Gordon Brown's little black book). From this moment the New Labour Project was to be constructed in earnest, with Blair and Brown as its joint architects.

For me, this was the renewal of social democracy, the necessity of which I had argued for in print and speech. It was not just an electoral tactic, but an essential revisionism. At this time my name regularly appeared in the 'ones to watch' newspaper features on the intellectual movers and shakers of New Labour. Yet this was misleading, as I was never an insider; in fact, Peter Mandelson once informed me that my role was that of a 'useful outrider'. I am not sure that I was content with that role, or whether I actively chose it. It would at least have been nice to be invited inside the tent. The nearest I got was a note from Tony Blair in 1995, saying he did not want to put me on the front bench at the moment – 'I think you are better (for me) doing what you are doing now. But you know I am a huge admirer of you and your time will come!'

From time to time I would be asked by Blair's office to supply material for speeches, usually to buttress points he wanted to make with historical references or quotations. On one occasion, just as I was finishing a Friday evening constituency advice surgery, Blair himself rang with a query. He was doing a big speech the following day and wanted to ask me, 'What is socialism, exactly?', and could I supply a couple of good quotes? This was refreshing and alarming in equal measure; and not a request that could have been made by any previous Labour leader. It was a reminder that Blair really was in a class of his own.

A request of a different kind came from Gordon Brown. The decision had been taken to change Clause IV, and Gordon asked if I would rapidly put together a collection of writings with him (helped by a researcher he would give me) that would demonstrate the rich variety of socialist thought.

As we talked he began tossing assorted volumes at me from around his book-filled room that he thought might be useful, most of which he had probably read. Here was a genuine intellectual, although his purpose was firmly practical. The book (a rather handsome anthology called *Values, Visions and Voices*) was duly produced and launched by Brown and Blair at the Labour conference. I had assumed (and hoped) that this collaboration would lead to a continued relationship with Gordon, but it did not. As his rivalry with Blair intensified, I suspect this complex, formidable, driven and unforgiving man thought I was in the wrong camp.

In fact, I was in a sort of no man's land of my own. Much of my Parliamentary activity at this time was taken up with pressing for various political reforms, such as the protection of whistleblowers and the curbing of patronage, and I was given a Parliamentary award for my work by the Campaign for Freedom of Information. I was also very critical of Parliament itself, and of its expenses, which did not make me very clubbable. In one debate on MPs' pay and expenses soon after I arrived in the place, I described the advice I had been given on my first day by a colleague on how I could maximise my travel expenses. (This involved buying a certain make of diesel car with a big engine so that you could claim the highest rate for engine size while also maximising miles to the gallon.) Leaving the chamber, having recounted the story, I was accosted by a senior colleague who warned me icily that I 'would never be forgiven for what I had just said'. It was my first encounter with the Parliamentary *omerta* on the matter of expenses. This same colleague, Stuart Bell, went on to preside over the Parliamentary expenses system that, a decade and a half later, exploded over us all.

It was an early indication of just how toxic this issue was.

I described in a *New Statesman* article in 1996 (under the heading 'Palace of Low-grade Corruptions', reprinted on pages 190–95) how I had endeavoured to pursue the issue, and the resistance I had met. 'What really matters,' I wrote, 'is that when the rest of the world is having to learn to live with the requirements of audit and performance indicators, the Westminster club will go to extraordinary lengths to avoid scrutiny of its own inner workings. That makes it ripe for assorted low-grade corruptions.' As it turned out, of course, also for some higher-grade ones. When I coupled this with an argument about the defects of Parliament, and Parliamentarians, as instruments of effective scrutiny, it is not surprising if I was viewed with suspicion and irritation by many of my Parliamentary colleagues.

By the time of the 1997 election, when Conservative disintegration combined with Blairite transformation had made the outcome certain, I was playing a leading role in the promotion of the New Labour cause. When Penguin wanted to produce a set of election specials, I was asked to do the *Why Vote Labour?* one (with David Willetts writing the Conservative equivalent). However, I had also written a widely-noticed Fabian pamphlet (with the title *Who Wins Dares*) in the run-up to the election in which I argued that it was not enough to win the election if it did not also mean a new kind of politics: 'There may be those who think that a governing project can be assembled and contained within the parameters of spin-doctoring, media-managing, polling and focus-grouping. It cannot. I am prepared to believe that these black arts are indispensable to the conduct of modern politics; but I am not prepared to accept that they provide a substitute for a governing vision.'

Worryingly, at least for my political career, words like 'thoughtful' and (worse) 'independent-minded' had started to become routinely attached to my name in the public prints. This made me doubt whether I would be given a job in the Blair government, despite my public profile and regular appearance on speculative lists of likely names. The journalist John Kampfner has recorded how, when he once mentioned my name to Peter Mandelson, 'Mandelson bristled and replied: "The trouble with him is that he thinks too much."' This was not a good omen. My ideal job would have given me a role in implementing some of the political reforms for which I had been arguing, or advancing the cause of public service reform. In the event, I was summoned to attend upon the new Lord Chancellor, Tony Blair's old pupil-master, Derry Irvine.

I had never met him before. He said he wanted me to be his Parliamentary Private Secretary, an elaborate name for the lowest form of sub-ministerial life. When I said that he did not know me, he replied, 'Tony has told me all about you.' I then pointed out that I was not a lawyer, to which he retorted that there were already too many of those. I had resolved that I would only take a proper job or nothing, but he went on to explain that I would not be a 'normal PPS' but 'more of a special adviser' and that he would arrange for me to have access to all the official papers. As Derry was also to preside over the Cabinet committee implementing the government's big constitutional reform programme, this was an attractive proposal and I accepted. It was further agreed that I could continue to speak freely on all other issues except those relating to the work of the department.

The problem was that it did not work out like this. Within

days, the official machine had clearly told Derry that there was no role of the kind he had offered me, and there was certainly going to be no routine access to departmental papers. He wrote to say that we should 'abstain from any mutual discussion' of constitutional matters, and that anything I said or wrote on such matters should make clear that it had no connection with my departmental role in relation to him ('the message needs to be unambiguous'). It was already clear that Derry and I had entered into a relationship that was going to cause difficulties for both of us.

Matters rapidly became much worse, as comments by me on assorted issues were invariably (and inevitably) trailed in the press as coming from 'Irvine aide', despite my insistence that they had nothing to do with him. His proximity to Blair made him an especially inviting media target. When, in the course of one interview, I said that I could see no reason why Charles should not marry Camilla at some point if he wanted to ('better a happy king than an unhappy one'), and that the Church would simply have to like it or lump it – all of which seemed to me to be pretty obvious – the balloon went up. Derry had to write me an official letter which began, ominously, 'Alastair Campbell has contacted me about your recent interview on the *Today* programme', and went on to demand a vow of future silence from me. Geoff Hoon, the department's minister in the Commons, told me that Derry had asked about the state of my mental health. Once Alastair had cracked the whip, I realised that (for both my sake and Derry's) I had to make my escape.

It was still the summer of 1997 and, on my return from holiday, I wrote to Derry to tell him of my decision: 'Having been offered something more than routine PPS-dom,

I find myself with something less. Of course, I could just settle for the status, and my regard for you personally, but that is not really my kind of politics. I think it may be sensible for me, and easier for you, if you dispense with my services. There need be no public fuss about it.'

Unfortunately, there was a different kind of public fuss going on by this time, which centred on the cost of the wallpaper with which the Lord Chancellor (who combined a prodigious intellect with a political innocence) was refurbishing his state rooms. He said that if I resigned just at this moment, when he was under attack, it would be linked to the wallpaper issue and be very damaging to him personally. I therefore agreed to stay on until things were calmer and quieter.

In the end I stayed, with ever increasing frustration, until the calm of the following summer, when I slipped away quietly. I was the first to leave the Blair government; but in my resignation letter I said, accurately, that I was 'a loyal and enthusiastic supporter of the government and this is a resignation only in the sense that it is a natural moment to take stock and move on'. But move on to what? I had reclaimed my freedom, but with no clear idea of what I was going to do with it. It was also the moment, although I did not see this at the time, when I had removed myself from the conventional political career ladder. Some years later I was told that this is how my action had been perceived in Downing Street, perfectly reasonably. Yet it had not been my intention. I retained an arrogant and politically naïve assumption that, despite casting myself adrift, my services would still be called upon at some point by Tony Blair.

It soon became clear that this was very unlikely, never

more so than when a message appeared on my pager one day that said: 'The Prime Minister is pissed off with you. Phone No. 10 at once.' The exact nature of that particular offence is long forgotten, although it doubtless involved expressing a view on something or other that was regarded as 'unhelpful', but what really shocked and appalled me was that some No. 10 apparatchik had thought it appropriate to put such coarse language in the name of the Prime Minister, who almost certainly knew nothing about it, and that it was acceptable to communicate with a Member of Parliament in this way. Although an enthusiastic supporter of the Blair government, I began to worry increasingly about its political style. In turn, the party managers began to worry about me.

The closed world of Westminster likes to put people into categories. Once in a category, such as 'maverick' or 'usual suspect', it is very hard to escape. Having abandoned one role, I knew I had to find another, but I also knew that it would not be easy. There were plenty of agreeable ways for a Member of Parliament to pass their days; however, that is not the same as having a role and there are inherent frustrations in being a government backbencher, at least if you want to avoid being either a toady or a malcontent. I sampled the Council of Europe, a kind of Siberian exile assuaged by sybaritic pleasures, but that just intensified the problem. I had aborted one kind of political career, and now needed to find another that would make it worthwhile to continue being a Member of Parliament (beyond the constituency work that will happily fill any vacuum).

I saw my opportunity when, in 1999, Rhodri Morgan vacated the chair of the Public Administration Select Committee to devote himself to Wales. I thought I had a good claim on the job, as it was a committee on which I had previously served and which reflected my interests in the operation of government, so I decided to try to get it, the first time I had actively pursued a job. The trouble was that these select committee posts were in the gift of the whips and they soon made it clear that this particular gift was not one that they were prepared to bestow on a troublesome character like me. (In fact, I was a serial loyalist with only occasional lapses.) I was outraged by this, not just personally but because I thought it was a corruption of Parliament by the executive. When I said this to Clive Soley, who chaired the Parliamentary Labour Party, he told me that I did not help my case by being seen as 'a kind of visiting professor'. This upset me, because I knew it was true, and I vowed to become less semi-detached. I realised that I had no political patrons to whom I could turn, a major disability, although when I approached Jack Straw he readily offered his support.

It was only some years later that I discovered that the post eventually came my way because of the intervention of Tony Blair, to whom I had also made indirect representations. As my informant, who had worked at No. 10, put it: 'He thought he owed you one.' It was hardly a triumph for Parliamentary democracy to have select committee posts decided by the Prime Minister (a matter to which I was to return later) but in this case I was grateful for the outcome. It meant that I had become Parliament's man, not the executive's, and it gave new purpose to my political life. It also meant that I was often described as someone who had deliberately eschewed one kind of political career for another. That was not quite how I had seen it at the time, but it was a retrospective narrative that I was happy to encourage. It was also more comforting for the question to be why you are not in the government rather than why you are. In my maiden speech in the Commons in 1992 I had declared: 'It is a fact – although it may be an unpalatable one – that this country has never taken the business of democracy very seriously. We have taken the idea of strong government and a strong executive seriously but not democracy'. So perhaps I had always been a Parliament man, really.

From the start I wanted to turn the select committee with the most boring name into the most interesting and effective one; and in the process to show that the scrutinising role of Parliament could be made to matter far more that it usually did. The committee (which we deliberately branded as 'PASC') had the advantage that it was not confined to a single department but could range widely across government. This meant that, for more than a decade, it provided a running commentary on the conduct of government at a time when it was a matter of considerable and continuing controversy. The profile of the committee steadily rose and it established a reputation for the vigour of its scrutiny, the independence of its approach and the quality of its reports. Even when we were being critical I wanted to ensure that we were also constructive, which helped to cement my close relationship with a succession of Cabinet secretaries, if not always with ministers. We came to be seen as a constitutional watchdog, and one that was quite prepared to bite when the occasion demanded it.

One such occasion arose immediately, as the committee was examining the proposed Freedom of Information legislation. The government had produced a bold white paper but then a weaker bill, and we set about strengthening it. The committee's work gave a focus to Parliamentary (and public) discussion of the proposals and prompted Labour rebellions in support of our amendments, much to the displeasure of the whips. After one vote, in April 2000, I complained in a letter to the Chief Whip about the conduct of the whips: 'Colleagues arriving to vote were told that one lobby was for the "intellectual wankers". A young colleague who had previously always supported the government was told "never to ask for anything again". Another loyal and respected colleague who could not support the government was told he was "pathetic" ... I simply cannot believe that this is how a mature party should treat decent and loyal colleagues on a matter like this. Not only is it wrong, but it must surely also be counter-productive to deal with people in this way.' I never received a reply, of course, but we did succeed in getting some important improvements made to the bill that made ours one of the strongest FOI regimes in the world.

This episode had another consequence, which was not appreciated at the time but was to have dramatic effects some years later. In the course of taking evidence on the FOI bill, it was pointed out to us that its provisions did not include Parliament and that this omission should be rectified. When we recommended changes to this effect, Jack Straw (who was handling the bill) accepted the recommendation and it went through the Commons on the nod. Without this provision the subsequent disclosures about MPs' expenses would not have been possible. Jack likes to say that it is all my fault; and I like to remind him of his role. The fact is that it took FOI to lift the lid on the murky secrecy of a Parliamentary expenses system that was in desperate need of scrutiny and reform.

I found myself in the curious position of supporting the government but developing doubts about its governing style, which I began to think would end in tears. Despite its crushing majority, there was an intolerance of reasonable dissent, a disparagement of Parliament and an obsession with presentation. This was not the sort of new social democracy for which I had argued, and which I had believed Tony Blair to stand for. I started to issue warnings, but without wanting to become a malcontent – not a stance that the party managers either understood or liked. In one article in 2000 under the heading 'I am still a Blairite, but is Blair?', I suggested that there was 'a problem at the centre of the Blair project' and that 'unless this problem is attended to, there will be tears before bedtime'. (See pages 91–6.) The problem, I continued, reflected itself in a political style 'that is often downright embarrassing. We have the sterile verblessness of ministerial speeches delivered *de haut en bas* without the flicker of original thought or the passion of real argument. This is a politics for middle managers.' When a whip phoned to express displeasure at this, I explained that I was just trying to be helpful.

One small incident added to my unease. Peter Mandelson had invited a small group of us, no more than about half a dozen, to meet him in his room at the Northern Ireland Office to discuss the state of the Project. He asked us to take it in turns to say what New Labour was all about. We fumbled our way through the familiar answers – improving life chances, empowering people, reducing inequality, combining economic efficiency with social justice and so on – until it was Peter's turn. He said the answer was to be found in a single word: change. That was the governing idea. I found this deeply disturbing, partly because I was a conservative in everything but politics, but mainly because it was so politically rootless and vacuous. If it simply meant that there was a standing need to be responsive to new circumstances, then it was trite. If it was intended to mean more than this, then it was alarming.

One of the advantages of having a Parliamentary power base as a committee chair was that I could ride some of my hobby horses. Among these was the need to bring Prime Ministers within the accountability framework of the select committees, something for which that great constitutional gadfly, Peter Hennessy, had long pressed. The Prime Minister was the only minister who did not have to appear before a select committee, not even once a year, and the knockabout that was Prime Minister's Questions was no substitute for this in terms of effective accountability. PASC took up the issue, but were always directed to other ministers. When we thought we had identified something for which the Prime Minister was uniquely responsible, in the shape of the annual reports that the government had started producing on its performance, the government's response was to abolish the annual reports. When I persisted, Tony Blair wrote to say that he could 'see no case for departing from the long-standing convention that Prime Ministers do not themselves give evidence to select committees'.

I transferred the campaign to the committee that brought together all the select committee chairs (under the exciting name of the Liaison Committee), pressing for an annual Prime Ministerial appearance. The rebuffs still continued. Robin Cook, then Leader of the House, asked me to abandon the cause as 'Tony has made it clear that he is never going to agree'. Then came the announcement that Tony Blair had decided to appear twice a year in front of the Liaison Committee, with the first such meeting to take place on 16 July 2002. It was a small victory for Parliamentary democracy; a new constitutional convention had been born.

As I had expected, Tony Blair glided effortlessly and notelessly through these two-and-a-half-hour sessions, charming a committee that was much too unwieldy to inflict any real damage on him. These virtuoso performances left the Conservative members wearily resigned to their fate – they were never going to win an election again while Blair was around. When Gordon Brown took over as Prime Minister, these jolly occasions turned into rather dour seminars. Each Prime Minister will handle things differently, while the task for the committee chairs is to sharpen up their own act.

On our own committee, with its membership of independent spirits from all parties, we got stuck into a range of issues where we thought reform was needed: from quangos to the House of Lords, and from the honours system to lobbying. We produced proposals for a Public Standards Commission that would bring coherence to the ethical regulation of government, and opened up the issue of prerogative powers that made governments too strong and Parliament too weak. We proposed pre-appointment hearings by select committees for key public appointments and ran a long campaign to give a statutory basis to the constitutional position of the civil service, during the course of which, uniquely, the committee drafted its own bill in order to push the issue along. It was a particular cause of satisfaction that this historic measure was finally enacted in the last hours before the dissolution of Parliament for the 2010 election.

Because the committee was not merely reacting to issues that had been generated by government but also pursuing its own agenda, what frequently happened was that resistance to our proposals at the time turned into at least partial adoption at a later date. On public service reform issues, for example, our analysis of the targets regime and its unintended consequences helped to produce a more sensible approach; while our advocacy of user rights in the form of a developing system of public service guarantees eventually found its way into Labour's manifesto for the 2010 election (by which time it was much too late). We even floated the idea of a lottery system for over-subscribed school places – after a visit to the United States – which has attracted more interest subsequently. Our proposals on House of Lords reform, involving a mix of election and appointment, were eventually adopted by both Robin Cook and Jack Straw as Leaders of the House and could have provided the basis for a durable settlement of this intractable issue. Our suggestions regarding the regulation of lobbying were rejected at the time but taken up when a new lobbying scandal demanded a response.

Not only was the committee conspicuously active, but it frequently found itself in the eye of the prevailing political storm. It went into battle with the government on behalf of occupational pensioners on the back of an Ombudsman report, and won. When special advisers like Jo Moore and Damian McBride misbehaved, it demanded tighter controls on their conduct (including the ability to sack them). When assorted ministers also got into trouble, it argued the case for an independent investigator of compliance with the ministerial code. None of this made us popular with the government, but it did show that Parliament was doing its job.

No political storm was more intense than that surrounding the 'cash for honours' affair (more accurately, 'loans for peerages'). The committee had previously undertaken a major inquiry into the honours system, and when these allegations about party donors being offered peerages and other honours appeared we decided to examine the issue. Then came the surprise announcement that Scotland Yard had also decided to investigate whether the law on the sale of honours had been broken. We were asked by the police to suspend our own inquiry, which – after taking legal advice – we did, above all because we did not want to run the risk that a Parliamentary inquiry might make it more difficult subsequently to mount a successful prosecution.

In the event, what was originally intended to be a short police investigation dragged on interminably. It was led by Inspector – later Assistant Commissioner – Yates ('Yates of the Yard' as he became known), who would come to my office periodically to brief me on how it was going and when it was likely to be concluded. He also wanted to assure me that the continuous leaks about the inquiry were not coming from him. He was impressive, sharp and determined, and we got on well. I told him that I did not think he knew what he had taken on and that, although the practice of rewarding big party donors with peerages was incontrovertible, it was unlikely to take a form that would pass an evidential test under the law. He told me that he was 'following the evidence where it leads' and we joked about whether he was ever likely to find a 'smoking gun'.

Finally, and I think inevitably, he could not; although he did believe that he had uncovered a seedy underbelly of political life that needed exposing. While the affair dragged on, it dominated everything, with arrests at dawn and, for the first time ever, a Prime Minister being interviewed by the police. To some (including Lord 'Cashpoint' Levy and his lawyers, who also contacted me) it seemed excessively heavy-handed, but press and public loved watching politicians getting their collars fingered by the police. Since then Mr Yates has had his own collar fingered for what seems like excessive inactivity on press phone-hacking.

The affair threatened to dominate Tony Blair's last period in office. At one point he asked to see me. He was bubbling with frustration and indignation at what was happening and the fact that it showed no sign of coming to an end. He was also upset at the way in which his staff had been treated. 'What on Earth can be done?' he asked. I said that in my view the investigation was unlikely to lead to charges, but that it had to run its course. I do not think he found this very reassuring, or helpful. My main concern was to prevent such a scandal happening again by beefing up the safeguards, and this is what the committee recommended once it was able to resume its own inquiry.

Then there was the other dominating issue of Iraq, into which I also wanted the committee to have a role in forcing a proper inquiry. I had not supported the war, despite my general support for the 'liberal interventionism' that Blair had espoused, simply because I did not think the case for it had been made and that it was likely to do more harm than good. However, what preoccupied me after the war was the need for Parliament to put in place an inquiry into what had happened. It did not seem adequate to me that Parliament should constantly bleat about the need for an inquiry but not have the means to establish one. The particular focus was

Iraq, but the point was a more general one about the position of Parliament in relation to the executive. The committee had previously proposed the mechanism of a Parliamentary Commission of Inquiry to investigate major issues that went beyond the resources and remit of particular select committees, but we now made this case again with particular reference to Iraq. Our pressure helped to get an inquiry, and then to make it public, but the need for Parliament to regain the initiative on inquiries of this kind remains.

Beyond committee work, there were other reforms to pursue. One of these was for fixed-term Parliaments, for which I introduced a bill in 2002, telling the Commons: 'If it were suggested that one runner in a race should be able to fire the starting pistol at a moment of his choosing and, moreover, that that runner should be the one who had won the race last time, it would be considered absurd and monstrously unfair, although no doubt there would still be those who would defend the practice as traditional and having the merits of flexibility. Yet that is precisely what we allow in relation to general elections.' There was little interest in that argument then, but it seems to have been accepted now.

Nor had I given up on MPs' expenses. In June 2002, giving evidence to the Committee on Standards in Public Life, I said: 'My guess is that any future difficulties with Members of Parliament are far more likely to occur around issues to do with the allowances that they now get ... If you have lax rules, I'm afraid that you will have lax use of money ... Unless you get hold of these issues now and think about them, they will come and hit us later on.' And hit us they did some years later with the force of a political tornado. It did not take unusual prescience to see what would happen, as everyone inside the system knew it was rotten. The problem was in getting something done about it. At the beginning of 2008 I wrote again to the chairman of the Committee on Standards in Public Life, requesting an 'immediate inquiry into the whole system of MPs' allowances', but this was rejected and it was only much later – when the ship of state was already sinking – that an inquiry finally happened.

Public outrage in the wake of the expenses scandal was entirely justified. MPs had enjoyed a system that invited abuse and many had readily accepted the invitation. They had nobody to blame but themselves for the opprobrium that descended on them – and, by extension, on Parliament and the whole political class – not least because they had consistently tried to resist disclosure and had blocked reform. Pointing out these obvious truths did not go down well with many Parliamentary colleagues, some of whom were fighting for their political lives. The retribution that came was brutal, but uneven. For every Member of Parliament who has gone to jail, there are others who are lucky not to have done. When the storm broke, the Parliamentary club huddled together in a paralysis of trauma. Recalling the nicknames that had sometimes been given to Parliaments in the past, I suggested at one PMQs that we might be remembered as the Moat Parliament or the Manure Parliament. Nobody laughed.

Yet there was something pathetic about an expenses scandal. For a whole variety of reasons – not least, the existence of an independent and impartial civil service – although there were some black spots, British government had a deserved reputation for propriety, certainly by international standards. The effect of the Parliamentary expenses scandal was to put this reputation at risk and to play into the hands of those (including those in the press) who peddled various brands of anti-politics. This is why it was both serious and pathetic at the same time – lacking the kind of systemic corruption familiar elsewhere, all we could provide was a scandal of MPs fiddling their expenses. Yet this was no less damaging to the reputation of the political system.

However, acting on the principle that a crisis is too good an opportunity to waste, it seemed to me that here was a moment when it might be possible to achieve some serious Parliamentary reform. All the party leaders were busily trying to out-bid each other in their zeal for political reforms of assorted kinds, in a desperate attempt to show the electorate that they had learned the lessons of the expenses scandal. The fact that many of the proposed reforms (such as changing the electoral system) had nothing at all to do with the scandal of MPs behaving badly did not seem to matter.

It was against the backdrop of this frenetic atmosphere that in June 2009 I wrote to Gordon Brown – by then Prime Minister – suggesting a way forward on political reform. Among my suggestions was a proposal for a 'new special committee on Parliamentary Reform, composed of authoritative reform-minded Members, set up for a defined period only, and with a mandate to come forward quickly with reform proposals'. I cited the need for the House of Commons to control more of its own business and to elect its select committees. I received no reply to this letter, although both Jack Straw and Harriet Harman (to whom I had sent copies) were enthusiastic.

Shortly afterwards Gordon Brown made a statement in the House announcing a raft of political reforms. As he rose to speak, Jack Straw came over and asked if anybody had told me that, as part of the package, Gordon was going to announce the government's support for my proposal and that I was to chair the reform committee. Of course, nobody had told me, but I was delighted nevertheless. It even made me wonder if I should have written to Gordon (and his predecessor) on assorted matters previously.

I knew the committee would have to move quickly before the fleeting window of reform opportunity opened up by the expenses scandal started to close again, which is why I insisted that it should be required to report by the end of the Parliamentary session in November. There had, uniquely, been elections held for places on the committee, and this had produced a strong core of reformers from all parties. We worked at a frenetic pace to produce a report by the date we had been set. This was made easier by the fact that the reform agenda was well-rehearsed, and some of us had been advancing it for a long time; what had been lacking previously was the political will and opportunity to make it happen. At its centre was an argument about the need to shift the balance between Parliament and government if Parliament was to become a more vital institution. It could now also be argued, in the face of the expenses scandal, that this might help to repair the damage that had been done to the institution's reputation.

In practical terms, we proposed a mechanism for enabling the House to take control of its own business, thereby breaking the total grip of the executive, and another for electing the chairs and members of select committees, to end the nonsense of scrutiny committees being appointed by those they were supposed to be scrutinising. These were the fundamental reforms from which many others could flow. One or two members of our committee also saw this as an opportunity to ride their own hobby horses. For example, Chris Mullin mounted a genial but tenacious campaign to get a recommendation that the Commons should sit in September, as he thought the summer recess was outrageously long. I suggested that, on the model of the 'Baker Days' in schools, we might perhaps call these September sittings 'Mullin Days' and that Chris (who was to retire) might send postcards from exotic places each September to his former colleagues.

In our report, rather portentously called *Rebuilding the House* (see pages 195–202), we said that the House of Commons was 'going through a crisis of confidence not experienced in our lifetimes', but that this also offered 'a rare window of opportunity'. In normal times our proposals would almost certainly have met organised resistance from the party machines, but these were emphatically not normal times. There was a little skirmishing, but the momentum behind the report ensured that it was accepted by the House. Not for the first time, a scandal had been a trigger for reform. One of the last acts of a discredited House of Commons was to lay the basis for a very different kind of Commons in the future, if it took full advantage of the instruments it now held in its hands. There are already some positive indications that this is beginning to happen.

In personal terms, I could not have wished for a more satisfying legacy. Long-standing health problems had caught up with me and I had announced a couple of years previously that I would be standing down at the next election. It was an unexpected bonus to spend the final months of my Parliamentary career in the intense activity of a reform enterprise that promised much for the future. Jack Straw was kind enough to say in the House, on the last day of the last Parliament, that I had been 'a paradigm of the best of the Members of this House who have shown that it is possible, by assiduity and imagination, to be profoundly influential from the back benches, on either side'. If that is even a little true, then it may perhaps offer encouragement to others.

‡

One of the many interesting observations in Tony Blair's memoir, *A Journey*, is his view of what it means to be a professional politician. 'To the professional politician,' he writes, 'every waking moment is, in part or in whole, defining. To them [*sic*], the landscape of politics is perpetually illuminated, and a light which is often harsh shines on a terrain that bristles with highs and lows of ambition, risk and fulfilment. They are in a constant fret about what may befall them as they navigate it.' This reminds me of the extent to which I was not a professional politician, and what a disability that was. Yet it captures, precisely and honestly, what the world inhabited by the professional politician is like. In this world everything is political. Every event, however trivial, is interpreted in terms of its political significance. Life inside this political bubble is so intense and enclosed that it can be difficult to understand how different it is from the world outside. One letter from a constituent (at the time of the shocking Baby P case that provoked intense public anger) made the point exactly: 'I don't normally get involved in the goings-on in the world, as we can't normally do anything about it but grumble and get on with life.' That, I suspect, gets pretty close to the typical British political sensibility, notwithstanding any episodic excitements. If politicians understood this better, they might be less inclined to get in a frenzy about the next headline and focus more on doing some durable good.

This also provokes some reflections on how the political world has changed in the past half century or so, since the time when I first started taking an active interest in it. There are at least two senses in which it has become much more professionalised. First, many more of the participants are people whose only career has been politics, which increases their relentless focus on the activity itself (and on their career prospects within it). This may be inevitable, but it is nevertheless striking (as is the almost total disappearance of the working class from the House of Commons). It also raises the prospect of a separate political class in which the leading players look and sound very much like each other, with its attendant dangers and disabilities. Such people may not have much experience either of real life or of running anything. All they know about is politics. It was Aristotle who identified the importance in politics of knowing 'where the shoe pinches'. It is one thing to learn about something; but quite different to feel it. The direct pressure of feeling was once strong in the House of Commons, but it is much less tangible now. One antidote may be to nourish another class of non-professional politicians to undertake the task of scrutiny and accountability that is indispensable to good government. This is a particular issue for Westminster politics, which fuses executive and legislative power. A more radical solution would be to consider whether there may now even be a case for trying to separate out these powers more.

There is a second respect in which the professionalisation of politics has advanced. The activity of politics is an inextricable mixture of high purpose and low cunning (or, at some times and in some places, of low purpose and high cunning). It is both deeply serious and a kind of game, purposeful and puerile at the same time, a combination which can give rise to confusion and disillusion (as well as to comedies like *The Thick of It*, which – unlike *The West Wing* – see only the game). Politics is now played with techniques of marketing and manipulation undeveloped a generation ago. It takes place inside a media bubble of round-the-clock 'news' that demands an unceasing war of position and rebuttal. Politicians who are good at this game (and look and speak the part) will prosper; others will not. An exemplary figure like Clement Attlee – a bald little man, of whom it was said that he would never use one word when none would do – would not get a look in now. This seems to me a serious loss.

Then there is the much-reported decline of trust in politicians over recent decades, which began long before the Parliamentary expenses scandal, which just served to make it a whole lot worse. We have to be careful here, though. There was no golden age. As Trollope wrote of politics in the middle of the nineteenth century: 'It is the trade of the opponent to attack, it is the trade of the newspaper to be indignant, it is the trade of the minister to defend; and the world looks on believing none of them.' There certainly used to be more deference, but that is not the same as trust. What there was, though, was much more secrecy; and it is doubtful that many of the commanding political leaders of the past (Gladstone? Lloyd George? Churchill?) could have long survived the kind of intense and intimate scrutiny that now goes with the territory. This is the paradox of transparency. When more is exposed to scrutiny (to increase trust), there is inevitably more to be concerned about (which diminishes trust). The result is that although political standards are almost certainly higher than they once were, and political conduct much more tightly regulated than it ever was, this has been accompanied by an erosion of trust.

Perhaps we now live in a post-trust age in a wider cultural sense. This is good if it produces a sceptical questioning of received wisdom and those who purvey it; but not good if it means a default position of cynicism and contempt. There are sections of the British media – nicely described as 'junk journalism' by Chris Mullin – that, engaged in a desperate race to the bottom, have given up on any serious civic role and pump out a daily diet of contempt for politics and politicians, as well as much general unpleasantness. Equally, alas, bile seems to be the default setting of much of the blogosphere. The sneer has replaced the argument. What is at issue here is not party bias – although that remains strong – but bias against politics itself. It is difficult to be sure about cause and effect, but it is likely that such a relentless onslaught of negativity and cynicism will make its malign influence felt. Wherever it comes from – from old media or new – the lazy rant against politicians and all their works just feeds the malevolent forces of anti-politics.

What is clear is that, compared with the post-war period, participation in the formal political system has declined sharply. After the 2001 general election I wrote a piece for *The Guardian* in which I said that during the election I could 'smell civic death in the air'. In 2010 there was relief that the turnout figure managed to reach a less than glorious 65 per cent, higher than the miserable figure of the previous two elections but almost 20 per cent lower than the first election of my lifetime sixty years previously – and this despite the prospect of a change of government and the boost from the first-ever televised debates between the party leaders. Millions of people have turned their back on even a minimum engagement with the formal civic realm. Generational change has produced a seismic decline in voting as a basic civic duty. The fall in party membership, and of identification with parties, is part of the same story. Only a politics of anti-politics is on the rise.

There is much debate about why this has happened (and whether it is offset by other forms of participation) and what possible remedies there might be. There are many favourite nostrums, but no agreed answers. In some ways what has happened is surprising, just as it might seem surprising that the general expansion of education and prosperity has resulted in a coarsening of language and behaviour rather than a gentle civilising of the population. Perhaps it is just easier being a satisfied consumer than a dissatisfied citizen. The internet brought the promise of a reinvigorated democracy, opening up the political arena with expanded participation and new transparency, but its transforming effects have not (so far) included the rejuvenation of our representative institutions. Then there is the blunting of the old ideological antagonisms that propelled many people (including me) into political activity; but these have been blunted for a reason and will not benefit from a process of artificial re-sharpening.

It is sometimes suggested that in a globalised world many issues are simply too far away for people to get a political purchase on, even if they wanted to. When Tony Crosland wrote his celebrated *The Future of Socialism* in 1956, he could say in the preface that he was not going to discuss anything beyond these shores. This would seem ludicrous now, when so much power on so many fronts lies elsewhere. As John Major rather plaintively put it in his memoir: 'Governments can cajole, entice or plead, but they can no longer control.' Bankers say they will go elsewhere if they are made to pay for the financial crisis, so financial regulation is only effective if it is international; climate change is inherently global. Even institutions like the European Union that are designed to get to grips with unaccountable global power are met with the charge (certainly in Britain) that they usurp a mythical national sovereignty. If the big issues (and the big power) really have gone elsewhere, it might seem rational for the domestic political space to contract. Except that the local and global sit together, and we have to get a political handle on both. Nor is this a new problem. Delivering newspapers one morning in 1962 before going to school, at the height of the Cuban missile crisis, the headline in the *Daily Telegraph* (the only *Telegraph* on my round, delivered to a gloomy bungalow) proclaimed: 'World on the Brink.' I remember thinking that I might not be able to come home that day as the world could be destroyed by nuclear warfare while I was at school. We required politics to save us then, and it is no less needed to save us now. Yet politics has to be able to show that it matters, that it can make a difference on the big issues and bring unaccountable power to heel, or people will increasingly give up on it and just cultivate their own gardens.

It may be that the kind of politics that dominated the twentieth century – with its roots in mass parties, organising ideologies and representative institutions – is in the process of being replaced by something else. The academic John Keane has recently coined the term 'monitory democracy' to describe this new dispensation. In this view, politics increasingly becomes the preserve of a class of professional politicians, sustaining themselves with all the techniques now at their disposal, and their activities are watched over by a network of scrutiny bodies of various kinds, both official and unofficial. There seems to me to be a good deal of truth in this description and there are many worse ways of doing politics. If we nevertheless feel uneasy about it – and what it means for representative democracy and democratic citizenship – then we had better try to do something about it.

It is not a matter of dumping representative democracy, as antiquated and irrelevant, but of making it work better. It has to become richer and thicker. Just giving someone a vote every few years and letting the politicians get on with it is not an adequate model for a mature democracy. Nor does it have to be, now that the contents of the democratic toolkit are so enlarged, offering new opportunities for communication and involvement. This is a challenge for our political institutions, but also for the conduct of our politics as a whole, which can itself be democratised.

We could start by doing politics in a rather different way. Even as a participant I was turned off by the ritual name-calling and reflex adversarialism that too often passes for political debate, so it is not surprising if the electorate is. The routine predictability of political exchanges (conducted in their own sterile language) is depressing. As Anthony King once remarked: 'Anyone switching on the radio in the morning, however blearily, can instantly tell whether the person being interviewed is a politician or not.' There is plenty to argue about – including big questions about the state and the market – but just playing the old tribal games does not help us very much. Honest grown-up argument that does not just involve trotting out a party line would be a tonic for our politics. I have long been a political reformer (and still am), but have become convinced that unless we learn to do politics differently, then merely institutional reforms will not work. This is emphatically not an argument for consensus, but it is an argument for some intellectual (and political) honesty.

Politics in Britain is already changing, rapidly and unexpectedly, as a result of the 2010 election. Old truths (about the first-past-the-post electoral system delivering majority governments and about the British not liking coalitions) have turned out to be convenient fictions. A new sort of politics is in the making, and people seem to like it (though this is not the same as liking what it does). The political world is turned upside down; what seemed like a temporary arrangement of political necessity begins to look like a durable alteration in the British way of doing politics. In the plural politics of coalition, differences are acknowledged and negotiated (posing a challenge for a media culture that lives off discovering 'splits' and exposing 'U-turns'). Manifesto promises become bargaining positions. Politics becomes more fluid and less monolithic.

None of this was planned. It happened because the electoral system could no longer prop up a party system eroded by a more fragmented electorate. For as long as the first-past-the-post electoral system produced a majority, its lack of proportionality could be overlooked on the grounds that it delivered a government that could govern and a clear line of accountability (in Bagehot's memorable phrase, a form of rule that was 'come-at-able'). Once this was no longer the case, then this intellectual support necessarily fell away. It used to be argued that electoral reform would be required to make politics change; it is now argued that it is *because* politics has changed that electoral reform is needed. Despite the emphatic rejection by referendum of the Alternative Vote in 2011, this argument is unlikely to go away. Parties doing business with each other, co-operating as well as competing, begins to feel like the norm rather than the exception. There is a real opportunity in all of this to do politics very differently.

Yet none of this will matter ultimately if the purpose of politics is forgotten, or the activity becomes so disparaged or neglected that it ceases to perform its democratic function. Some of the most profound aspects of life have nothing to do with politics: 'How small, of all that human hearts endure, that part that laws or kings can cause or cure', as Dr Johnson put it. We should protect ourselves from the political obsessive (as I undoubtedly once was) and keep politics away from those parts of life where it does not belong. Yet when all this is said and done, the fact remains that politics is the place where a society grapples with its common concerns – and that place needs to be kept in a good state of repair.

That requires us to be citizens, not just consumers. This was the classical ideal of an engagement with public affairs – the realm of *res publica* – that naturally sat alongside the world of private, family and business concerns. That is what a citizen did. Not to take an interest in public matters was not to be a fully rounded human being. It was an abdication of social responsibility not to be prepared to share the burden of public office. We could decide to give up on all this, to retreat into our own gratifications and the satisfactions of the market, and contract out the public realm to somebody else – some think that is what is happening now and what the culture of our times encourages – but this means giving up on the continuing public conversation about the nature of a good society and the terms on which we live together that politics enables us to have.

It is this conversation that sits behind all the immediate issues that provide the daily diet of political argument – all the taxing and spending decisions and all the policy choices – and gives them context and meaning. Michael Foot wrote of Aneurin Bevan that he 'converted the small change of politics into large principles', and that is what political leadership should endeavour to do. Too often we seem just to have the small change, with the large principles wheeled out only for special occasions; making the connection, in a way that is authentic, is the real political challenge.

Governing is tough, and in many ways it has become much tougher. It is not surprising that politicians often express frustration (as Tony Blair did in his 'feral beasts' speech) with a climate of commentary that suggests all problems are straight-forward and only politicians' idiocy prevents them being tackled. The more complicated truth is that many problems are intractable; and that policy frequently involves adopting a least-worst course of action. This is not something that newspaper editors or academics have to face up to; but it is what politicians have signed up for. However, they do not help themselves, or the intelligent conduct of politics, by playing the game of pretending that they have all the right answers or that their political opponents have all the wrong ones.

The pressures at the top of politics are now relentless, making it difficult (but ever more necessary) to carve out a strategic space in which directions can be set and stuck to. The days of Harold Macmillan taking to his bed with a Trollope in the afternoon are, sadly, long gone. At the same time, the old solidarities that structured life in the early post-war period – war, class, work, community, behaviour, family and faith – have weakened and fragmented. The social underpinnings of collective life have become badly frayed. As a constituency Member of Parliament, this was brought home to me on a daily basis. People turn to the state because somebody has to pick up the pieces, but it can only do so inadequately. David Cameron's 'big society' is offered as a response to this; although it is difficult to see how his 'broken society' provides the materials for it. When I went to visit a little Baptist chapel in my constituency that was celebrating its centenary, I was told how it had been built by miners in a matter of weeks. They came up from the pit at the end of their shift and got on with building their chapel. This is the kind collective self-help that really does represent a big society.

There is wide agreement that some fundamental rethinking is required, but less consensus on which political traditions can best contribute to this. Neither the state nor the market has covered itself in recent glory. As yet it is unclear what the new solidarities that provide the basis for collective action (and political choice) might be, or how they might be formed. The daily political knockabout goes on, and there is no shortage of issues to fight about, but at the same time there is an absence of any kind of theory that can provide the basis for a new political direction to fit the condition in which we now find ourselves. We should be honest about this, rather than pretending that old certainties are still intact, and in an open and enquiring way set about the task of remedying the deficiency. Unless we are content for politics to revert to a mere game between the Ins and

Outs of a political class – which for my generation it was not – the need for the kind of intellectual reconstruction that can frame political choices is both necessary and urgent.

What is clear, though, is that we want good people to take an active part in political life (there are plenty of bad people who will always want to). It seems to me that far too little attention is paid to the process of political recruitment that provides the small class of professional politicians from which governments are drawn. We could start by deciding what we think 'good' means – in terms of competence and experience, certainly, but also (and perhaps especially) of integrity and judgement – and then make sure that there is a party (and public) recruitment process that properly tests this, weeding out the worst kind of political careerist. It is hard – probably too hard – to remove politicians once they are in, just as it is difficult for the public to know what politicians are really like or what they get up to. In my experience some of the very best people (in all senses) are to be found in political life; but also some others (many fewer, fortunately) who could not really be safely trusted to walk a dog. The mystery is not how the latter were elected, but how they were selected. How we get politicians, and how we get rid of them, should be taken much more seriously than it currently is.

This takes us back to Tony Blair. At the end of his memoir he declares his belief that 'the way we run Westminster or Whitehall today is just not effective in a twenty-first-century world'. That is worth listening to, coming from a long-serving Prime Minister. Then he goes on to say that 'the debate … focuses exclusively on the issues of honesty, transparency and accountability as if it were a character problem. It isn't. It's an efficiency problem.' The trouble with this is that good government is about efficiency *and* integrity, exercising power as well as holding power to account – good government requires good accountability. These dual responsibilities should not be seen as alternatives, as they too often are, but as the indispensable constituents of a well-functioning polity. If Tony Blair had seen this more clearly, instead of just being irritated and frustrated by what he saw as distracting process issues, then he may have avoided some of his more obvious difficulties.

There will never be a shortage of politicians (though there may be a shortage of good ones). Far more serious is the need to ensure a culture of democratic citizenship that makes everyone, in some sense, a citizen-politician. This is the only real antidote to the development of a separate political class. It requires a vibrant civic culture, a sustained and continuous civic conversation; yet what we have is much closer to a civic crisis. The causes go deep, and are not confined to this country, but there are specific features of the British political tradition – the top-down adversarialism, a fragile public realm, an enfeebled Parliament, an unrepresentative electoral system, weak local democracy, a corrosive media culture – that have contributed to the malaise. Each will need to be remedied if the civic tradition is to be reconstructed.

It is in the nature of citizenship that it has to be regularly practised if it is to be kept in good condition. Inactivity soon produces atrophy. That is why it is worth exploring ways in which opportunities for democratic involvement can be enlarged and a culture of citizenship nourished. The alternative is to leave the activity of politics to a professional political class and to settle for the role of subject-consumer. This would be to abandon a whole conception of what it means to be a citizen. The writer Raymond Williams once said that 'culture is ordinary'. In a healthy democracy doing politics would be ordinary too, which is how it seemed to me when I first encountered it, those many years ago.

PART TWO

WRITING ABOUT
DOING POLITICS

What follows is a selection of pieces I have written over the years – before, during and after my time in the House of Commons. Each bears in some way on the activity of politics and reflects what I have thought about, observed and – on occasion – taken part in. In putting them together, I have come to see how my writings combine a belief in the indispensable value of politics with a profound dissatisfaction with the way it is usually conducted. It has become a wearisome cliché to espouse a 'new politics', but that has, nevertheless, been my running theme.

This should not be misunderstood, however. It certainly does not mean a bloodless kind of politics. When The Times *said, on my departure from the Commons, that I 'always put the interests of the House above tribal politics', it was not entirely accurate. My political origins were fiercely tribal and, when faced with the kind of rosy-cheeked public schoolboy who assumes he is born to rule, I can effortlessly lapse into the most unworthy and unseemly tribalism. But it is the bogus point-scoring partisanship, the ritual posturing and positioning that is really only a political game, that turns normal people away from politics altogether, and this must not be confused with the clash of ideas, values and interests that is the real stuff of politics. It is the former that I have railed against. If politics is about conflict and competition, it is also about compromise and co-operation. One without the other (as in the United States at present) is a formula for disaster.*

Nor should a new politics be identified with various kinds of mechanical fixes to the political system. Institutions matter and procedural reforms can be useful, but they are not a panacea, as the briefest glance around the world demonstrates. The fact that the young people massacred in Norway in 2011 were at a political summer camp suggests a democracy in vibrant health; yet the country has recently been lamenting its political malaise. I am a political reformer, and a range of reforms are discussed in the pieces here, but that makes it even more necessary to say that, in my view, what really matters is how politics is done. This emphasis on the culture of politics was the theme of the Political Quarterly *annual lecture I delivered in 2009 when I was introduced to the lecture audience by my old friend Peter Hennessy.*

Doing Politics Differently

I am taken back to a summer evening, about twenty years ago, when Peter and I were on a boat moored on the Westminster embankment to celebrate the publication of a book by Ben Pimlott, our much-missed friend. Peter asked what I was up to. I told him that I had just been selected as the Labour Parliamentary candidate in a winnable seat. His reaction is forever etched in my memory. 'Oh you poor boy,' he exclaimed. 'Just make sure you get yourself on a select committee; then it won't be quite so bad.' I have followed Peter's advice, and it has not been so bad.

Peter clearly thought I was wholly ill-equipped ever to run

anything, and this is a view that has since been shared by others. When, in the early days, I read in a newspaper that Peter Mandelson had said of me, 'He thinks too much', I realised the true worth of the other Peter's advice. During my first week in the House of Commons, I was stopped in the members' cloakroom by Donald Dewar, also much missed. He wanted to offer me some advice. 'Don't fall into the John Mackintosh trap,' he said. John Mackintosh was the academic Labour MP, elected in 1966, also an editor of the *Political Quarterly*, who died too early. I asked what that trap was. 'People thought,' replied Donald, 'that he was only here so that he could write a second edition of his book on the British Cabinet.' This was good advice, but I fear that I did not altogether manage to follow it.

My original intention was to call this lecture 'In Defence of Politicians'; however, this was vetoed by the organising committee as too implausible. But let me briefly tell you what I had in mind, as it leads to where I want to go. I had hoped that my old patron Bernard Crick would be here, and it is very sad his recent death means that he is not. Bernard's brilliant book, *In Defence of Politics*, had a huge and lasting impact on me (as it has done on so many others) when I first read it as a student forty years ago. It was both a compelling argument for the centrality of politics as a civilising activity (in his words, 'a great and civilising human activity ... something to be valued almost as a pearl beyond price in the history of the human condition') and a warning about the kinds of people, doctrines and forces that threatened this activity. I wanted to tease Bernard by suggesting that the defence of politics necessarily involved also, but less obviously or appealingly, the defence of politicians.

I mean, of course, politicians as a category, not individual politicians, or the way politicians do politics; not politicians who abuse power, or tell lies, or use public money for private purposes. But if we want to defend politics, then we do have to defend politicians. The class of people is intrinsic to the activity. It is possible to say that you like football but do not like footballers; but it is not possible to defend politics without, in some sense, defending politicians. I absolutely do not mean, by the way, that politics is, or should be, the preserve of professional politicians. As Crick argued, politics is what citizens do. We badly need to expand the arenas in which citizenship can be practised. But when all this is said, the fact is that political systems require politicians.

It is sometimes said that there are two kinds of politicians: those who want to exercise power and those who want to control the exercise of power. Both are essential, though one tends to be regarded as nobler than the other. It is because I have specialised in the latter – the noble world of scrutiny and accountability – that I want to emphasise the importance of the former. It is easier to ask questions than to answer them, and easier to hold to account than to exercise responsibility. That is why I come to defend politicians, in all their forms.

Somebody has to do it. Somebody has to take on the messy business of accommodating conflicting demands and interests, choosing between competing options, negotiating unwelcome trade-offs, and bear the responsibility for decisions that may often represent the least bad course of action (like bailing out banks). This does not have to be done by pressure groups, or by newspaper columnists, or by professors, or by voters. But somebody has to do it, and that somebody is politicians. They give voice to our hopes, but they also – inevitably – feed our disappointments. This is so, even if their name is Obama.

This is why I am suspicious of all those – even some of the enthusiasts for greater citizen participation – who seem to argue that all will be well if only the political class is somehow cleared out of the way. This line of reasoning unites the *Daily Mail* and Monbiot. At bottom, this is a version of the anti-politics that infects our age, and which a certain sort of newspaper serves up daily to malign effect. Their message is that all problems are simple and only the fact that politicians are knaves or fools (or both) prevents solutions. It is not surprising, as the latest survey commissioned by the Committee on Standards in Public Life shows, that it is the readers of such newspapers who are most cynical about politics and politicians. I do not know why the Prime Minister decided that the editor of the *Daily Mail* was the most appropriate person to conduct a review of the thirty-year rule. But it is surely beyond parody that Mr Dacre should introduce his review by lamenting 'a corrosion of … trust between politicians and people over the past few years' and expressing a hope that his review will help create 'a more mature democracy in which there is a greater trust between the electors and the elected'. It is scarcely surprising, given the cultural force of anti-politics, that we have disappearing voters and collapsing trust. Anyway, that is the lecture I am *not* going to deliver.

I am going to be critical of some of the ways in which we do politics, which contribute to our difficulties; but because of this I want to insert a little perspective. Most of the issues we face here – from declining voter turnout to how we manage our public services – are mirrored elsewhere. On international surveys of 'good governance' like those conducted by the World Bank and others, we are in the premier league, about mid-table, behind the Scandinavians. It is also worth recalling that thirty years ago the British political system, for so long seen as an exemplar of stable constitutionalism, was being widely described as a basket case of ungovernability, 'a country on the verge of political breakdown' as one leading political scientist put it. So whatever criticisms are made now, they are of a very different order from a generation before. Even the much-discussed decline in trust has to be set against the fact that distrust of politicians is nothing new; that standards of conduct are now exposed to a transparency that reveals what was formerly concealed; that there is now a whole regulatory apparatus surrounding standards that was entirely absent until relatively recently.

So in many respects we *are* doing politics differently. There is much less voting, much less joining of parties and much less activity within parties. The hollowing out of formal politics has been replaced, in part, by the rise of informal politics, but also by a professionalisation of the political process. Members of Parliament now promote themselves to their constituents using public money that they have voted to give to themselves for this purpose. Experience of life and work is no longer seen as the pathway to politics, just early apprenticeship to the political class. There is a permanent election campaign, with parties fighting a daily (even hourly) war of position in the voracious media environment. New technology enables new sorts of campaigning. My own moment of epiphany in this respect was on a visit to Washington a few years ago, when a young Conservative MP in our group announced that he had just e-mailed a third of his constituents before breakfast.

What his constituents thought about this is another matter. By the way, I had it explained to me the other day that when we MPs ask – on the leaflets paid for by taxpayers – for the views of our electors on issues of concern, it is really in order to acquire their e-mail addresses. There are now political trade journals dedicated to the art of campaigning. The impression is that of the triumph of process over product.

Of course, the context of politics has changed in even more fundamental ways in recent times. We have become more constitutionalised. Together, membership of the European Union and the introduction of the Human Rights Act have severely dented the traditional Westminster model. Devolution has transformed territorial politics and created a kind of quasi-federalism. The result of all this has not been a new constitutional settlement, but a sense of movement without destination – what Anthony King has called 'a new constitutional unsettlement'.

If we wanted to do politics *very* differently, there are plenty of models to choose from. For example, a separation of powers would transform the relationship between executive and legislature. With or without a directly elected executive, if ministers appointed officials the nature of our political process would radically change. A different kind of electoral system would produce a more pluralistic and coalition-building kind of politics. A written constitution would constrict the realm of politics and politicians and enlarge the realm of law and judges. My point is not to recommend, or reject, such proposals; merely to observe that politics would be done very differently if proposals of this kind were adopted. But if they were adopted, it would mean that something pretty extraordinary had already happened to our politics.

This brings me, at last, to my main theme: the relationship between structures and cultures in politics. In particular, I want to ask if we do politics in the way we do because of the political structures we have, or whether we have the political structures because of our particular kind of political culture. In turn, this leads to the question of whether, if we want to do politics differently, this is a cultural project or an institutional one (or both). I realise I shall disappoint those who think that the remedy for all our political ills is their favoured set of institutional reforms – to the electoral system, say, or to the House of Lords. I do not believe this is the answer, even if I favour the particular reforms. For example, there is dismal evidence that more proportional voting systems do not increase voter participation, and I am baffled by the logic that holds that a disinclination to vote at eighteen is to be remedied by votes at sixteen. There are, alas, no magic bullets.

A couple of years ago I met an engaging politician in the United States who had represented downtown Boston for the Democrats for over thirty years, and in that time had seen off all opposition. 'When I was starting out,' he said, 'I campaigned under the slogan "Give Youth a Chance". Now my campaign slogan is "There is No Substitute for Experience".' His uninterrupted tenure had been secured by his ability to ensure that electoral districts were drawn in a way that protected his vote. When it was put to him that in Britain this practice would be regarded as unfair and undemocratic, and was done by an independent commission, he said that he had heard of this crazy idea, which would certainly never be adopted while he was Speaker of the State Senate. This is both culture and structure. Usually this story is told differently – presenting a civic energy in the United States (first identified by Tocqueville) that contrasts with a world-weary entropy here. As Ferdinand Mount puts it in his recent memoir: 'What I brought back from America was not anything resembling a new idea, what I brought back was the habit of optimism.' Culture and structure again. That is why some years ago Jonathan Freedland wanted to 'Bring the Revolution Home', but it was unclear whether this was a cultural revolution or an institutional one.

But why should we want to do politics differently anyway? Let me remind you of some of the ways in which we do politics now. A government proposes something; this is automatically opposed by the official opposition; and the minority parties also oppose it, but on different grounds from the official opposition. This adversarial pantomime is played out in the Commons then on our television screens, as the rival talking heads repeat the scripted battle lines. Meanwhile, viewers and voters yearn for a proper conversation among grown-ups. Each side, every day, seeks to press its own narrative of events. Currently this is 'The crisis is a global one and Gordon Brown is leading the world in sorting it out' versus 'Gordon Brown promised an end to boom and bust and he is directly responsible for the mess we are in.' The more that the ideological territory on which the parties compete has narrowed, the more vigorously synthetic becomes the battle. I once heard Tony Blair tell a private meeting of senior civil servants that they should understand that any government would face the same problems and the same range of solutions; but this was the same Tony Blair who would return to the Commons to rally his troops with apocalyptic versions of the party dividing lines.

There is now a complete mismatch between the party tribalism that dominates Westminster politics and what has happened to the world outside. What happens at Westminster looks increasingly like an old kind of party game played in a time bubble. And it is a game. That is why it is now largely recorded only by sketch writers; and why the BBC's dutiful reporting of Parliament does not quite know whether to play it straight or to interpret the game. Part of the game, of course, is the stultifying tendency for all differences of expression, however trivial, to be reported as 'splits'; and all policy changes as 'U-turns'.

It also means that consensus is always elusive. The daily war of position prevents it. Every issue – even, as in the Baby P case, the death of a child – has to be fed into the adversarial mill. Belief in consensus is sometimes proclaimed, but only as a drunk occasionally affirms a belief in sobriety. It endures only until the next drink, or the next political opportunity. Thus, consensus on the banking crisis lasted for about forty-eight hours, and the calls for some kind of political coming together in the face of economic emergency are destined to remain unanswered. Consensus is not always desirable, but conflicts should be *real* ones, and on issue after issue progress is prevented by the habitual politics of disagreement. 'Conflict where necessary, agreement where possible' should be the watchword. Instead, we have conflict where possible, agreement only where unavoidable.

But there is another aspect of how we do politics that has, perhaps, even more serious consequences. It can be seen in action every day in the House of Commons, where ministers are required to answer for everything that happens in every street in the land – from every bus service to every crime to every school. Answers are provided and actions are promised. Ministerial responsibility requires no less. It is, of course, a governing conceit, but its effect is to suck ever more power to an already over-extended centre. If ministers are going to be held accountable for everything, then it is not surprising if they want to control all those things for which they are going to have to answer. Nor is it surprising that there are then complaints that when levers are frantically pulled at the centre, nothing much seems to happen down the line. This spiral of centralism, with all its consequences, is intrinsic to how we do politics.

We arrive, therefore, at our current position, in a disaggregated world of agencies, quangos, agreements, contracts, partnerships and all the rest of the modern governing toolkit where people no longer know who provides the services on which they depend and so just hold 'the government' responsible for everything. At the same time, public antipathy to our old friend the 'postcode lottery' means that governments are pressed to ensure that the same service is available to everybody, wherever they live.

This takes us back to cultures and structures. It is familiar to describe the British political system in terms of a strong central executive, giving considerable power to a governing majority with few formal checks and balances. This has frequently been commented upon by foreign observers accustomed to more elaborate constitutional arrangements. A recent US ambassador to this country has described how he 'kept looking for constitutional checks and institutional balances that could stay the will of a British government. But I could find none.' So far, so familiar. The question is whether a political system of this kind is an authentic expression of the British political culture; or whether the political culture has been formed and nourished by a particular set of governing arrangements.

Here is how the *Guardian* journalist Hugo Young once described the British view of democratic politics: 'The British do not passionately care about democracy. As long as they get a vote every few years and the children don't starve, they are prepared to put up with almost anything politicians throw at them... This preference, which is for strong government over accountable government, is to be found throughout the British Parliamentary system.' In some ways this echoes what R. H. Tawney once wrote about how Britain 'went to the ballot-box touching her hat'. For Young this was a fact; for Tawney a challenge. But is it right? And what does it tell us about the relationship between culture and structure?

There is certainly a striking congruity between this stripped-down understanding of democracy – the alleged preference for strong government over accountable government – and the institutional underpinnings of British politics. There is an electoral system that only poorly represents the public, but which delivers governments and clearly identifies who the rascals are. There is an absence of significant checks and balances and of formal constitutional frameworks. Some would say there is a carelessness about liberty – although it is a very one-eyed kind of liberalism that does not recognise that threats to liberty can come from places other than the State, and that people look to the State to protect them from such threats. There is a capacity for strong and untrammelled executive action in the British system, most evident of all in moments of crisis: at the outset of the banking crisis, while the US Congress met night and day before a rescue package was agreed, in this country government acted and Parliament was not even sitting to hear what had been decided.

However, the fact that there might seem to be a strong link between culture and structure in our politics does not tell us about causation. All we know is that there is some kind of fit. There is our particular history, of course, in which the prerogative power of monarchs was transferred without decisive interruption to the hands of elected executives. There is also the fact that dominant traditions on both the left and right in Britain for most of the twentieth century have preferred strong government – the left because it delivered state power for progressive purposes; the right because it was the guarantor of order and authority. This is our inheritance, but that need not mean that we are forever imprisoned by it. Cultures and structures can change. At least at the level of rhetoric, there is now a professed desire on all sides to do politics differently. Even though eyes understandably glaze over at the mention of a 'new politics' or a 'new localism', and words like 'empowerment' and 'engagement' atrophy in politician-speak, something is in the air. Left and right compete for this new political territory. Its institutional shape remains undefined, but there is, perhaps, a sense of a political project in the making.

We are a long way, though, from those intense and rich debates about the State and democracy that were conducted in the early part of the twentieth century, which prefigured a very different kind of institutional landscape. These arguments deserve re-reading now, especially those between the Fabian old guard of the Webbs and the young Turks of guild socialism led by G. D. H. Cole. I was much influenced by Cole, who argued that representation had to be 'specific and functional' not 'general and inclusive'. Parliament was the worst offender against this principle since it 'professes to represent all the citizens in all things, and therefore as a rule represents none of them in anything'. An immersion in the ideas of Cole was not an ideal preparation for being a Member of Parliament. But these ideas were hugely influential in their time. Thus Clement Attlee, the architect of post-war collectivism, declared in 1923: 'No form of society will be satisfactory that leaves the worker a wage-slave.' Although these ideas resurfaced occasionally thereafter, from the 1920s they were replaced by a dominant collectivism. Their protagonists were doubtless naïve in imagining a permanently participatory citizenry, but not wrong to want a version of democracy that was somewhat richer than a periodic ability to replace one set of rulers with another. Democracy is about culture as well as about structure, and unless there are sites where democratic citizenship can be practised and exercised we should not be surprised if a kind of civic stasis sets in. Some may think that is the condition in which we now find ourselves.

In practice cultures and structures interact, in a variety of ways. For example, the effect of freedom of information legislation was not merely to release more documents but to alter a culture of secrecy that had long been embedded in British government, and in turn to stimulate a public expectation about transparency. So we should not be content to say that politics is organised as it is in this country because that is what the political culture decrees. The relationship is much more dynamic than that, and we can do something about it, unless of course we are content with the tribalism, adversarialism, game-playing, executive dominance and top-down centralism that characterises our way of doing politics.

In a book many years ago I described this as a 'dominocracy', which I thought would catch on. It did not, which is why I am trying it again now. Even within the parameters of the plausibly possible there is much that can be done; and I want to spend the rest of my time briefly suggesting what some of this might be.

There are, perhaps, three levels of democratic government, all important. The first is the ability to kick the rascals out, the democratic bottom line and never to be underestimated. The second is the ability to kick them while they are in, in a continuous process of accountability. The third is the ability of people to contribute actively to their own self-government.

On the first level, the kicking out, we do rather well, symbolised by the brutality of the post-election removal vans in Downing Street. It is true that votes cast are not accurately matched by seats won, even occasionally that losers can win and winners lose, and that electoral outcomes are determined by a relatively small number of marginal seats. That of course is the case for electoral reform, of some kind; although it might also make the business of rascal-removing rather less straightforward (and even keep some of the rascals in office permanently). It is also true that the ability of Prime Ministers to choose the most propitious moment to go to the country can affect the result. This is the case for fixed-term Parliaments, as well as the joyous relief this would bring from endless speculation about election dates; but this was a notable (and no doubt inadvertent) omission from Gordon Brown's constitutional reform proposals.

From time to time it is announced that the process of rascal-removing has become stuck, as one party remains in power for an extended period and it seems unlikely that the main opposition party can ever put itself in a winning position again. Thus John Mackintosh could write, in 1962, just two years before Labour ended thirteen years of Conservative rule: 'It is hard to escape the conclusion that the Labour Party is unlikely to return to power and that the government of the country will remain in the hands of the Conservatives for the foreseeable future.' Similarly, in the early 1990s, distinguished academic experts on electoral trends were to be found suggesting that Britain had 'gone Japanese' and settled into a fixed pattern of Conservative one-party rule. Entirely plausible at the time, but soon followed of course by the Labour landslide of 1997. In more recent times some have wondered if the Conservatives would ever win again. But the rascals do get removed, even with a lag. If there *is* a cultural preference for governments that can govern, coupled with a periodic capacity for throwing one government out and replacing it with an alternative, then that is what people get.

The second level, that of kicking governments when they are in, raises more difficulties. Of course the media does this all the time, more or less satisfactorily. But what about our democratic political institutions? This is where we come up sharply against the executive dominance, of governments routinely in control of the House of Commons and buttressed by the tight disciplines of party, that is the hallmark of the Westminster system (even allowing for the evidence of some increased rebelliousness, and the permanent need for leaders to carry their parties with them on contentious issues). Here it seems to me that the key question is whether a system of strong government can really be balanced by a system of effective accountability. Or is it the case that the way we do politics is inevitably structured by the nature of our governing arrangements?

Those of us who want Parliament to matter more worry away endlessly about this question. We know that governments should legislate less, but better. We know that legislative scrutiny is often hurried and unsatisfactory. We know that the Commons should control more of its own business; that its select committees (and those who chair them) should not be chosen by those they are meant to be scrutinising; and that a sovereign Parliament should be able to launch its own inquiries into big issues (like the Iraq war, or the origins of the banking crisis), with proper access to persons and papers, without waiting for the government's permission. Governments need to be able to govern, and to expect to get their business, but this need not (and should not) mean that Parliament is reduced to a role of 'heckling the steamroller' as Austin Mitchell once nicely called it.

In fact, for those Members of Parliament with an eye on preferment (and that is almost everybody) it is not so much heckling as caressing. It is a funny kind of legislature in which the ambition of most members is to join the executive (or shadow executive). That is why we need to control the executive's tentacles, and we could start by reducing the number of ministers and culling Parliamentary Private Secretaries. If Attlee could manage with many fewer, then so should we. The difficulty has never been in deciding how Parliament could be strengthened, but in getting its members to summon up the political will to do anything about it. For me the most dismal moment came in 2002, when Robin Cook, as a reforming Leader of the House, proposed that the House's select committees should no longer be chosen by the whips but on a free vote, the majority voted for the whips. That is the measure of the challenge, if we are really to match strong government with effective accountability.

The role of the House of Lords is relevant here too, because in my view it has an indispensable function as a house of scrutiny. This should be the key consideration in proposals for the reform of its composition. I have always favoured a mixture of election and appointment – enough election to secure legitimacy, enough appointment to secure independence and expertise. But the very worst outcome would be a second chamber that was a clone of the first. Most people, when asked, say they favour an elected second chamber; but the same people say also that they want an independent house. These may be inconsistent preferences. Nor is it a zero-sum game in which a stronger Lords means a weaker Commons: the real task is to strengthen scrutiny in the system as a whole.

The constitutional reforms since 1997 have been important, but they have not been intended as a serious revision of executive power. Here reforms are, at best, incremental: for example, in making statistics independent of government, in freedom of information, and bringing the Prime Minister within the scrutiny of select committees. This last, by the way, was a mission of Peter Hennessy's which he passed on to me. When I first raised it I was told, on the highest authority, that it was constitutionally impossible. Then Tony Blair announced – in the same week that Robin Cook told me that the Prime Minister was never going to agree to it, so I would be well advised not to keep going on about it – that he would appear twice a year in front of the chairs of select committees, and it has now become a constitutional fixture.

That is how our system works, and it is a matter of capturing advances and bottling them, so that strong government does have to encounter stronger accountability. This is all about kicking them when they are in.

I turn, thirdly and very briefly, to the wider terrain of self-government, a deepening of democracy in which citizenship is actively practised in a variety of settings. When J. S. Mill wrote that 'participation, even in the smallest public function, is useful,' he identified this developmental character of citizenship. This is the world of micro-democracy, what Demos has called 'everyday democracy', and it is here that we need to try things out, especially in the organisation of public services. The new public management has not been matched by a new public involvement. Experience of public services will shape people's feelings about the public realm. Working-class communities used to have a rich fabric of participation in small public functions, largely through the institutions of the Labour movement, but this has now gone. We badly need to develop a new fabric, if people are to learn to do politics in settings that are close to them.

An inescapable part of this should be a vibrant system of local democracy. This is where citizenship can be practised and democratic experiments – like local referendums and neighbourhood councils – tried out. Everybody pays lip service to the need for a rejuvenated local government, with power and money and the accountability that goes with this. But it does not happen. After devolution to Scotland and Wales, England remains uniquely centralised. In a more sensible (and consensual) world we would have had a royal commission (remember those?) on the governance of England, with political agreement to act on its recommendations. That is what a real commitment to a 'new localism' would involve, if only we did politics differently.

Then we come to the matter of party. After I had given a talk to the local Rotary Club in my constituency recently, in which I had been exhorting the assembled Rotarians to throw themselves into civic life (in the spirit, say, of Joseph Chamberlain's Birmingham), someone came up to me afterwards to say that he would really like to get involved in the council but that he could never join a party. He was speaking for many others of course. The political parties are the gatekeepers of civic life, but only a tiny fraction of the population now belongs to one, or ever wants to. Fifty years ago one in eleven of the electorate belonged to a political party; today it is one in eighty-eight (or 1.14 per cent). This poses a huge challenge. We know that parties are indispensable for organising coherent political choice, but also that they can be a barrier to wider participation. I offer no solution, except to say that parties need to become very different kinds of organisation, outward- and not inward-facing; and that we should continue to explore ways in which people like my constituent can contribute to public life.

You may remember a notorious remark by Peter Mandelson, in a speech back in 1998, when he said: 'It may be that the era of pure representative democracy is coming slowly to an end.' He was denounced for seeming to suggest that representative democracy could be replaced by focus groups. In fact (and I never thought I would find myself saying this) he was wholly misrepresented. For what he went on to say was this: 'Today people want to be more involved. Representative government is being complemented by more direct forms of involvement, from the internet to referenda … Not to mention more citizens' movements, more action from pressure groups. That requires a different style of politics …' In other words, traditional representative democracy does have to be supplemented with new forms of politics if it is to be kept vigorous. For those of us who are children of the politics of the 1960s, this is our credo.

But it is supplemented, not supplanted. Here I start to come back to where I started. We have to make our representative democracy work better, not think it can somehow be replaced by something else. It cannot, for the reasons I touched on earlier when talking about the essential nature of politics, and politicians. There is undoubtedly a huge problem in our civic life currently, a real sense of malaise and disconnection. In a piece in *The Guardian* after the 2001 election I said I thought we were in a civic crisis, and I think we are. But it will not be solved by versions of anti-politics (from whatever source): that is, at best, a symptom of our difficulties.

Nor do I think that a shopping list of institutional reforms is the answer, though I support many and the committee I chair regularly suggests new ones. There is always a tendency to think that a problem can be solved by a new piece of machinery. That is why I have wanted to talk about cultures as well as structures, and why I have come to think that the former is often more decisive than the latter in terms of how organisations actually work. I am sorry if this sounds too fluffy, and insufficiently muscular, as a conclusion. But the fact is that we *can* do politics differently now, if we want to; and by doing so we could make a positive contribution to the emaciated quality of our civic life.

What might this mean? Well, politicians could play it

straight. Journalists could play it fair. Parties could resist the rise of a political class. Ministers could make sure that Cabinet government works. MPs could decide that Parliament matters (and clean up their expenses!). Interest groups could say who should have less if they are to have more. Civil servants could tell truth to power. Governments could promise less and perform more. Intellectuals could abandon their 'mechanical snigger', as Orwell called it. Social scientists could start writing in good plain English. The blogosphere could exchange rant for reason. Electors could decide to become critical citizens.

None of this requires a written constitution, a bill of rights, proportional representation, or an elected House of Lords, however desirable these might or might not be. But it does require a change of culture.

Whatever else it is, as Bernard Crick spent a lifetime trying to explain, politics has to be a continuous civic conversation about how we live together and what we want to achieve. At the present moment it seems to me that we need a particularly vigorous conversation about this. We are all participants in it, or should be.

And of course we can always do our politics better. As it was once said: 'He that goeth about to persuade a multitude, that they are not so well governed as they ought to be, shall never want attentive and favourable hearers.' That was Hooker. The year was 1593.

(*The Political Quarterly,* July 2009)

‡

Doing politics differently is not just something that concerns politicians, though. It should concern the journalists who report

*on politics and the academics who write about politics as well.
I had all these in my sights when I was invited to speak at the
awarding of the Orwell Prize in 2001 (given to those writers
who best fulfil Orwell's injunction to 'make political writing
into an art'). I used to make all my students read Orwell's
magnificent essay on 'Politics and the English Language' (which
should be compulsory for anyone intending to engage in politics)
and it provided the peg for what I wanted to say. The Guardian
published an edited version.*

Bad Language

It was in April 1946 that George Orwell's essay 'Politics and
the English Language' appeared in *Horizon* magazine with
the memorable description of much political writing as stale
phrases 'tucked together like the sections of a prefabricated
hen-house'. His was the definitive demonstration of the connection between bad writing and bad politics.

Orwell helps us to identify dangers which, if not attended
to, threaten the future of that progressive tradition of which
he was such a distinguished representative. In drawing attention to these dangers, I want briefly to bite the three hands
that have kept me moderately well fed for most of my life.

First, the academy. In particular, that section of it represented by the so-called social sciences. This is now giving
us entire fields full of nothing but prefabricated hen-houses.
When I became an editor of *The Political Quarterly*, a journal
whose credo is clear argument in plain English, I started col-
lecting particularly fine examples of such prefabrication from
articles that were sent to us.

Here is one example, typical of many others, from a political scientist: 'It is possible to offer a discussion of the "Pacific

Asian model" in terms which gesture to an ideal-typical polit-ical-economic configuration, related to social-institutional structures, and associated cultural forms.'

Is anybody supposed to read this kind of stuff?

Academics are writing more and more about less and less, and in a mutilated language that cuts them off from the public arena. Is it because they really have nothing to say, or because – even if they had – they have forgotten how to say it? Where are the social science equivalents of those science writers who have looked for and found a huge public audience for their intelligently accessible books? Where are the successors to public intellectuals like Bernard Crick and David Marquand, who repudiate narrow academic bound-ary lines in pursuit of the big picture that can make sense of the details? Where, in other words, is the commitment to public philosophy that was the academic contribution to that old progressive tradition with its well-trodden path from the university common room to the *Manchester Guardian*? Its absence is today's *trahison des clercs*.

Second, the political class. The entire energies of today's political managers (in all parties) are devoted to closing down, or sealing off, free-range political argument. These are our thought police, the on-messengers of yet more prefabri-cated hen-houses.

This is the world of verbless vacuities, of mindless 'mod-ernisations', of 'level playing fields' and 'rolling outs', of robotic repetition of words and phrases that have long lost any connection with meanings. They glaze the eyes not only of the receivers but of the deliverers. They are, in Orwell's words, the stale tea leaves that block up the drain, preventing any fresh thoughts or arguments getting through. Now the practitioners of this kind of politics, the thought policemen armed with their shiny, modern toolkits, these destroyers of political language, are not bad people.

In fact they are usually good people, who want to do good things. But they are killing politics. And they have to be stopped. Third, the media class. My charge here is that the media class has become the accomplice of the political class in closing down serious political argument.

The old distinction between fact and opinion has entirely disappeared, in the broadsheets no less than in the tabloids and with the broadcasters not far behind. News is routinely spun, by journalists as much as by politicians (and often in collusion). Stories are no longer expected to be true, even by those who write them. Speculation and suggestion is all. What matters is what sells.

In this environment, a sensible politician keeps his head down. If he is asked for his views, it is not because they might be thought interesting but because they might provide a journalistic opportunity to insert a cigarette paper of difference between these views and those of someone else. The story becomes the difference, not the issue. Faced with this, the politician naturally comes to prefer a protected life inside the prefabricated hen-houses. The result is that, together, journalists and politicians are squeezing the life out of serious political debate.

So that is my charge sheet: academic abdication, political suffocation, and journalistic collaboration. It would be bad enough if only one of these was happening, but together and in combination they are threatening the basis upon which a serious public life can be conducted, and on which the progressive tradition was built.

We are not yet in Orwell's Room 101 (except as a television show), but there is a sense in which we are now in the building. The only remedy is resistance. Orwell demands no less of us.

(*The Guardian*, 6 April 2001)

‡

Perhaps this is why I found the political style of the early Blair ascendancy so difficult and frustrating. I welcomed the fact that the Labour Party had at last come to its senses, but not that it was accompanied by a controlling kind of politics that was intolerant of independent thought and obsessed with ensuring that everyone just recited the party line (usually expressed in mutilated English). Even allowing for the need to learn costly lessons from the party's fractious past, this was a reaction too far. Already in my mid-forties by the time I entered the Commons, I had spent the previous twenty years teaching students to see politics as a dynamic and civilising activity requiring all ideas and positions to be contested and interrogated, and this made it difficult to accept that the only role I was required to perform was as a cheerleader for the regime – even if it was my regime. I wanted to be a loyalist, but not a speaking clock. Some of these frustrations were already evident in this piece I wrote for the New Statesman *in 1997, in the heady first year of the Blair government, which argued for a radical kind of politics to match the moment.*

Controllers versus Visionaries

Let's start with two outrageous predictions. Tony Blair will turn out not to be immortal. And Labour will not be in power for ever. All we have is an opportunity, nothing more, and if we blow it we are unlikely to get another one.

By 'we' I mean the progressive left-centre of British politics, for so much of this century divided and defeated, but representing much of what is best in the British political tradition. This tradition has been the engine of practical improvement for most people. Its values of decency and fairness are widely shared. Yet it has failed to establish for itself a durable political ascendancy. It believed, mistakenly, that it had done so after 1945, until the post-war 'settlement' came so dramatically unsettled in the 1970s.

The May election result was certainly an extraordinary achievement. After the 1992 election the right believed it could always win and the left believed it might always lose. Number-crunching pundits lined up to tell the same story. Behind Essex Man stood the gurus of Essex University. Yet, in a magnificent victory of politics over sociology, the Conservative Party decided to disintegrate, while Labour became seriously New.

But this landslide is not yet a permanent settlement and may never be. Electorates can give and electorates can take away, these days with alarming speed. Political support has to be actively and endlessly reinvented if it is to last.

It may be fun to watch the Conservative Party behaving like the old Labour Party, but it would be a serious mistake to think we are witnessing its death agony. The Conservative Party has only ever existed in order to be in power and it will not be long before it remembers its central mission. Unable to settle big issues, it will take scalps wherever it can.

What we have is an opportunity, albeit one of historic proportions. Much will turn on the respective roles of three groups. I will call them the Sneerers, the Controllers and the Visionaries. The Sneerers are those people who may like to claim a general *bien-pensant* centre-leftness, but who can be relied upon to affect a condescending disdain for the actual business of converting a cultural attitude into a political project. The influence of such people, who are not to be confused with critical participants, is entirely corrosive, and always has been.

They cheered on 1 May and began to sneer on 2 May – on the op-ed pages, in the university common rooms, at the dinner tables – and they can be counted upon to continue to do so. This has long been their role, which is why the left-centre has failed in recent times to be nourished by an organic intelligentsia – and why the current initiatives to do something about it are particularly important, especially at a moment when the rest of civil society is receptively energised by the transformed political environment.

Far more important, though, are the Controllers and the Visionaries. It is scarcely too much to say that the eventual fate of the Blairite Project will be determined by the roles of these two groups. The Controllers inhabit a world of fixing, spinning and news managing. Their vision extends to the next bulletin. They are impatient with dissent, fresh thinking and loose cannons. Their version of inclusive politics involves getting powerful interests on-side and keeping them there. They dislike Cabinet government and prefer more direct command structures. When they get it wrong, as they did on the party-funding fiasco that brought the long honeymoon to its abrupt end, they can sink the ship.

It is only to be expected that the fratricidal shambles that characterised Labour's not-so-distant past should have produced this reaction. We should rejoice in the fact that the party became awesomely professional; if there are to be practitioners of the black arts, it is better that they should be on the side of the angels. The problem arises only if it comes to be thought that all this is what government is about.

The Visionaries are those who see the potential to effect a lasting transformation of the political landscape. The long-discussed realignment on the centre-left is actually happening, though not in the ways traditionally foreseen. This situation calls for audacity, exploiting historical opportunities and wrong-footing opponents who think it is still business as usual. When Blair defied the conventional wisdom of party managers and went for broke on Clause IV, or surprised everyone with his post-election deal with the Liberal Democrats, he displayed exactly this capacity. More of the same will be required if the momentum is to be sustained.

Even those of us who have long advocated a more pluralist, inclusive and collaborative kind of politics have found ourselves outflanked by the pace and scale of events. The joint Cabinet committee of Labour and the Liberal Democrats to underpin the political reform programme is a dramatic constitutional innovation. Its offspring, an electoral commission, seems to have survived a difficult and protracted birth. These arrangements will be attacked and tested (by those Liberal Democrats who would rather be free to play their local political games; by those Labour people who dislike such association and are increasingly the target for such games); and leadership on both sides will be needed to keep the show on the road. This is where strategic thinking needs to prevail. Yet in many ways such mechanistic arrangements are the least interesting part of what is happening. Far more significant is the change in political culture. A routine and sterile adversarialism is finally, if still tentatively, being replaced by something more grown-up. Parties discover that it is possible to compete and to co-operate. Parliament begins to reform itself in ways, that will make it more than a continuous election campaign. The constitutional reforms both reflect this process and accelerate it.

But even this does not go to the real inclusiveness that is at the heart of the Blair Project – and which will make it or break it. Its central audacity is to seek to dislodge ancestral affiliations and to build new structures of support on a 'radical-centre' platform that is defined as the modern common sense. This is not a political tactic but a hegemonic project. When set against this, other versions of collaborative politics look positively prehistoric. There is room for argument about whether this can be achieved (if at all) as a uniquely Labour project, or whether it will require a broader underpinning. That is what the big strategic issue of electoral reform is all about, and why it will be so important to get it right.

This project must not fall into the hands of the Controllers, who will think the task is to assemble a soggy consensus and avoid upsetting powerful interests. Nothing could be further from the truth. Unless it remains clear to people what this government is for, especially when the going gets rough, it will fail – and all larger ambitions with it. A party needs friends, but a radical party also needs some good enemies.

A radical party of the left-centre should find them wherever its twin goals of modernisation and justice are blocked. The blockages might come from assorted directions: business that wants to ignore its social obligations, professional groups that seek to avoid accountability, public sector bureaucracies that give inadequate public service.

Modernisation without justice was the hallmark of Thatcherism. Justice without modernisation distinguished old Labour. In combination, they represent not the end of ideology but its reinvention.

(*New Statesman*, 12 December 1997)

‡

This was not only a matter of political style, but also of political substance. I took the 'Third Way' seriously (I sometimes thought I was one of the few people who did), not just as an electoral strategy but as a way of genuinely changing the terms of political trade. It provided the basis for a new social democracy, but this required a confident and concerted ideological offensive, which involved making enemies as well as friends. In a further New Statesman *piece in 2000, which provoked both attention and trouble from the party managers, I asked whether Tony Blair was really this kind of Blairite.*

Am I a Blairite?

I am a Blairite. At least I always thought I was. It's the description that routinely precedes my name in the newspapers. I did spot a reference to me as a 'former Blairite' recently though, and even one alarming citation as 'left-wing' (prompting a subscription demand from the Campaign Group). Then a journalist phoned last week to ask if he should include me in his list of assorted Labour malcontents.

I clearly need to work out what is going on, if only because it may have a wider significance for current arguments about the state of the Project. Beyond the lazy journalism, and the fact that the space for any kind of independent thought and opinion in British party politics has now become suffocatingly narrow, there is a real sense of this being (in Blair-speak) a genuinely defining moment for the New Labour enterprise. We now know more about it than once we did, which sharpens the questions we can ask about its future direction.

I became a Blairite (even before Blair, I like to think) because I wanted the left-centre to become the dominant force in British society, as I believed was possible if Labour was reformed and modernised. Drawing on the rich intellectual resources of the 'liberal socialism' that was forged in the early part of the last century, as new liberalism mingled with ethical socialism, the opportunity existed to put together a powerful modern progressivism. This would combine markets with social justice, rights with duties, and subject both State services and market operations to public interest disciplines. A new language of community, emphasising society as a common enterprise in which we all had a stake, would be developed to articulate and integrate these arguments into a coherent public philosophy.

Above all others, Tony Blair seemed to have the vision of what was required, and the courage to bring it about. His determination to do battle on Clause IV, when others urged evasion, signalled his intent. Here was a politician who, like Mrs Thatcher, was going to make the weather. And so it proved. Labour found a new language and a new audience, confirming that the idea of a progressive majority in Britain was not a chimera.

Where stands all this now? Some of those who supply critical answers may be safely ignored. They never shared the vision in the first place and simply prefer the role of permanent oppositionists. Others want to play off Old Labour against New, the Heartlands against Middling Britain, already forgetting the elementary lesson that a progressive majority requires just that, a majority. Then there are those who give only grumbling and grudging credit to the government for all the many good things it is doing, which is why it is better placed than any previous Labour government at a comparable stage. Yet, when all this is properly said, something is clearly not right. There is a problem at the centre of the Blair Project, which even the ill-mannered ladies of the Women's Institute could not fail to notice.

Unless this problem is attended to, there will be tears before bed. Blairite true believers therefore have a duty to attend to it, while there is still time.

It is a problem of definition. Unsure of what it is, Blairism lacks the confidence to become what it might be. Its fuzzy centre leaves the party uncertain and the electorate suspecting hollowness and spinnery. What is lacking is the sense of a central mission or purpose. There is much tacking, but not enough steering.

There are policy initiatives galore, but somehow the big picture that would make sense of the parts never comes into sharp enough focus. The obsession with presentation has been at the expense of theory and strategy. It is ironic that a government that has made presentation so central should have left people so uncertain as to what, at bottom, it is really all about.

Perhaps, as some suggest, a Mark Two Blairism has replaced the original Mark One. How else to explain the distance between the expansive, risk-taking, realigning, history-shaping instincts of the one and the cautious, controlling temper of the other? One makes the weather, the other dishes out umbrellas. Or perhaps there was a confusion in the original, which I (and others) did not fully see at the time. I thought the Project was to make our ideas into the dominant ideas of the society, in an enterprise of advocacy and persuasion and example, not to take the dominant ideas we found lying around after the Thatcher years and make them into our ideas. This is a fundamental distinction. My big tent was designed to be capacious and inviting enough to attract people in, not a smother blanket that pretended that everybody was already inside. A different kind of politics derives from each. No amount of windy rhetoric about change and modernisation can bridge that gap.

My first real doubt came a year or two ago when Labour's junior education minister received a standing ovation from the assembled public school heads of the Headmasters' Conference after announcing that partnership had now replaced antagonism. This was seen as a great presentational triumph at the time. It reminded me of Tony Crosland's remark that if we simply abolished grammar schools and left the public schools alone then we would have made matters worse rather than better. When the recent Oxbridge row erupted, we had a response but no strategy. This is not an argument for finding enemies, but it is an argument for finding a strategy that clearly expresses social democratic values. Then people will at least know what we are about.

Some argue that the whole point is that they should not know. That we should only redistribute by stealth. That even the civic purpose of taxation should not be mentioned in case people get the wrong idea about us. That radical ideas (for example, on NHS funding) should be ruled off-limits because they might frighten the horses. That we can make a constitutional revolution without exciting people about the new democratic possibilities. That inequalities can be removed and opportunities opened up without touching the taxes, schools or privileges of the rich and powerful. That social inclusion is a strategy for the poor, but not for the wealthy. That lions and lambs can forever graze happily together on the sun-kissed uplands of the Third Way.

A durable progressive majority can never be assembled on these terms. It is not just that it is misconceived, but that it simply will not work. You can never deregulate enough to satisfy the deregulators, never cut taxes enough to mollify the tax-cutters, never out-Widdecombe the right, never permanently appease the *Daily Mail*, never love business enough to make it love you enough. The only alternative is to be what you are, or should be, which is the party that makes public services work, prevents a market economy becoming a market society, opens up opportunities, extends democracy and strips privilege of its sting.

This is inconsistent with timidity or vacuousness. It requires a clarity of purpose and a confidence of message. It requires people to know, and to engage with, what you are doing. It also requires some philosophical supports. A mantra about what matters being what works is no substitute for a coherent public philosophy.

The perceived theoretical vapidity of New Labour may in part be a reflection of the times, but it comes at a price. It has, for example, produced a pensions policy that is intellectually impeccable, morally defensible, economically sensible – and politically disastrous.

It has also produced a political style that is often downright embarrassing. In contrast to the new politics that was promised, involving an active engagement with civil society, we have the sterile verblessness of ministerial speeches delivered *de haut en bas* without the flicker of original thought, the passion of real argument or the utterance of memorable phrase. This is a politics for middle managers, not for a party of radicalism and reform with ambitions to reshape the political landscape.

Fortunately, between them William Hague and the jeering ladies of the WI have come to the rescue. From now on there is simply no alternative to being positive and confident. The big picture has to be brought back into focus. Seventy years ago R. H. Tawney identified what he saw as Labour's gravest weakness: 'It does not achieve what it could, because it does not know what it wants ... Being without clear convictions as to its own meaning and purpose, it is deprived of the dynamic which only convictions can supply'. I am a Blairite because the new social democracy born out of Labour's renewal both corrected this historic weakness and opened the way to a progressive majority in Britain. I just hope that Tony Blair is still this kind of Blairite too.

(*New Statesman*, 13 June 2000)

‡

These were the years when there was much discussion about the formation of a 'progressive majority' that would break the historic grip of Conservative politics and turn present electoral success into durable power. Roy Jenkins was one of those urging Blair to seize the moment, do a deal with Paddy Ashdown, change the electoral system and realign British politics. Blair flirted with a bold stroke of this kind, but drew back in the face of Labour's ancestral loathing of the Liberal Democrats (matched only by Conservative loathing of them). I was less interested in party fixes than in getting progressives to work together in a spirit that recognised their common intellectual and political inheritance instead of playing the usual party games. They were not the same, nor did they need to be, but they did all spring from a confluence of socialist and liberal traditions that had set the framework for progressive politics in Britain. Some think that the arrival of coalition politics after the 2010 election may be the harbinger of a very different kind of realignment. Or it may, eventually, revive interest in the tradition of 'liberal socialism', which I wrote about in 2001, among those who want to assemble a new progressive coalition.

Liberal Socialism: Then and Now

Progressive movements need progressive ideas. Those who think that a progressive century can be secured by political fixes of various kinds (even by a fix of the electoral system) are wrong. Such devices and contrivances may be desirable, or useful, or both, but they do not go to the heart of the 'progressive dilemma' that made the centre-left weaker than it should have been for much of the last century.[1] If this next century is really to be different in this respect, the centre-left has to win the battle of ideas.

It took the Blair government some time to understand this, which was curious in view of the central role of ideological revision in the renewal of the party. Only when backs were to the wall, suddenly and unexpectedly, did the government discover its authentic voice, arguing rather than accommo-dating, and confronting people with fundamental political choices. What had previously seemed politically risky had now become a political necessity. The big tent might have become somewhat smaller, but it had also become a good deal stronger. Instead of the suffocating assumption that everybody was already inside it, there was a bracing invitation to enter. Policy particulars were reconnected with the big picture and the grand narrative.

This is a reminder that a progressive movement requires a proselytising mission. When William Morris used to insist, against the mechanical Marxists and the no less mechanical Fabians, that the real task was to 'make socialists', this was his message. It is still worth listening to. A focus group makes no converts. That requires a continuing enterprise of argument and persuasion. Paradoxically, all the modern complexities and blurring of old ideological dividing lines make this task more rather than less necessary. The fragmentation of traditional certainties may mean that the joining up of analysis and argument is more difficult, but it is also even more of an imperative. In a world without reliable maps, compass points become more essential. Without them we are liable to wander all over the place, radiating uncertainty about who, what and where we are.

Again, the experience of the Blair government offers an instructive lesson here. For much of its life, the government seemed preoccupied with demonstrating what Labour was not. It was not a party that screwed up the economy, or taxed people until the pips squeaked, or waged war on business, or gave in to the unions, or was soft on crime – and so on. Much of this was quite understandable, in view of the party's recent past and the political price that had been paid for it. There were many ghosts to be laid. But for as long as this remained a reckoning with the past rather than an engagement with the future, so it was harder to forge a positive identity. Ghost-busting only takes you so far.

This suggests a further point, of a more far-reaching kind. To compress a long story, much of the recent history of the left has involved a process of adjustment, adaptation and accommodation to individualism and market liberalism. On tax, ownership, welfare, regulation and much else, old territory has been abandoned in order that new positions can be occupied.

Far from being a distinctively British phenomenon, the British experience sits squarely within the general trajectory of parties of the centre-left across Europe.[2] We might describe this process in the simplest terms as going with the flow, a response to the social and economic currents that seemed to be reshaping the political landscape.

Yet such going with the flow, necessary as it may be for political adaptation and ideological repositioning, has also to be combined with efforts to staunch the flow and redirect it into new channels. This requires a robust engagement with the battle of ideas, often of a fundamental kind. The more clamorous the welter of private interests, the more pressing the task of defining a public interest. The more rampant individualism is, the more necessary it becomes to resolve its contradictions. The more differentiated society becomes, the more important it is to strengthen the conditions of social unity.

Nor are these abstract propositions, for they make themselves felt on all sides. The failure to provide everybody with a stake in society leaves many to kick over the traces. We demand the right to drive our cars until gridlock descends, then realise we should have developed a high-quality public transport system. Many of the things we need most in this age of individualism – not least, a decent environment – are obtainable only by collective action. We resist paying taxes to the State, but then discover that what we most want for ourselves and our families – such as excellent schools, good health and social care – is not available when we need it.

These are elementary propositions, but it is the continuing duty of the centre-left to propound them. They do not impede the proper and necessary revisionism that should be a permanent feature of progressive politics, but they do constitute a standing reminder of some basic linkages and connections. The neo-liberal right has a mission to show that collective action fails. The left has to show that it is indispensable for a good society, which includes enabling individuals to secure what they want. The forms and mechanisms of collective action should change and develop as circumstances require; but its point and purpose is a durable truth. The socialist (or even social-ist) argument has always been both moral and empirical: fairness is morally right, but a fair society will also work better. This is another linkage that has constantly to be argued, and given practical illustration.

The progressive failure of the last century, which needs to be remedied in the next, was an inability to mobilise such propositions into a politically serviceable public philosophy capable of winning support over an extended period. This would have required the Labour movement to become more than a labour movement. It would have required the left to see its mission as empowering people rather than making them supplicants of a central (and centralised) State. It would have involved new relationships between individual endeavour and collective action. It would have fostered a social market in which economic competition was combined with social obligation. For all its huge achievements, Labour in the twentieth century failed to assemble a progressive coalition of this kind and eventually paid a heavy price for not having done so.

Yet the materials for it were there at hand, right at the beginning of the last century. When Tony Blair, commemorating the fiftieth anniversary of the 1945 Labour government, invoked the heritage of 'liberal socialism', this was his reference point.[3] His immediate political message was about the electoral cost of the fragmentation of progressive forces, and the need to rectify this if the next century was to be different from the last, but the reference point involves more than this. It means putting progressive liberals alongside progressive socialists (Hobhouse and Tawney, Keynes and Cole, Beveridge and Attlee...), not to show that they inhabit the same tradition – which they do not – but to demonstrate that there is an intermingling of progressive traditions that is capable of producing something richer and more vital than the constituent parts. In simplest terms, they need each other.

In this sense liberal socialism represents the original Third Way. Its source is the meeting between 'new' liberalism and ethical socialism in the early years of the twentieth century. It was a peculiarly British encounter, involving an intermingled progressivism that has good claim to be regarded as the richest repository of applied social thinking that modern Britain has produced. 'Liberalism has passed through its Slough of Despond,' declared the liberal theorist L. T. Hobhouse in 1911, 'and in the give and take of ideas with Socialism has learned, and taught, more than one lesson. The result is a broader and deeper movement in which the cooler and clearer minds recognise below the differences of party names and in spite of certain real cross-currents a genuine unity of purpose'.[4] Here was the basis for a broad progressivism beyond the confines of party.

Both traditions were the product of internal revisionism. The new liberalism was a break from the laissez-faire individualism of the old, having discovered that individual freedom could often be enhanced rather than diminished by collective action. Ethical socialism was a rupture from an economic determinism that repudiated bourgeois democracy and moral choice. These twin revisionisms found much common ground; but this is less interesting than the nature of their dialogue. For it was out of this dialogue, with its different perspectives and preoccupations, that a richer body of ideas was nourished that fed into progressive politics in Britain. If it failed to be organised into a coherent governing force, this was not because the theoretical ingredients were unavailable.

The conversation between new liberals and ethical socialists ranged widely. The socialists thought that liberalism was still too soft on capitalism; the liberals thought that socialism was too trusting of the State. Socialists pressed for equality, while liberals cautioned about the effects on liberty and enterprise of pressing too far. Liberals wanted to diffuse power in the name of diversity and citizenship; socialists thought that an equity of common citizenship demanded central provision. Liberals worried about the dangers of bureaucratic collectivism, socialists about the perils of leaving people unprotected. Socialists talked of communal duties, liberals of individual rights. The liberal emphasis on political and civic freedom was countered by the socialist emphasis on economic and social freedom. Liberals thought that socialists were too preoccupied with class; while socialists believed that liberals were too in thrall to individualism.

This is a bald summary of dense arguments. The point is not that the protagonists were lined up on opposing sides but that the dialogue produced a body of social thinking, fusing and mingling its constituent strands, that informed progressive politics in Britain. At least that was the promise. Hobhouse wrote:

> If, then, there be such a thing as a Liberal Socialism – and whether there be is still a subject for inquiry – it must clearly fulfil two conditions. In the first place, it must be democratic. It must come from below, not from above. Or rather, it must emerge from the efforts of society as a whole to secure a fuller measure of justice, and a better organisation of mutual aid. It must engage the efforts and respond to the genuine desires not of a handful of superior beings, but of great masses of men. And, secondly, and for that very reason, it must make its account with the human individual. It must give the average man free play in the personal life for which he really cares. It must be founded on liberty, and must make not for the suppression but for the development of personality.[5]

In other words, it required a genuine synthesis of liberalism and socialism as the creative product of a process of mutual learning.

The ideological battleground of the twentieth century left little political space for a synthesis of this kind. Yet it was there to be drawn on when imaginative minds tried to think their way out of the ideological impasse in which they found themselves. For example, G. D. H. Cole responded to the totalitarian experience by explicitly invoking a 'liberal socialism' as the basis upon which the left could be reconstructed after the Second World War, with democratic freedom at its centre. This was grounded in the Western liberal tradition, of which the socialist view of freedom was a natural extension and complement. It valued tolerance and diversity, hated bureaucratic monoliths, and was fiercely libertarian and democratic. The only kind of socialism that was worth having was one that incorporated the best of liberalism. The direction of the contemporary world 'should make even Socialists wary by now of tearing up by the roots any small man's refuge that is left in a world so ridden as ours by hugeness. It should make them regard the farmer, the shopkeeper, the small manufacturer, not as obstacles in the way of universal centralisation, but as valuable checks upon a dangerous agglomerative tendency. Politically, this opens up the possibility of immense innovations ...'[6]

So much for the pedigree of liberal socialism. Its ingredients were assembled at the beginning of the twentieth century, as ethical socialists met new liberals. Although the meeting shaped much subsequent progressive thought in Britain (for example, the way in which R. H. Tawney famously tied together equality and freedom, and tied both to an idea of community), the twentieth century was brutally hostile to such nice synthesis. It was an age of polarities – capitalism versus communism, class against class, equality or liberty, state or individual – and social democrats struggled to find convincing third ways between competing positions.

British labourism, despite its practical achievements, was notably unsuccessful in the task of theoretical construction. Yet the materials were at hand, in rich abundance, once the collapse of the old polarities opened up a space where a public philosophy of liberal socialism could flourish.

That space now exists. Having promised so much at the start of the twentieth century, liberal socialism might finally deliver that promise at the start of the twenty-first century. The conditions are propitious.

There is an openness and interchange among progressive forces of an unprecedented kind, as old tribalisms and sectarianisms collapse, and in the face of issues and alignments that do not fit neatly (or, in some cases, do not fit at all) into traditional ideological categories. In this sense the new politics is not a glib phrase but an accurate description of the need for politics to be conducted differently. There are two main reasons why this provides an opportunity for the liberal socialist synthesis to come into its own. The first is rather general and theoretical; the second more particular and practical.

In general terms, liberal socialism provides a basis upon which a progressive approach to politics can be constructed. Some of its elements can be briefly sketched. A market economy is distinguished from a market society. Both State and markets need to be made to work in the public interest. The balance between rights and duties should be carefully weighed. Citizenship is about empowerment and not just about provision. Collective action nourishes a good society, but it is not for the state to tell people how to live their lives. Enterprise should be encouraged, while security is guaranteed. There can be too much regulation, and too little. The demands of equity need balancing against the claims of diversity. Unjustified inequalities should be removed while cherishing individual liberties. Economic dynamism and social justice are conjoined.

Such liberal socialist propositions, wholly unexceptional in their nature, define the territory of contemporary political debate. Yet their real test – and opportunity – comes in their ability to open up innovative policy thinking. Once the old categories and polarities are escaped from, it should become easier to follow policy ideas where they lead. It is not difficult to identify some areas and issues where this is required. Once choices are extended beyond State or market, other providers of services become possible, thereby extending experiment and diversity. Traditional battles about levels of taxation become less significant to the extent that it becomes possible to construct more direct and transparent connections between taxes paid and services delivered. Redistribution that confers endowments upon individuals to improve their lives and advance their careers offers a practical liberty.

Sponsoring new forms of bottom-up community provision in place of top-down statism strengthens the frayed bonds of citizenship. Extending democracy to new areas lifts the curse of centralism. Finding a version of Europe that has democratic resonance replaces a version that conspicuously lacks it.

There is much here for liberal socialists to do. Out of that original meeting between the new liberals and the ethical socialists, there came a connecting tradition that integrated equality and liberty, community and individual, solidarity and individuality, enterprise and justice, State and market, centralism and localism, responsibilities and rights, collectivism and citizenship, into a rich synthesis that has informed progressive politics in Britain. It also carried with it innovative policy implications. Yet, in the last century, its political promise was not fulfilled. If the next century is really to be a progressive one, liberal socialism will have to come into its own.

(In Lawson, N. and Sherlock, N. (eds),
The Progressive Century, [2001])

‡

Politics without ideas is barren. Slogans should convey ideas, not substitute for them. The late Guardian *journalist Hugo Young once wrote that the only big idea is that there is no big idea. This is certainly true now. Neoliberalism is a busted flush, but there is an absence of developed alternatives. Social democracy has had the economic rug pulled from under it. The result is that we inhabit a kind of intellectual and political limbo in the face of daunting forces over which we seem to have little control. As the historian Tony Judt put it in 2010 shortly before his death: 'Today, neither Left nor Right can find their footing.' When the governor of the Bank of England, speaking about the fallout from the banking crisis, said that he was 'surprised that the degree of public anger has not been greater than it has', he confused a lack of anger with an absence of a convincing means of political expression for that anger.*

Is David Cameron's 'big society' a big idea? Certainly not in terms of its own neglected antecedents. That is why I have included, perhaps eccentrically, a piece written nearly forty years ago about a period of intellectual and political history almost a century ago. At that time there was intense argument and debate about how the State could tame the market without becoming oppressive itself, and how self-government could become an active reality in all spheres of life. Leading the charge were those who called themselves Guild Socialists.

Guild Socialism Revisited

'*On s'engage et puis on voit.*' Lenin's fondness for this particular Napoleonic maxim was not widely shared by one group of socialists who appeared in Britain during the second decade of the twentieth century. For them the struggle did not, except in a very limited way, determine its outcome. The proper revolutionary method did not consist primarily in engaging the enemy, with the course of the war determining the nature of the victory. For the Guild Socialists (as this group was called) the problem was rather that of devising and pursuing the sort of struggle which seemed most likely to issue in the victory whose essential details they had already established. Merely to overthrow capitalism and to smash the State was not difficult, but neither was it enough. Capitalism had not only to be displaced but replaced, and it was just this which Guild Socialism claimed competence to do. Not only was it necessary to achieve socialism; it was also vital to be clear about the essential nature of that socialism. Unless this was done, capitalism might indeed be destroyed, only to be replaced by 'a new sort of collective tyranny of all over each'.[7] In other words, the problem for Guildsmen was to win the war without losing the peace.

History has not been kind to Guild Socialism. The conditions which sustained the Guild idea during and immediately after the First World War largely disappeared in the changed circumstances of the inter-war period. The Guild movement took its place as a brief early-century interlude, a current isolated from the mainstream of British socialist development, to be recalled patronisingly or with derision according to taste. It began to take on the air of a museum piece, its antique charm preserved by an occasional dusting, but deemed irrelevant to the needs of a modern socialism. Of course the very name 'Guild' enormously eased the path to the museum, where it could be arranged alongside such relics as William Morris, Hilaire Belloc, and the Arts and Crafts movement, sad monuments of protest against the inexorable logic of modernity. The Guild movement was labelled 'a Romantic hangover', exhibiting 'a kind of pristine, almost schoolboy-ish innocence.'[8]

Since this article will take a rather different view of Guild Socialism, at least in its theoretical aspects, perhaps some of the conventional criticisms should be conceded immediately. Many of the Guildsmen did indulge in the sort of woolly and over-confident idealism which is the occupational hazard of young middle-class intellectuals. Their class origins made them suspect to many sections of the more militant workers (to the rest they were generally unknown). To the syndical-ists, for example, Guild Socialism appeared as 'the latest lucubration of the middle class mind'.[9] Further, it is certainly true that the theorists of the Guild idea did get bogged down in some interminable and intricate system- building as they attempted to work out the structure of the future Guild society. Partly this was not their fault for, as Cole – the worst offender – often pointed out, Guildsmen were forced into details in answering the objections of critics. But it did often give the impression of a group of people 'gaily starting a revolution armed with split hairs', as S. G. Hobson described it.[10] There are more substantial criticisms to be made and some to be answered, but that must follow an examination of Guild theory itself.

Neither as theory nor as movement did Guild Socialism arise in a vacuum. It is intimately related to a number of theoretical and social developments which are both too important to ignore and too large to discuss at any length. The state was challenged in theory and defied in practice. 'A certain tendency to discredit the State is now abroad', noted

Ernest Barker on the outbreak of war. While Maitland established the historical pedigree of the association, and Figgis asserted the rights of the Church, Laski and Cole pushed the new pluralism along more radical paths. The claim of the State to sovereignty was found to be unsound, perhaps dangerous, as theory, and to be belied by the facts of social life. Hence the State was 'but one of the groups to which the individual belongs',[11] one element in the social complex of associations, functions, and loyalties.

Here was a challenge not only to the State itself, but also to all those theories and attitudes which embraced the State and its bureaucracy. Belloc is central here, more central perhaps than was fully realised by those people, including many Guildsmen, for whom the 'Servile State' became a ready slogan. Here was not simply a protest against increasing State regimentation, a plea for a return to a pre-industrial system of diffused property ownership, but also and more significantly a perceptive anticipation of the lines of possible future social development. In essence, collectivism would set out to achieve socialism but would instead create servility, 'a society wherein the owners remain few and wherein the proletarian mass accepts security at the expense of servitude'.[12]

Socialism demands socialisation to achieve sufficiency and security for the workers; capitalism opposes socialisation but accepts State action giving economic security to the proletariat (and benefits for itself); this process completed, the argument for public ownership is seemingly obsolete, for sufficiency and security have been achieved anyway. What has really been achieved, of course, is a State regime of free possessors and unfree non-possessors – the Servile State. There is clearly more to all this than the usual picture of

Belloc as just an old-fashioned individualist moaning about the National Insurance Act would seem to suggest.

At a less rarefied level men unversed in the subtleties of pluralist political theory challenged the State in their daily working lives, armed perhaps with the intellectual equipment of syndicalism and industrial unionism. While the government worried about 'labour unrest', the leaders of official Labour warned the 'community' about the perils of a doctrine which 'considers the working classes only'. [13] The impact of war was decisive, linking State and capitalism as never before in a system of regulation anathema to the growing forces of unofficial labour. Antipathy to the State increased enormously. [14] At the same time official Labour seemed irretrievably lost in the coat-tails of Liberalism, 'drifting into futility', in Beatrice Webb's phrase.

It was in this sort of environment, intellectual and social, that the Guild idea flowered and developed. For some years it did indeed seem to be 'the idea of the hour', as Barker described it. As to the use of the word 'Guild' except for A. J. Penty, who 'restored' the term in 1906, the Guild movement was never medievalist. It did claim some affinity of spirit with the medieval guild in its desire to reunite man and his labour, in its concern with the production of good commodities in free conditions, and in its localism; but the theorists of Guild Socialism were concerned to transform the industrial world, not to abolish it (though the Storrington Document, the Guildsmen's manifesto, did claim that the Guild system would enable the workers 'to place machine production on its trial') – a job requiring more than a 'false medievalism' as Cole called it.[15] Guild theory made three essential claims: it was to provide a critique of the existing system of industrial capitalism, to outline the basic requirements of an alternative social system, and to suggest the best method of transition from one system to the other. The use of the word 'system' is important, for Guild theory did operate at a system level, with its emphasis on social interdependence making any piecemeal social engineering impossible. One contemporary critic saw this as the fundamental error of Guild Socialism: it committed 'the Fallacy of the Present System' in asserting that all problems are related at a system level.[16] As a system theory it was also a general theory. While focusing on the industrial system, it claimed competence as a comprehensive social theory, its principles applicable to the ordering of every area of social life – or at least to those areas which could legitimately be ordered. In one sense, though, it was a particularist theory, claiming to bring together the truths of continental syndicalism and native collectivism in a synthesis uniquely suited to English tastes and conditions.[17]

The essential Guild charge against the capitalist system was fairly straightforward. The fundamental characteristic of capitalism was its treatment of the worker as a commodity, as a mere factor of production. (Hobson coined the term 'wagery' to describe this capitalist characteristic.) The wage-system was not simply a method of remuneration (as the Fabians liked to maintain), for it involved 'a determinate relation between him who gives and him who receives'. Guildsmen liked to compare this modern wage-slavery with traditional chattel-slavery, to the latter's advantage. The older form of slavery at least did not separate man from his labour – it was a unitary dependence, unlike its modern counterpart which maintained the fiction of citizenship in one area of social life only to negate it in another. Guild theory accepted the main categories of Marxian economics, but was more concerned to probe those human consequences of economic exploitation which we now like to describe in terms of 'alienation'. The Guildsmen are the grand diagnosticians of alienation. 'The sense of being owned is deadening,' wrote Cole.[18] Guild theory also subscribed to the essentials of the Marxian analysis of the capitalist state and of capitalist democracy. The existing state was the servant of capitalism, and political democracy was a fraud unless rooted in genuine economic democracy. But here again Guildsmen sought to trace the human consequence of this bare analysis. They found two types of citizenship, active and passive, distributed according to one's place in the wage-system, and that 'in no conceivable circumstances is it possible by political means to change passive into active citizenship'. Guild sociology centred on the concept of status, in many respects the key word in the Guild vocabulary, for if a man was deprived of his humanity in the workplace, treated as factor rather than actor in the production process, how could he enjoy status or dignity in the wider society? Guild psychology demonstrated that he could not, for 'economic subjugation brings in its train certain definite psychological results, which, in their turn, colour and dominate politics'. The outcome is the passive society, sustained by the psychology of servility.[19]

If this sort of analysis was correct, if the status of the worker in relation to the wage system was really the fundamental issue of capitalism, then clearly orthodox socialism had lost its way somewhere. Guildsmen were vigorous in their assertion of just this. For them mainstream socialism was mistaken about both product and process, being wedded to collectivism and to the political method. Collectivist socialism had hold of the wrong end of the stick; it was rigidly distributionist, attentive to men as consumers but deaf to their claims as producers. It attacked the symptom, poverty, while ignoring the disease, slavery. 'Socialists have all too often fixed their eyes upon the material misery of the poor', wrote Cole, 'without realising that it rests upon the spiritual degradation of the slave'.[20]

Collectivism sought equality and efficiency by heaping more powers upon the state, the likely result of which would simply be a transfer of authority from the capitalist to the bureaucrat, with little change in the status of the worker. Indeed, with capitalism finding the State increasingly useful, a real State Capitalism would emerge, and it mattered little whether this new formation was to be called the 'Servile State' of Mr Belloc or the 'Selfridge State' of Mr Cole.

The failure of socialist orthodoxy in its conception of the end to be achieved was compounded by its failure of method. Attacking the effects of the wage system rather than that system itself, it had lost itself in the world of politics when only economic action in the workplace could bring about genuine emancipation. In Hobson's neat phrase, the British Labour movement displayed 'a soft head for economics and a soft heart for politics'.[21] It failed to realise that economic power precedes political power – this last statement becoming so insistent in Guild propaganda that it was sometimes reduced to the formula 'EPPPP'! The Labour Party could never achieve socialism for it relied on politics to do what politics was inherently incapable of doing. Guildsmen were fervent in their attack on official Labour, prompting an otherwise sympathetic Lansbury to comment on one occasion on 'this holy horror of politics', which he did not share.[22] These failures of perception and method on the part of socialist orthodoxy were often seen by Guildsmen as the product of a general limitation of mental and spiritual outlook in minds of the Fabian variety. There is a story that A. J. Penty finally broke with the Fabian Society upon discovering that Pease, its secretary, had selected the winning design in the architectural competition for the new London School of Economics by calculating the floor space in each of the plans submitted and picking the one with the highest total. Here (it was said) was the Fabian mind in action. Cole put the point exactly: the Fabians 'know', he said; 'if they could but imagine, their souls might still be saved'.[23]

Guildsmen claimed for themselves knowledge and imagination, and sought to construct a new social system on the basis of both.

In describing the proposed structure of Guild society it is important to distinguish – as Guild theorists sometimes seemed not to do – between essential structural principles and the last details of Guild organisation. It is, for example, less useful to dogmatise about the precise composition of Cole's 'democratic Supreme Court of Functional Equity' than to be clear about why such a body should be thought necessary and what its role in a living Guild system should properly be. Guild society was designed to remedy that loss of citizenship inherent in the capitalist wage system to which collectivism offered no solution. At a theoretical level, this entailed a new (albeit 'classical') conception of democracy and a special view of the state. Democracy was a statement and claim about man's proper relationship to his social world. For this claim to be genuine, democracy had necessarily to be a general theory of society and not merely a limited theory of political government. In other words, the democratic principle applies, as Cole said, 'not only or mainly to some special sphere of social action known as 'politics', but to any and every form of social action'.[24] Stated bluntly, if the people of Leicester had the democratic right to elect Ramsay MacDonald to the House of Commons, they also had the right to elect their leaders in their place of work and to exercise a continuous scrutiny over their performance in office. It was this lack of economic and social democracy which nullified the exercise of political democracy. Further, if democracy was ever to become more than a slogan, it would have to be organised along functional lines. Each main function in the social whole had a claim to representation, as did each participant within each function. There had to be as many representative bodies as there were distinct functions, each body being internally democratic. Such a system required a new view of representation too, for it was a false theory which claimed that one man could 'represent' another, when all that could in fact be represented was the functional purpose in which men take part. For representation to be effective in practice and sound in theory, it must be directly linked to a function. In other words, it must always be – in Cole's terminology – 'specific and functional', not 'general and inclusive', or misrepresentation was bound to result. Clearly Parliament was the worst offender in this respect. As an island of democracy, it 'professes to represent all the citizens in all things, and therefore as a rule represents none of them in anything'. [25]

Guild theory was largely concerned in working out the implications of this theoretical position in terms of an actual system of co-ordinated functional democracy. The principle of function served to subject all social institutions to the test of social purpose. The main concern was with industry, not because economic life should be the central area of human concern but because it had become so owing to the perversion of its social function. Its true function consisted in production for use under democratic conditions, whereas its perverted function centred on production for profit in conditions of wage-slavery. The Guild system would recognise industry as a distinct social function, and would recognise the claim of the worker as producer to a share in the exercise of that function. Each industrial Guild, composed of all the workers in that industry, would be an essentially self-governing association (though the industry itself would be owned by the whole community), internally democratic, and responsible for its members in good times and bad.

This Guild scheme of workers' control had one or two especially interesting features. For example, the Guild was to include all the workers by hand and brain in each industry, not just the manual workers as with existing trade unions. Guildsmen were singularly free from illusions about the need for technical expertise in the conduct of industry, and went to great lengths in pointing out the benefits to be expected from the Guild system for the professional and technical middle classes. Expertise would receive proper respect in a democratic factory, for 'a mass vote on a matter of technique understood only by a few experts would be a manifest absurdity'. The Webbs could breathe easily again. Cole even suggested that under the Guild system the supervisory personnel would probably turn out to be 'largely the same people' as were then doing that job.[26] Yet the atmosphere in the workplace would have changed dramatically, for in an important sense the right of the workers to dismiss the manager was more significant than the actual exercise of that right. Democracy ceases to be an act and becomes a process; and often it was suggested by Guildsmen that the absence of industrial conflict in Guild society would be a sign of social health, an indication that men had been able to turn their attention to other (and higher) things.

The precise nature of the Guild conception of workers' control raises some of the most interesting features of Guild Socialist theory, and brings us into an area of controversy between the major Guild thinkers themselves. Industrial democracy was necessary to meet the legitimate aspirations of men as producers, but because industry was an essentially social function its operation was of legitimate concern to consumers too. How then was it possible to speak of 'control' by the workers when such control had necessarily to be less than total? This was not a problem for Hobson, who denied that production and consumption were distinct interests, needing their own representation – the Guild was quite able to look after both. He criticised Cole's insistence on the need for the separate representation of consumer interests as serving to 'subject the producer to a supervision almost as galling as under capitalism'. Hobson looked to the Guild system to achieve two main things – to release the worker from the bondage of wagery, and to release the State from the bondage of economics. This entailed full industrial self-government, without such interference by the State as would infringe the rights of producers and contaminate the State's own true purpose. In Hobson's view, the State had become perverted through its association with economics. By eliminating this association, Guild Socialism offered the 'possibility of a puri-fied political system concerning itself with the national soul'.[27]

Cole's position was rather different, and shifted somewhat

over time. It began with a frank recognition that syndicalism, while valuable in asserting the genuine claims of the
producer, was ultimately defective and inadequate as a general social theory. Therefore the problem for Cole became
one of devising the social machinery which would effectively and justly reconcile different sectional and functional
interests – above all the interests of producer and consumer.
His first solution was to install the State as the functional
representative of the consumer interest, negotiating with
the Guilds in those matters (e.g. price, quantity, resource
allocation) which went beyond the internal work process
and concerned the wider community. But in his final and
most elaborate portrait of Guild society, *Guild Socialism
Restated*, the State, as a narrowly political body, had lost its
role of consumer representative, a task now assumed by a
new range of specially created consumer organisations (e.g.
the Collective Utilities Council). The book presents a picture
of a working Guild society as a general social system and
not merely in its industrial aspect. For example, in addition
to the Guilds of producers and the corresponding organisations of consumers, there were to be Civic Guilds for such
activities as education and health, and these in turn would
be paralleled by Cultural and Health Councils to represent
the citizen point of view, with all these various bodies being
co-ordinated at local, regional, and national levels. The aim
was to show, albeit in 'ideal' form, what a system of functional democracy would really look like. It was clearly not
only the factory that would be transformed.[28]

Cole's view of the state is particularly interesting, though
it can only be touched on here. Like Hobson, the early Cole
held that the role of the State had been perverted by its

alliance with capitalism, but that in Guild society politics would triumph over economics and the State would find its true role as 'the alert and flexible instrument of the General Will', which is close to the sort of mystical language that Hobson liked to use about the 'purified' State. But this view soon changed. The State became simply one piece of functional machinery and, as we have seen, it even lost its function of consumer representation. Sovereignty was possessed not by the State but by the whole community – it was diffused among all the functional associations. In Cole's final formulation, the traditional State machine seems to have disappeared altogether from the functional universe. But what of those functions of coercion, co-ordination and the like normally associated with the State machine? These become the province of a National Commune, where the whole range of functional bodies is represented. But the very existence of such a body led to the charge that here was no true pluralism at all, for sovereignty is kicked out of the front door only to be smuggled in again at the back. This argument has some force if rigid definitions of 'pluralism' and 'monism' are accepted.

It remains to say something about the method of transition envisaged by Guildsmen from capitalism to the future Guild society, for this was a distinctive and much criticised aspect of their doctrine. Clearly the 'great change', a phrase Cole liked to borrow from Morris, would not be brought about by the middle-class intellectual Guildsmen themselves (as they frankly acknowledged, calling themselves a 'movement' only in a deliberately self-conscious way). Ideas and theory were vital, but only in creative fusion with a great mass movement: the working class had to make the social revolution itself, for neither the Fabian Society nor the Labour Party could or would make it on its behalf. 'Labour is perfectly right', wrote Cole, 'to mistrust any person or any movement that tells it what great things can be done for it by someone else. It should trust only those who tell it what great things it can do for itself.'[29] It was natural for Guildsmen to embrace the trade union movement as an embryonic Guild organisation, destined to lead the working class to industrial self-government, especially at a time when trade unionists themselves were busy pressing the issue of control. No longer were the unions to be no more than defensive organisations within capitalism; they were to be the positive agents of social transformation. Hobson even asserted that 'no strike is worthwhile that does not aim specifically at some form of control'.[30]

Clearly the working class had to prepare itself for its new offensive role. Its experience of the industrial struggle, linked to a great expansion of working-class adult education, would, it was hoped, convert trade union consciousness into class consciousness. Trade union organisation would have to be drastically reshaped on industrial lines both to fight capitalism more effectively and in preparation for its role in Guild society; and for both these purposes the new big unions would have to attract increasing numbers of white-collar workers. But how were the unions to wrest control from the capitalists? The distinctive Guild answer was 'encroachment', for if capitalist power was rooted in the workshops it was there that it would have to be challenged and undermined by the gradual usurpation of capitalist functions by the organised workers (for example by the 'collective contract', whereby employers were forced to come to terms with the workers as a body in matters of pay and production). The aim was to weaken capitalism by steadily depriving it of its social functions. It was not suggested that a mere accumulation of encroachments in the outposts of capitalism would itself be enough painlessly to inaugurate the new society, but it was suggested that such a policy would serve to make the ultimate confrontation 'as little as possible a civil war and as much as possible a registration of accomplished facts and a culmination of tendencies already in operation'. Evolution might not obviate revolution, but it should certainly precede it. There could be no slavish imitation of the largely irrelevant Russian example, nor could Parliamentary action do more than support the industrial offensive of the organised workers, easing a transition which it had no power to accomplish itself. Despite the threat it posed of a new State capitalist bureaucracy, nationalisation was likely to be a necessary precondition for the Guild system in most industries, so it was necessary for Guildsmen to press the Guild idea in relation to nationalisation if not actually to press for nationalisation itself. One thing above all was clear – whatever the nature of the final confrontation with capitalism, it was necessary to start right away on laying the foundations of the future Guild society. This meant essentially, in Cole's words, that 'the problem of transition to Guild Socialism is ... primarily a problem of Trade Union development'.[31]

The critics of Guild Socialism have been both numerous and various. Bruce Glasier of the ILP declared that the Guildsmen were striking at the moral foundations of his beloved socialist movement (by the time the ILP got round to adopting a Guild position it was, characteristically, too late for a mass movement). Beatrice Webb was upset by the 'frightfulness' of the Guild Socialist rebels who 'do violent arid dishonourable acts just for the sake of doing them'.[32] More recent critics have tended to concentrate on the movement's utopianism, its alleged lack of realism about both ends and means. It was too democratic for the ordinary man, whose apathy would just produce a new Guild bureaucracy.[33] Its chosen instrument, the trade unions, was hopelessly inadequate in both consciousness and organisation to perform the role expected of it. Even if 'encroachment' was pursued as a conscious policy, neither the State nor the employers would just retire gracefully from the ring. A working Guild society would anyway be extremely inefficient, unable to deal with sectional interests, and lacking the expert central direction necessary to a modern economy. The sum total of such criticisms was a view of Guild Socialism as a sort of historical aberration, out of touch with the aspirations of ordinary people and irrelevant to the real needs of the modern age.

In fact, Guild Socialism was never so naïve as this type of criticism seeks to suggest. If it had great hopes for the trade unions, it also had few illusions about them. The claim was not that the organised workers were ready to assume power – indeed, the trade union movement was 'an appalling chaos of contending atoms'[34] – but that the business of making them ready had to be actively undertaken. It was claimed that a merely defensive role for trade unionism would neither succeed in shifting the balance of economic power away from profits towards wages nor produce any fundamental change in the status of the workers. It also claimed that Parliamentary action alone would prove impotent in this respect, with a Labour government acting as a brake rather than a spur to radical social change, and that a series of nationalisations would become sound capitalist economics; nationalisation itself would leave the position of the worker unchanged, and capitalism would erect what Cole called a 'barrier of reforms' to soften and conceal the conflict of classes. Clearly, Guildsmen had a conception of social development which has proved far more imaginative than that offered by most of their contemporaries.

They also offered an active alternative for the Labour movement which was 'romantic' only in so far as it was fundamental, demanding a revision of orthodoxy in relation to both process and product. Socialism was to be won by the industrial struggle of the organised workers themselves, and this meant a policy of 'more quarrels on the right things' for the trade unions. At the same time, the distributionist thinking of socialist orthodoxy had to be rejected, along with the statism basic to British political life. Guildsmen offered instead the vision of an active democracy. Labour was strict in its commitment to democracy as a method of change, but for Guild Socialism democracy was also and primarily a condition to be achieved.

This involved a view of capitalism as a power relationship, defining men in relation to each other as owner and owned. It also involved a view of man himself as someone capable of active participation in his social world and, indeed, of such participation being in a real sense 'natural' to man. No doubt it was naïve to think that it was possible to instil joy in labour by democratising the conditions under which it was performed, but not to hold that genuine industrial democracy would do much to transform man's view of himself and of his work, and stimulate his interest in the wider society. Guild Socialism was a statement not only about the rights of man but about his nature too. To have a conception of the end to be achieved was not mere utopianism if it encouraged effective action that would bring about reforms without the movement becoming reformist. Cole asked a question at the very beginning of his first major book which captures both the spirit of Guild Socialism and the permanent concern of his own thinking long after the Guild movement had disappeared: 'What is the Labour movement capable of making of itself?' [35] For Guildsmen this clearly implied voluntarism, emphasis on will and imagination as opposed to the determinism of Marx or the sterility of Fabianism. Above all it brought the issue back to fundamentals. Was the aim to provide people with a decent standard of life, to remove some of the inequities of capitalist distribution, leaving man as passive beneficiary of this new capitalism, or should people be trusted with the free organisation of their own social life, rejecting the power relationships inherent in both capitalism and State bureaucracy?

In the inter-war years there was little place for a doctrine which looked to socialism for the 'intensification of man' – as the *New Age* put it – rather than for immediate remedies for economic ills. Cole turned to economics, the Labour movement to politics, the intellectuals to other things (and later perhaps to Marxism). But in recent years, in a world of political bureaucracy and industrial concentration, interest in Guild Socialism has revived, not because it offers a blueprint but because it marked a genuine attempt to think out what a socialist democracy might look like and how best it could be achieved. If incomplete, it was also suggestive, confirming Cole's own verdict that '*les systèmes meurent; ce qui restent, ce sont les sentiments et les idées.*'[36]

(*Journal of Contemporary History*, 1974)

‡

This piece reflects my own youthful enthusiasm for these ideas, which still seem to me worth exploring – in spirit if not in their convoluted detail – if we are serious about the democratic diffusion of power. It may be that the materials for a civic enterprise of this ambition no longer exist. What is clear, though, is that, set against this kind of 'big society' thinking, the purpose of which was to empower people in relation to both market and State power, the current version seems woefully thin and anaemic. That is why it is seen by many people as merely an exercise in State-shrinking. Historically, the British version of democracy (on both left and right) has been very top-down and this has made it difficult to nourish other traditions. That is what I wanted to do when, in 1996, I wrote about 'reinventing' democracy.

Reinventing Democracy?

Unlike the Webbs on the Soviet Union, it is unlikely that the question mark in my title will one day disappear. The desire to 'reinvent' democracy is restless and endless, rooted in the visionary ambition of the idea of self-government, of people ruling themselves; that is at the heart of what democracy is.

A certain modesty of approach is therefore appropriate. Each generation in each place will come to the question afresh, trailing its own historical and ideological baggage. We may all be democrats now, but we may well not talk in the same way or even mean the same thing. It is always useful to recall the cross-national survey conducted by UNESCO after the Second World War that found both universal affirmation of the democratic ideal and widespread uncertainty about the meaning of what was being affirmed. Confusions and ambiguities abound. Democracy is both an achievement of the past and a project for the future. It needs defending, but also extending. These false opposites have been the source of much confusion in the past, not least on the left. It is important to follow the democratic argument where it leads, but this does not remove the need to have a reliable map. It is an argument about power and provides a popular answer to Aristotle's old question about 'who rules'. But to be operative it also has to be disaggregated. We need to know what kinds of power are relevant to it (and which are not); and in terms of what criteria (for example, accountability, participation, representation, and openness) it is being assessed. This process does not dissolve the central self-governing vision of democracy, but it does force us to define the kind of democracy that we want to be visionary about.

So much for the preliminaries. The discussion here now returns closer to home. The modest aim is to make some connections between these wider considerations and aspects of current arguments about democracy in Britain, with an eye on the larger world beyond. I want to identify some issues, get some bearings, ask some questions – and perhaps fly a few kites and even tread on a few toes. There is a real sense in which the democratic argument in Britain now is too easy for those of us on the political left-centre. The purpose here is to try to make it a bit more difficult.

The Clever State
Why is it too easy? Let me suggest two reasons. First, there is a nicely available symmetry in being able to trump the fashionable argument about the 'reinvention' of government (set text from the United States by Osborne and Gaebler,

but with the Conservatives in Britain claiming their public service programme as its leading practical edge) with an argument about the real need being to reinvent democracy. Where this latter argument becomes too easy is in its implied suggestion that a reinvented democracy is an alternative to a reinvented government rather than a necessary complement to it. It becomes easier still if what is meant by reinvention is really only a traditional restoration. We need to reinvent both the way in which government works and the way in which democracy functions – and to do this together as part of the same process.

An instant balance sheet of the Conservative public service programme might conclude, on the positive side, that it has moved the emphasis from those who provide services to those who consume them and that it has opened up new models of service delivery; but also that, on the negative side, it has been transfixed with quasi-market models, has eschewed all collective means of user empowerment and has eroded public accountability to a point where nobody seems to be responsible for anything anymore. Yet the appropriate response from the left is surely not to want simply to return to the world before 1979. Rather it should want to develop its own version of reinvented government. There is a general point of some importance here. It might be expected that those who most believe in using the State to achieve public purposes would also be those who are most active in ensuring that the State achieves such purposes as effectively and efficiently as possible. That was certainly the promise contained in that old Fabian slogan of Measurement and Publicity, a commitment to innovation, evaluation and emulation.

Yet this is not what has happened. Labour has not in the

past been much interested in exploring new forms of public service delivery (or new forms of democracy). Its concern with what went in to services in terms of resources was not matched by an equal concern with what came out of services in terms of performance. No doubt there are good and bad reasons for this. But producer capture is not an invention of the right; nor is the recognition that the State (and those who run it) is a powerful special interest group in its own right. If the left's critique of the market is indispensable, then so too is the right's critique of the State. The argument here is that the left needs to know this, precisely because it is most committed to an effectively performing State. So too with the organisation of democracy. The right has identified the blunt infirmities of traditional electoral representation as the rationale for its substitution in a range of areas by an individualised consumer democracy. In its proper dissatisfaction with the latter, the left is too prone to succumb to an uncritical embrace of the former.

What the left should embrace is what I want to call the clever State. The clever State will display a restless ingenuity in devising new forms of government to enable it to perform better; and equal ingenuity in devising new forms of democracy to give practical expression to the promise of self-government. These are not different enterprises, but part of the same project and inherently interconnected. New forms of democracy, in which citizens come to exercise more direct control over the activities of the State, will do more than anything else to ensure that the State serves their interests rather than its own. This may be unsettling to, and resisted by, those interest groups clustered around the state, but this is necessary and unavoidable. Of course the neo-liberal right will insist that the clever State is a chimera: only markets are clever, whereas the State is inherently bureaucratic, unresponsive, self-regarding and self-aggrandising. The left has to prove this wrong, not least because people's willingness to pay taxes for public provision of services will increasingly depend upon their belief in the effectiveness of such provision and in their sense of ownership in relation to its character. The clever State is one which reconnects citizens to it, but this needs to be done in new ways.

One example makes the point. When elected parent governors arrived in schools in the 1980s, they met the hostility of the teacher unions, resentment from many local party machines (especially Labour ones) and suspicion from much of the local educational establishment both inside and outside schools. Yet this citizens' army carried with it the potential to transform the school system for the better, putting parental issues on the agenda and giving parents a greater sense of ownership of schools themselves. It is not surprising (though it seems to have surprised the Conservatives) that governors have emerged as vociferous and informed defenders of their schools against those who would undermine their effectiveness. In the clever State, democracy and efficacy are mutually enhanced.

There is not a single model. Indeed, one of the hallmarks of the clever State is that there is a hugely variegated landscape of organisational forms. The trouble is that the traditional left was not much interested in exploring this landscape, with the result that opportunities were missed and high political prices eventually had to be paid. When A. H. Halsey told the North of England Education Conference in 1977 that schools should become self-managing, old municipal socialism preferred not to listen. The unpopularity of the former nationalised utilities could have been transformed (and their journey into privatisation prevented) if the form of public ownership had been translated into the reality of popular ownership, for example through their conversion into consumer co-operatives. Current issues present similar challenges. The quango State invites an imaginative response that involves something more than either a swap of appointees or a return to traditional forms of public service organisation. The distinction between a commissioning (or contracting) function and a providing function is an important one in thinking about public services, and the confusion of these functions has often contributed to a lack of effectiveness. This is true of education, where it would be sensible to divide the role of local education authorities into a contracting authority (for which new forms of democratic representation should be considered, including direct election) and a provider association for schools (with their own form of representation on this body). Again, both democracy and effectiveness would be enhanced. On another front, the current attempts to rethink the welfare state should have as one of their central purposes the construction of welfare institutions that plausibly carry with them some sense of citizen ownership. This is one of the real merits (if not the current reality) of the national insurance principle, which is also why it is worth exploring hypothecated forms of taxation; but it is also a merit of State-sponsored compulsory mutual schemes of the kind advocated in some quarters. The clever State will range widely in its search for appropriate models.

What it will not do is to be content with the traditional position of the left, which preferred to rehearse the familiar antinomies of State and market rather than to explore ways in which the State might be redesigned to improve government and reinvigorate democracy. There was a brief period, in the early part of this century, when there was vigorous and imaginative debate on the British left about alternative forms of democracy that would be required in the developing collectivist state. Between them G. D. H. Cole and R. H. Tawney defined the problem of combining community purpose with self-governing institutions that remains at the centre of the democratic socialist project. Yet for too long this issue was not actively pursued and explored, allowing the right to associate the left with an unreconstructed statism. It is time to renew that earlier debate, not in simplistic, naïve or Utopian ways but as an essential part of the contemporary task of inventing a clever State.

Terrain, Traditions and Techniques

I turn now, more briefly, to a second reason why the democratic argument is perhaps too easy in Britain at present. It is too easy to convert it simply into the familiar agenda of constitutional reform. That agenda is indispensable. The democratic deficit is so yawning, the need to constitutionalise British government so long overdue, that the running together in the circumstances of Britain now of the wider democratic argument with the narrower focus on the reform of the constitution is almost inevitable. I yield to no one in my enthusiasm to reform the British political system from top to bottom. Its unreformed condition, the product of a particular history and culture, mocks the requirements of a mature democracy and impedes our ability to tackle a range of problems. Yet the fact remains that, so obvious, urgent and available is the reform agenda in this area, that it too easily allows us to make it the universal answer to almost every democratic discontent. And that is, at bottom, an evasion.

Might it not even be a substitute for other agendas that we find more difficult and intractable? Does the new certainty on the left about the centrality of political reform really serve to hide its new uncertainty about so much else? Are we sure that the real issue is not the purpose of government rather than its process? Is there not also an irony in the embrace by the left of an old-fashioned liberal constitutionalism concerned with setting a limiting framework around democratic government? There is enough force in such questions to make it important not simply to duck them. They require hard answers, not easy evasions. Then there remains the toughest question of all: if and when a serious programme of constitutional reform is enacted in Britain, would not the wider problems of a 'reinvented' democracy still remain? The short answer is that they would, for they are general problems of the kind identified earlier. The political reform agenda is local and domestic. Its necessity invites us to make it identical with the larger task of democratic reinvention. That invitation has, sadly, to be rejected.

On this wider front, the prospects can seem thoroughly gloomy. We do not need to buy all the currently fashionable rhetoric of globalism to know that the contemporary world looks an unpromising place if the purpose is to refashion the instruments of collective self-government. If old arguments in support of direct democracy seemed to have been trumped by the problem of size in the big state, then arguments in support of almost any kind of effective democracy can easily seem to have been trumped by the problems of both size and power in the big world. It is a world of big states and big corporations, but it is also a fragmenting world, a post-enlightenment world, a world out of control, a world stalked by forces that threaten much and promise little. Or so it can easily appear. It is a world that invites us to take refuge in an ideology of personal survivalism, or to surf off into a cyberspace of virtual and personal democracy. As we lock our doors we hang out the 'gone surfing' sign. Technological panaceas are not the only responses that fail to convince. We are told that the role of pension funds and insurance companies means that we are now all the owners of the modern economy, but we sense that this is really an invitation to exchange the aspiration to self-government for its chimerical form. Faced with trans-national power, we respond by imagining schemes of global governance; but know that this could all too easily be a kind of politics with the people left out. Nearer home, Europe exemplifies the problem. If we want to be cheerful, we have a duty to be gloomy as well.

Let us get some bearings by returning briefly to that core democratic idea of self-government, of people ruling themselves in the classical sense of ruling and being ruled at the same time. This vision was transmuted (and abbreviated) in modern times into the struggle for electoral democracy. Different political traditions responded in different ways to this development. The conservative tradition was hostile, fearful that the untutored masses would subvert order, authority and property, but also coming to understand that a conservative statecraft could find something to its advantage in the new democratic environment. (Thus Lord Salisbury in 1892: 'The French are always defending their worst proceedings by saying their Chamber won't stand for this and won't stand that. It may be an advantage that we too should be able to flourish an inexorable Chamber in their faces.') Liberals were anxious democrats, happier when democracy had been firmly disciplined as representative democracy (as it was by J. S. Mill) and embedded in a secure framework of constitutionalism. The liberal triumphalism that marked the end of the Cold War and collapse of communism felt like a huge historical sigh of relief, a final emancipation from anxiety. Modern neo-liberal conservatism gives a new twist to the story, of course, in which democracy is again seen as a problem – the carrier of inflationary expectations and a standing invitation to monetary indiscipline and a bloated state – requiring robust management. If some liberal conservatives have wanted to circumscribe such proclivities constitutionally (Hayek, for example), others have been content to manage them politically.

All this is shorthand, of course; but the broad lines of the picture are clear enough. And what of socialism? The short answer is that socialists have both embraced political democracy and wanted to go 'beyond' it into the more expansive realms of social and economic democracy. A Fabian might believe that political democracy would be the inevitable instrument of a wider democracy, a Marxist might believe that political democracy was a sham without a wider democracy, but all kinds of socialist were interested in that wider democracy of social and economic power. If this was what conservatives and liberals feared, it was what socialists wanted and (at least for a long time) expected. This had a number of consequences, one of which only will be mentioned here. It meant that socialists were not much inclined to explore political democracy itself, preferring to move it on to other things. In Britain this had a further consequence of some significance. As Sam Beer argued a generation ago in his *Modern British Politics*, the combination of a socialist tradition that saw democracy as the instrument of state collectivism and a conservative tradition that domesticated democracy in terms of its own Tory paternalism left little space for other and more active versions of democratic self-government. It was a powerful and suffocating combination. Its effects are writ large across the face of British politics and British society. Democracy became the name for the condition of being governed.

It is against this background, both general and local, that any process of democratic reinvention has to be conducted. Unless we are content to watch the further erosion of democracy's role as the legitimating basis of government in the West (and the evidence suggests that such erosion is marked and accelerating), we would do well to devote some thought and energy to how this role can be reinvigorated. In this sense the reassertion of an active understanding of self-government is not merely an exercise in political theory but an urgent and practical task for the times. What matters is not to argue for one reading of democracy against others but to nourish a reading that can speak to the times. If people come to feel that they are able to exercise ever less power over the forces that control their lives, no amount of democratic rhetoric will be able to fill the gap of credibility and legitimacy that is opened up. At best this will produce a sullen and cynical indifference, at worst something much nastier.

So what is to be done? There is no blueprint available. Different political traditions have their insights to offer. It is right to see democracy as the means of majoritarian action, but it is also right to see it as needing a framework of constitutional limitations in the interests of pluralistic liberty (which Bobbio refers to as 'this constant dialectical interplay between liberalism and democracy'). It is right to see electoral and political democracy as fundamental, but it is also right to want to apply the democratic principle to other centres of power. The emphasis of the democratic enterprise will also necessarily be shaped by the circumstances of time and place. Thus the main emphasis here is on Britain, although the connections go much wider. In seeking to reinvent democracy, we need to focus both on the terrain and techniques of democracy. The question to be asked is whether we can extend its terrain and improve on its techniques. The rest of this article offers some brief reflections on both of these fronts.

The Responsible Society

In wanting to open up new democratic terrain, the core justificatory principle is that major arenas of social, economic and political power – power over people's lives and power that shapes the life of society itself – should be harnessed to a doctrine of democratic responsibility. This is a responsibility that acknowledges a framework of obligations and accountabilities, recognises a range of legitimate stakeholders and seeks ways in which these stakeholders can have an effective voice. An approach of this kind will not be impressed by attempts to construct iron walls between 'public' and 'private' centres of power (for such walls turn out to be remarkably flimsy when closely examined) but will instead want to apply the doctrine of responsibility to both.

There are two clear implications for current political argument in Britain. The first is that the case for political reform should properly be understood (and presented) as one part of a wider argument about the nature of a responsible society. This does not in any way diminish its centrality or urgency, but it does anchor it in a wider democratic argument to which it properly belongs. The need to constitutionalise the British polity is part of a larger need to constitutionalise other terrain too. Irresponsible political power sits alongside irresponsible social and economic power on the reform agenda. Political insecurity connects with social and economic insecurity as the contemporary challenge to be engaged with. The attempt to construct a new politics of rights and responsibilities involves the political system but also includes much else. There is an integrated and intercon-necting argument here and its durable strength will come from the extent to which it can be assembled in this way. This meets the second implication of approaching matters from this direction. For what it identifies and throws into sharp relief is the central ideological divide in contemporary British politics. This is between what is essentially a doctrine of irresponsibility on the political right, in which the power of global markets is gleefully mixed with domestic ideological proclivities to sustain a politics which strips away securities, mocks social solidarities and erodes communities. In this new world of market liberalism, the very notion of respon-sibility is dissolved since it speaks to a relationship between human beings in their social setting that is rejected. They simply have to roll over and take what is coming to them, from forces and powers over which there can be and should be no control. Indeed when they are told that they have to become Asians, they are being told that they have to cease even to be themselves. In advancing a politics of democratic responsibility, the left is able to meet this argument head on and clarify the central political choice of our times.

But where else does it lead? What new democratic terrain does it open up? What are the 'sites' of responsibility and self-government? There is no single or simple answer, nor should there be, but there are several promising directions of advance. There is the pivotal choice to be made between the kinds of capitalism on offer in the world, a choice that is at the centre of the contemporary political battle. The argument for a 'stakeholder' capitalism is important precisely because it is the carrier and expression of a doctrine of responsibility in relation to the organisation of economic power. It stands in stark opposition to a doctrine of market irresponsibility. Arguments about the 'private' governance of corporations should not be divorced from arguments about the 'public' governance of states. One of the unintended effects of the privatisation programme in Britain has been to reveal how inadequate is the public/private distinction in relation to the privatised utilities and how unbalanced is any conception of the shareholder as the only legitimate stakeholder. If the policy task in relation to these industries is to develop a conception of the public interest company in the private sector, or to convert them into mutual or cooperative enterprises, the implications of doing this go much wider. Issues of corporate governance are here to stay.

For a long time the old socialist belief in 'economic' democracy was out of fashion, and in some of its versions no doubt deserved to be. Modern exponents of varieties of market and associational socialism build on these older traditions, but even without such visionary excursions there is promising work again to be done. We have learned enough from successful enterprises around the world to know that rigid hierarchies are as bad for companies as they are for states. Teamwork and partnership pay. But they are also right; the world of work should not be an arena of un-freedom in a responsible democracy. It is extraordinary that there are still those who believe that such modest developments as works councils should be regarded as a threat to market prerogatives rather than an opportunity for constructive partnerships. In these matters the State should properly seek to promote democratic virtue, just as it should actively promote and sponsor a variety of forms of ownership including co-operative and self-managing models.

Yet the world of work, so central to traditional socialist thinking on the application of democracy, is only one site (and for many not the most important) where a politics of democratic responsibility and self-government now becomes a serious project. The rich and dense fabric of associational life out of which the Labour movement was born – the world of co-operatives, trade unions, mutual and friendly societies, clubs and chapels – has to be reinvented in modern form. If this sounds like compulsory voluntarism then perhaps it is. We desperately need some new little platoons, just as we need some new forms of civic collectivism. A world in which the individual stands alone in the face of the big State and the big corporation, at the mercy of bureaucrats and markets, is not a world in which the civic virtues will flourish.

The trends may not seem promising. The movement from voluntarism into State provision is familiar, but it is supplemented by another movement from mutualism to markets (as with the building societies). Yet on all sides the need to find new ways to reconnect people to civic life is compelling. There is no shortage of sites or opportunities, if we are prepared to devote some energy and imagination to the task. Nor is there an absence of examples of what may be possible, if we are willing to learn from them and build upon them. New forms of neighbourhood and community organisation, animated by dynamic social entrepreneurs, are showing what can be achieved in some of the most desperate inner urban areas.

Forging new tools for community self-government is likely to prove an indispensable part of any durable regeneration strategy in such places. Neighbourhoods, estates, schools, workplaces: this is just the beginning of a list of the sites in which a new politics of democratic responsibility can and should be developed. In framing and re-framing a whole range of institutions and services, the opportunity should always be taken to explore the self-governing options (as with the self-governing pensions corporation in Australia). An empowering State will forever be searching for new ways in which citizens can exercise responsibility for their common life.

A flourishing and active democracy will be immensely variegated both vertically and horizontally, a civic arena of many levels and a rich variety of channels. The desire for uniformity (sometimes mis-described as a desire for equity) should not be allowed to snuff out democratic diversity. If the terrain of democracy is understood as multi-tiered, then it makes sense to think in terms of the democratic organisation of power at the most appropriate level. Instead of operating with a political equivalent of the 'lump of labour' argument, democracy should properly expand to enable it to follow power where it goes. It needs to flow upwards and outwards, beyond the nation to Europe and beyond; but it also needs to flow downwards and sideways, into a rich micro-democracy of associational life. The preference should always be for doing things at the lowest level that is efficiently possible. Understood in this way, sovereignty ceases to be a fixed and formal lump to be lost and becomes instead an array of democratic opportunities to be gained.

If we turn from terrain to techniques, there is also an abundance of democratic possibilities waiting to be explored. There is a good deal of intellectual vitality on this front currently, aimed at enhancing those democratic components of representation, accountability, participation and openness. A quick trawl would include online information flows, the postal voting experiment in Oregon, the development of deliberative polling techniques, the establishment of citizens' juries to consider public policy issues and (as in New Zealand) new opportunities for citizen-initiated referendums. It is not necessary to embrace all such techniques with indiscriminate enthusiasm to acknowledge that traditional forms of representative democracy may not be the last word in democratic development.

Indeed, what is remarkable is how undeveloped democratic forms have remained in the face of the enormous growth in both public and private concentrations of power during the twentieth century. It is almost as though we have been operating with a settled mental assumption that democracy had been 'achieved' at that moment in the past when mass enfranchisement had been secured. Yet democracy is properly seen as a continuous process not merely as an occasional event. If its bottom line is the ability of people to kick their rulers out, it should also include ample opportunities for kicking them while they are in. One study comparing elected and non-elected members of assorted public bodies threw up the alarming conclusion that, while those who were not elected worried away at being representative and account-able, the elected members simply assumed that the fact of election had absolved them from any need to worry about such matters. Yet it clearly does not. Walt Whitman's phrase about the 'never-ending audacity of elected persons' remains a text for our times.

Doing Democracy Differently

An equal audacity is now needed in devising new and sup-plementary democratic techniques. It is not possible here to do more than fire off a few suggestions, in the British context, about possible lines of advance. One indispensable task is to ensure that our central democratic institutions work better than they do now. These institutions are basic and vital, what-ever we may wish to supplement them with, and they need to be in good working order. Yet they are conspicuously not.

Parliament is nothing short of a scandal in this respect, its unreformed condition making a mockery of the functions of representation and accountability it is supposed to perform. It needs a fundamental procedural revolution to make it less a poodle of the executive and more a robust democratic creature in its own right. The key reforms that are needed are well understood and much rehearsed – above all in relation to the legislative process – but this simply serves to highlight Parliament's blind refusal to take reform seriously. Yet the fact is that any wider process of democratic reform will count for nothing unless our central representative assembly is itself reformed.

A similar argument can be made about local government.

It is crucial to restore and renew the role of our key local representative institutions, for they express our common civic life and are the carriers of our public purposes. They have been grievously eroded by the recent onslaught on them and it is therefore a proper task to restore their constitutional integrity on a more secure basis. However, what is improper is to make an unquestioned coupling of 'local government' with 'local democracy', for the need and opportunity for new democratic techniques is even greater at the local level than at the national. This is true of electoral reform, that pivotal innovation in democratic technique as far as Britain is concerned, for it is in local government that one-party states are able to stay in power (at least in normal times) courtesy of an electoral system that guarantees their permanence. However, local electoral reform needs to be seen alongside a range of other reforms to the workings of local government (of the kind identified recently in the report of the Commission for Local Democracy). On electoral reform in general, three points may be added. First, as Labour's Plant Committee argued impressively, it is ludicrous to get hooked on a particular voting system. It is horses for courses. Second, notwithstanding the above, those systems which enhance civic participation and promote citizen choice should be preferred to those which do not. And, third, it may be necessary to move to the kind of pluralist politics that would be delivered by electoral reform before it is possible to secure the radical institutional reforms described earlier.

But improvements in democratic technique do not stop at such alterations to the way in which our major democratic institutions work. A wide and exciting range of mechanisms are available, some at least of which are being actively explored in different contexts, whereby citizens may contribute to the democratic process in ways which enhance and supplement the traditional forms of representative democracy. There is no single model, nor should there be; but there is a repertoire of techniques available for exploration and development.

A quick list, in the context of Britain, might include the following. New forms of both territorial and functional representation (with a reconstituted House of Lords as an ideal place to start). An escape from the belief that election and appointment in their traditional forms exhaust the range of representative possibilities. The reform of the quango State provides an opportunity to develop new forms of representation and accountability appropriate to particular services and functions. It may even be possible, and desirable, to explore contexts in which lot or random selection (sometimes described as statistical representation) would cease to be merely a classical democratic memory and become an innovative democratic presence. The putative public service consumerism of the citizen's charter programme would become less a charter for managers (a description conceded by William Waldegrave when he was its guardian) and more a real charter for citizen consumers, with secure and enforceable individual rights (with means of redress) in combination with new collective mechanisms of user empowerment. User councils could be developed for all public services, not just for those without an elective basis (the rationale for Community Health Councils in relation to the NHS) and constituted in a variety of innovative ways. New forms of partnership between lay and professional voices in service provision and evaluation should be developed (as in advocacy schemes and locality planning). User groups will be strengthened, and unrealistic expectations about continuous citizen participation avoided, if they are serviced wherever possible by a nucleus of professional support. The technique of citizens' juries (as with deliberative polling) should be developed as a regular and expected part of the decision making and planning process wherever it has a role to play. Not the least of its merits, which may commend it even to those whose main priority is not to extend democracy, is that it may serve to prevent the planning process being dominated by special interest groups claiming to speak for the public.

Then there is the referendum, the potential of which has yet to be explored seriously in Britain, where the act of decision clarifies and disciplines choices in a way that ersatz devices do not. We should start worrying a lot less about whether referenda are compatible with the sovereignty of Parliament and begin thinking seriously about what they may add to democratic legitimacy. This is as true at the European level (why not a pan-European referendum on further integration?) as it is at the national (why not a referendum on the current proposal that British Summer Time should be extended, for example?), while the scope for local referendum is even greater. Local people in local areas could decide whether they wanted a comprehensive or selective system of schooling, for example, while the ceaseless struggle between the centre and local authorities over spending levels could be decided by means of local referenda if councils wished to spend (and tax) above a standard level. There will no doubt be argument over the particular examples, but what is not in doubt is the availability of an array of techniques – of which the referendum is only one – capable of nourishing the democratic process in innovative ways.

One final point of a more general kind. We live in an age of deep uncertainties. Old structures and paradigms (not least ideological ones) disintegrate in front of our eyes. Democratic politics is the means whereby we have to define new common purposes and translate them into collective choices, but it has to be a kind of democratic politics that engages openly and honestly with this new world. This has radical implications for the practice of politics, especially so in Britain. The kind of politics that merely trades in false certainties, closed cultures and rival dogmatisms is wholly inappropriate in a world charged with the task of thinking and acting its way through the challenges it now faces. Politics is a struggle of powers, interests and ideas; but it also needs to be a process of mutual learning. Pluralism is a kind of politics that diffuses power and shares political territory; but also has to signify a vigorous and deliberate plurality of ideas and opinions from which political learning can take place. This means a new approach to both the structures and culture of politics. Reinventing democracy now means reinventing politics too.

(In P. Hirst and S. Khilnan (eds), *Reinventing Democracy*, [1996])

‡

Representative democracy requires democratic institutions, and these need to be kept in a good state of repair if they are to do their essential job of holding power to account. My experience of the House of Commons was that it was not in a good state of repair for this accountability function. In too many ways it was prepared to settle for the form of accountability (as in

147

the knockabout of Prime Minister's Questions) rather than the substance (through sustained scrutiny). In the mid-nineteenth century Bagehot described the House of Commons as 'the greatest discussing and inquiring machine that the world has ever seen' and I wanted this to be true in the early twenty-first century too. That necessarily made me a Parliamentary reformer, and the reform theme was one at which I kept coming from a number of directions. In a piece from 2004 I identified both the need for reform and the political difficulties in achieving it.

Reforming Parliament

I was told last night that the scene of noise and uproar which the House of Commons now exhibits is perfectly disgusting. This used not to be the case in better, or at least more gentlemanlike, times; no noises were permissible but the cheer and the cough, the former admitting every intonation expressive of admiration, assent, denial, surprise, indignation, menace, sarcasm. Now all the musical skill of this instrument is lost and drowned in shouts, hootings, groans, noises of the most discordant that the human throat can emit, sticks and feet beating against the floor. Sir Hedworth Williamson, a violent Whig, told me that there were a set of fellows on his side of the House whose regular practice it was to make this uproar, and with the settled design to bellow Peel down. This is the *reformed* House of Commons. Charles Greville, 4 April 1835.

What of our own reformed House of Commons? It might seem odd to discuss 'prospects' of reform when the House of Commons has surely been living through a period of deliberate and sustained reform, as part of the Blair government's modernising constitutional agenda. The House sits at different times. A second debating chamber has been added on. More bills are considered in draft. Business is routinely programmed. Select committees have acquired more resources and tasks. Merely to recite these headline changes (and the list is far from exhaustive) is enough to register the fact of a significant reforming period. Indeed, there are those who suggest it has all gone too far, an echo of the Victorian judge who declared: 'Reform! Reform! Aren't things bad enough already?'

I want instead to suggest, firstly, that the process of reform has not gone nearly far enough; secondly, that reforms so far have lacked coherence and have sometimes been contradictory; thirdly, that there are inherent constraints on Parliamentary reform; and fourthly, that the prospects for radical reform will depend upon what happens on other fronts. A few preliminary observations will help to frame these arguments. There is the fundamental fact that in Britain the executive is particularly strong and Parliament commensurately weak. Behind the constitutional rhetoric about the sovereignty of Parliament there lies the reality of executive dominance in a political system which concentrates power rather than divides it. This is the British version of 'strong government', the product of a particular history and associated set of constitutional arrangements, given added force by the twentieth century development of disciplined political parties.

Any discussion of Parliamentary reform has to be anchored in this underlying reality. Too often it is not, which explains why it can seem to go round in circles without ever really getting anywhere. The difficulty has never been to draw up an agenda for reform, nor to describe the institutional disabilities that make reforms desirable. A raft of reports, articles and pamphlets on these matters stare down from the bookshelves, and there are doubtless many more in the making. The real question is not what it might be desirable to do, but why it has proved so difficult to do it. Unless this is properly understood, and the implications grasped, the enterprise of reform is not likely to advance very far.

Means and Ends

Central to the issue of reform is the question of mechanism. How, and by whom, is a reform project to be mobilised? The short answer is that, in a Parliamentary system of government where the executive is drawn from the majority party, it requires executive leadership, or at least compliance. This means a government that is well disposed towards Parliamentary reform, usually expressed through a Leader of the House who drives a reform initiative. This was the case with the Crossman reforms of the 1960s and the St John Stevas agenda for select committees after 1979. The government (and Prime Minister) of the day has to be content for such reforms to be put in place, certainly not to be hostile to them, and this enables a reform-minded Leader of the House to take the initiative. The House itself lacks an effective mechanism of its own to do this even if it wanted to, not being in control of its own business, and therefore waits for executive leadership. Even then, success is not guaranteed.

The period since 1997 is instructive in this respect. The Blair government had included Parliament in its constitutional reform agenda, but it was not clear what this would mean in practice. There were both worrying and hopeful signs. On the worrying side, Tony Blair told his new Parliamentary army in 1997 that their essential job was to be 'ambassadors' for the government in the country. The whips took this literally, putting in place a rota to enable Labour MPs to spend regular weeks away from Westminster, and taking MPs off select committees in order to join Parliamentary 'campaign' teams. This was a brutal reminder of the realities of British political life, and of Parliament's role in an executive-dominated system. It was certainly not an encouragement to Parliamentary scrutiny, or to reform initiatives designed to make Parliament count for more.

Its purpose and effect was to encourage MPs to face away from Westminster rather than towards it. They were helped in this by a supply of professional campaign materials, new technologies and a significant increase in allowances to pay for more staff and support services. It is not yet fully realised what an impact this has had on the activities of Members of Parliament (of all parties). In the United States the 'incumbency factor', fuelled by some of the same ingredients, is now huge. It is likely that a similar trend will establish itself in Britain, as office-holders use their vastly increased resources to try to keep themselves in office in a permanent election campaign. Activity at Westminster is increasingly seen as providing materials for this campaign of constituency self-promotion, the fuel for relentless local campaigning activity, a process which the parties (whether in government or opposition) foster and encourage.

In other words, Westminster becomes merely instrumental, much more so than was once the case (though there was no golden age). It could be argued that this development is merely a recognition of reality. If Parliament is weak in our system, and if there are few rewards (either for governments or MPs) in seeking to make it stronger, then it might seem perfectly rational to conscript it for other purposes that clearly are thought to matter (above all, getting oneself and one's party elected or re-elected). In this sense, the prospects for Parliamentary reform have become even less promising in recent times, as the activities of MPs have been directed elsewhere. It could be argued that there are some gains in this, as the role of MPs in their constituencies has grown considerably, not just in the familiar caseworker sense but as community catalysts and political entrepreneurs. But it has undoubtedly been at the expense of Parliament itself.

If all this forms part of the worrying side of the recent account, the more positive side is that the Blair government not only came in with modernising ambitions for Parliament but identified the problem of mechanism by setting up a new Modernisation Committee to act as the instrument of reform. It is under the auspices of this committee, steered by various Leaders of the House, that most reforms have happened, although the Liaison Committee has exercised its own influence in relation to the select committees. This is not the place to evaluate what has been done, except in so far as this relates to what more might be done in the future, but it is relevant to say something about the process involved.

What Kind of Modernisation?

There is an inherent ambiguity about the term 'modernisation', certainly as applied to Parliament. Two main meanings may be discerned, with very different (and often contradictory) implications for action. First, there is the kind of modernisation favoured by governments (and many of their supporters). This is the kind that wants to process business more efficiently and predictably, at more agreeable hours. As such, it is essentially executive-minded, although it wins adherents from those who are frustrated by Parliament's archaisms and so well disposed towards change. Second, there is the kind of modernisation that wants to shift the existing balance between executive and legislature in significant respects, notably by strengthening Parliament's scrutiny function. This is much less attractive to governments, because of its potential to make life more difficult for them and does not connect with the career paths or reward structures of most Members of Parliament.

It is not surprising, therefore, that the former kind of modernisation has enjoyed more success than the latter during the recent modernising period. As the Leader of the House most committed to radical reform, Robin Cook sought to build a coalition of support for change among both kinds of modernisers, but there were always intrinsic tensions between them. In significant respects, they wanted different things, and Cook eventually found himself out on a limb as the party machines conspired to ensure that radical excess was curbed. It should never be forgotten by those who parrot the glories of Parliamentary sovereignty, or denounce wicked governments for blocking reforms to strengthen Parliament, that when a Leader of the House provided MPs with an opportunity to decide on a free vote whether they wanted the composition and chairs of their select committees chosen by the whips and the party machines (as at present) or by themselves, they voted for the former option. This is more revealing about the real obstacles to serious reform than innumerable texts on the subject or routine polemics on the tyranny of the executive.

That is not to say that the recent modernising initiative has only delivered on one side of the account. The picture is a mixed one. For example, the way in which the programming of legislation has come to resemble the guillotines it was intended to avoid is clearly a loss for scrutiny, as many amendments to bills now go entirely undiscussed, but the extension of pre-legislative scrutiny through the draft bill procedure is a considerable gain for effective scrutiny (so that when it is not employed, as with the recent Human Tissue Bill, serious problems with legislation are too easily overlooked). As for the contentious issue of sitting hours, when the House sits is less important than what it does when it sits. In general, modernisation-as-efficiency has had more success than modernisation-as-scrutiny, despite the attempt by a reforming Leader of the House to combine the two.

This outcome was made more likely by the way in which the Modernisation Committee originally set about its business. It contains lessons for the future. If the new committee was to serve as the mechanism for a sustained process of reform, it would have been sensible at the outset to identify what the purpose of modernisation was. What would a reformed or modernised House of Commons look like? What were the key objectives to be pursued? Was reform required to enable government business to be processed more efficiently or to strengthen Parliament in relation to the executive? By not engaging with such questions initially, so that there was no underlying analysis or purpose behind particular proposals, there was no yardstick against which to measure progress.

Eschewing a general framework for reform, the work of the committee inevitably lapsed into ad hoc-ery.

This also meant that no real connection could be established between proposals being made for the Commons and the debate about the reform of the House of Lords. The debate was fatally flawed by not being anchored in a reform project for Parliament as a whole. If government was too strong and Parliament too weak, and if this was reflected in a scrutiny deficit, then both Commons and Lords had a role to play in an enterprise of constitutional rebalancing. In the absence of a coherent approach, Commons reform was dogged by the lack of general purpose and Lords reform collapsed in abortive fiasco. If reform of both Houses is to be returned to seriously, then the chances of success will be greatly improved if there is a common prospectus.

How is this to be engineered? It was suggested earlier that executive support is probably essential. There is no 'voice of Parliament' that can be collectively orchestrated. Parliament is a place where the parties do permanent battle, and this fundamental reality trumps attempts to build up Parliament itself. Members of Parliament do not inhabit a career structure in which service to Parliament, distinct from party, brings reward. The doctrine of Parliamentary sovereignty provides the legitimating cloak for routine executive dominance. There is little point in cultivating fantasies about any of this. It is much better to recognise what makes Parliament like it is than to chase illusions about what it might be. Those accounts which say that Parliament should do this or that to make itself more effective fail to understand that there is no 'Parliament', in a collective sense, at all. If there was, we would be living in a different kind of political system.

Advances and Retreats

If the above is put too brutally, it is as an antidote to the polite commentary that puts it too coyly. Reform is inevitably an uphill slog in such a system, and it is best to recognise this frankly. It is a matter of exploiting cracks and getting wedges into doors, which is easier when governments do not offer too much resistance. Sometimes the wedges can be significant ones, as with the select committee system or draft bills, which then provide the basis for further strengthening and extension. Often it can be a question of exploiting a favourable climate of opportunity before the political weather changes. Since it is unlikely that even a reforming government will want to see a radical alteration in the terms of trade between executive and legislature, at least in normal political circumstances, relentless pressure and ingenuity on the part of those who want to strengthen Parliament is essential.

Sometimes it can bring unexpected advances. An example makes the point. For some time I had been pressing the case (first through the Public Administration Select Committee, then through the Liaison Committee) for the Prime Minister to appear before a Parliamentary committee on a regular basis, as other ministers do. This was a clear gap in Parliamentary accountability which needed to be filled. In my correspondence with Downing Street on the issue, I was repeatedly told that it was an established convention that Prime Ministers did not appear before Parliamentary committees (not true by the way, as there were pre-war precedents and the post-1979 select committee system could and should have included the Prime Minister).

The exchanges reached the point at which Robin Cook, as Leader of the House at the time, took me on one side and asked me to drop the proposal once and for all as the Prime Minister had clearly decided that he was never going to agree to it. A few weeks later came the announcement that the Prime Minister had decided to appear twice a year before the Liaison Committee as an expression of his commitment to Parliamentary accountability. One convention was thereby replaced in a splendidly British way by a new and opposite one, which future Prime Ministers will be expected to adhere to.

Such advances need to be banked, and built on. They come in increments, usually after pressure and often against resistance, but enough increments begin to alter the terms of political trade. Another example of the process is the Parliamentary vote on the Iraq War, conceded after intense political pressure. This blew a hole in the power of the prerogative that enables governments to wage wars (and make treaties) without the ratification of Parliament. Here again it will be difficult for governments in future to remove the Parliamentary wedge from this particular executive door, as the Foreign Secretary has explicitly acknowledged. This in turn makes it more likely that, at some point, a wider Parliamentary incursion into the range of prerogative powers will be able to be mounted, building on what has been secured so far.

So we find an ebb and flow of forces, some tending to diminish Parliament since the continuous election campaign that now exists either conscripts Parliament for its purposes or by-passes it altogether, while other pressures try to insert Parliament more firmly in the picture. Fortunately, there are now factors at work that strengthen the hand of those who want to see Parliament play a more active and central role. Foremost among them is the mounting feeling, both in

Parliament and outside, that Parliament needs to matter more, and that its present condition and conduct are not healthy for our democracy. This presents a real opportunity for reformers, with some prospect of converting a reform agenda that is by now well rehearsed into a programme of sustained action.

The Parliamentary Mismatch

Above all, there is the ever more apparent (and embarrassing) disconnection between the Parliamentary game and the way in which issues are handled or discussed by everybody else. The Commons sits in a tribal time warp (or pretends to, which is even worse). The yah-boo adversarialism is just the unlovely manifestation of a whole approach to politics that is demeaning to those who are expected to engage in it and a disservice to those they represent. It is also a waste of the talents and experience of large numbers of Members of Parliament who are wanted only as cheerleaders and foot soldiers. When party counts for less in the electorate than it once did, and when old ideological divisions are blurred in the face of new realities, Parliamentary politics increasingly takes place in its own bubble. People look in, are sometimes amused and entertained by it, but it feels like a game from another planet.

Consider for a moment how the game works. A government proposes something. The official opposition opposes it. The third main party also opposes it, but on different grounds. These adversarial polarities are then paraded in Parliament and repeated in the media. The formulaic predictability of this pattern of behaviour engages the participants and disengages everybody else. It is also foolish, because it prevents sensible agreement in some areas (such as the finance of higher education or pensions policy) where consensus is desirable and invites damaging policy discontinuities. This is not an argument for some kind of soggy consensus, but simply for a more grown-up way of doing politics. Nor is it an argument against the indispensable role of party; but party should structure political life, not suffocate it.

At present there is an embarrassing mismatch between how Parliament operates (as with the sterile adversarialism of the legislative standing committees, mercifully kept from general public view) and how issues are discussed or handled in the outside world.

There comes a point at which such acute mismatch has to be remedied, unless the institution is content to slide into irrelevance. There is no shortage of ideas about what can be done, exciting participative technologies on hand, innovations in Scotland and Wales to learn from, and much else besides. A lack of reforming materials and suggestions has never been the problem, nor is it now. It all comes down to incentive and will. The failure of a reform-minded House after 1997, with a massive governing majority, to carry through a coherent programme of Parliamentary reform that would genuinely shift the balance in relation to a dominant executive, even with a seriously reforming Leader of the House for some of the period, shows just how difficult the task is. Yet it becomes more pressing, not less, if Parliament is to become fit for purpose. Good scrutiny really does make for good government.

If Parliament abandons functions, or does not reclaim them, they will still be performed, but by somebody else. The media will take over political debate even more completely. If Parliament does not control its own business, it will have it controlled for it. If representation is ineffective, other channels will be found. If inquiries are needed and Parliament is incapable of mounting them effectively, then they will be conducted elsewhere. This is why there needs to be relentless effort to keep, or insert, Parliament into the picture. It is a continuing struggle, and there is no prospect of it abating. This is why, just to take one example, the Public Administration Select Committee demanded that the government should restore to the Ministerial Code the requirement that policy announcements should be made to Parliament first, which was agreed. Continuing vigilance and pressure are required on every front.

A major front concerns the ability of Parliament to conduct effective investigatory inquiries. As was widely observed at the time, the contrast between the Hutton inquiry (with no formal powers at all) and a Parliamentary select committee in terms of the ability to undertake an investigation into the matters under consideration was stark. This has reopened the whole issue about the powers available to select committees to get access to persons, records and papers, and the ability of committees to undertake such inquiries effectively. Parliament should insist on equipping itself with what it needs for the purpose, which includes owning the rules (the so-called Osmotherly rules) under which civil servants give evidence. The clear lesson of the Hutton experience is that Parliament either has to equip itself with the means to undertake effective inquiries or it should leave the field to others.

There was much Parliamentary frustration in the wake of Hutton about the weaknesses that had been exposed in the select committee system, but whether such frustration will be converted into a resolute determination to do anything about it remains to be seen.

Changing Context, Changing Prospects

This returns the discussion to some of the fundamental issues with which it started. The preceding paragraph lapsed into the familiar rhetoric about 'Parliament should insist etc.' when the whole point is that there is no Parliament, in that collective sense, to insist on anything. There are simply Members of Parliament who have preoccupations and inhabit a career structure in which attention to the sustained strengthening of the institution is not a central priority. Nor are there effective mechanisms through which a reform process can be driven, despite recent innovations. So the only alternative is to keep plugging away, mobilising such mechanisms as do exist, and exploiting opportunities as they arise.

There is no point in inventing an imagined Parliament that does not exist, nor is likely to exist in any immediately foreseeable future, and judging all reforms against that impossible phantom. Equally, there is no point in exaggerating the significance of assorted reforms that are made, without a realistic appraisal of their practical effect. In a system of Parliamentary government in which the executive sits in the legislature, and routinely controls its operation, there are inherent limitations on Parliament's ability to develop a collective character and to act as an effective instrument of scrutiny and accountability. The real question – and test of reform – is whether it is doing as well as it might do in this situation. Framed this way, the prospects for further reform can be more realistically assessed.

Of course if the context changes, then the prospects are inevitably transformed. How could this happen? If a government lacked a secure Parliamentary majority, then Parliament would clearly count for more. Whether this would merely produce turbulence and instability or a strengthening of Parliament as an institution is difficult to say. Previous experiences of such situations are not encouraging. However, it is at least possible that coalition partners (if it came to that) might press the case for institutional reforms to make Parliament work differently, sharing power rather than concentrating it. This is certainly more likely than a single opposition party coming to power with a secure majority and implementing a major reform programme, whatever that party might say in opposition. Proximity to power is the standard cure for an excess of reforming zeal in any party as far as Parliament is concerned.

The development which would transform the prospects for Parliament is a changed electoral system, perhaps as a consequence of the sort of political circumstances just described, when coalition partners exact a price for their co-operation or a major party decides that its long-term fortunes are better served by a shift away from a simple plurality voting system. There have been moments in the past when such developments have seemed possible, if not likely, including the establishment by Tony Blair of an electoral reform commission under Roy Jenkins. Such moments may come again, and now in a context where there are already a considerable variety of electoral systems in the United Kingdom. Their effects are precisely those anticipated, pluralising power rather than concentrating it and creating a new kind of relationship between the executive and the representative institution.

This is not intended as an argument for electoral reform for Westminster, simply a statement that a changed voting system would have transforming implications for Parliament. If Parliament is like it is because our political system is like it is, then a change that would fundamentally alter the political system would necessarily have major implications for how Parliament operated. There would be even more radical implications if a new political environment of this kind prompted demands for a wider process of constitutional stocktaking, rebalancing and codification. For example, if it was decided that powers should be separated out more fully and formally, as a matter of constitutional principle and practice, then a directly elected executive figure would be required to do business with a separately created Parliament. That would clearly be the end of Parliamentary government as we have known it, but it would also be the beginning of a new role for Parliament.

At this point, the line between a sober consideration of realistic prospects and an exuberant flight of political fancy becomes blurred. Yet it serves as a reminder of the extent to which a seriously reformed Parliament is dependent upon the nature of the wider political environment. As this changes, so too will Parliament. Some of this change will be planned and predictable, but much of it is likely to come through events that are unplanned and unpredictable. Today's heresies are tomorrow's axioms. This emphatically does not mean that it is not worth attending to the reform possibilities in the circumstances in which Parliament finds itself now; it is simply that a change in those circumstances will inevitably transform the prospects for fundamental reform.

Facing Up to the Challenge

It is worth registering, in all this talk of reform, that Parliament performs some functions extremely well. It provides an arena in which the party battle is conducted on a continuous basis, and where brute accountabilities are demanded and identified. It makes, and destroys, reputations. It is a forum in which every issue under the sun makes its appearance. Members of Parliament are tireless in the service of their constituencies and constituents. None of this should be dismissed lightly in the cause of reform. Yet Parliament's failings are serious too, and now require to be remedied. Above all, it fails in the task of continuous scrutiny and accountability. It is content to exchange transient appearance for durable substance, and daily adversarialism for grown-up debate. Both structures and cultures need attention. It may be too much to say that it is an institution in crisis, but there is a growing feeling that it is falling down on the job expected of it by the people it represents.

This leads directly to a final point. Parliament remains our central representative institution. Whatever other channels there may now be to debate issues, represent views and enforce accountabilities, Parliament still sits at the apex of formal representation and accountability. At least, that is what it is expected to do, and why it is crucial to make sure that it does. At the end of his most recent anatomy of power in Britain, under the question *Who Runs This Place?*, Anthony Sampson writes: 'The will-o'-the-wisp of power has led us from one institution to another, and eventually to institutions abroad. But the ultimate responsibility must end up where it began – in Parliament, whose members alone can represent the interests of the British people, with all their growing diversity.' That is the indispensable point and the unavoidable obligation. If we understand this, and respond to it, then the prospects for serious Parliamentary reform are much brighter than they sometimes seem.

(*Parliamentary Affairs*, October 2004)

‡

There are particular difficulties in making sure that the Commons does its accountability job effectively in a political system where a Parliamentary majority forms the government. When that majority is a crushing one (as it was during the Thatcher and Blair years) the difficulty is compounded. It has become familiar to describe the British political system as one in which the executive is particularly strong and Parliament correspondingly weak. The question for me was whether this balance could be shifted in a way that managed to combine effective government with effective accountability. That was the question I tackled, in a piece (previously unpublished) in honour of Peter Hennessy, in 2009.

Parliament and Executive: Shifting the Balance?

Despite writing at inordinate length about Whitehall over the past thirty years, I am Parliament's man by instinct. I dislike the executive dominance that disfigured our system of government for most of the twentieth century; I rejoice when the legislature, to borrow a phrase beloved of Roy Jenkins, has 'risen to the level of events.

Peter Hennessy.[37]

Here, from Parliament's man, is the ambivalence that is intrinsic to any serious account of Parliament. On the one side, there is the Parliament of those 'great Parliamentary occasions', of dramatic debates, stirring speeches, titanic clashes and history-shaping votes. This is the Parliament that is the great assembly of the nation, the site of a continuous civic conversation, where ministers are held to vigorous account by the people's representatives. On the other side, there is the Parliament of executive domination, elective dictatorship, party control, adversarial pantomime and supine irrelevance (and now including fiddled expenses). So which is it?

It is, of course, both; hence the inherent ambivalence. Two MP diarists point the contrast. In a passage that Peter Hennessy says always makes him 'glow', the Liberal MP Alexander McCallum Scott described leaving the House one night in 1917 at the height of the Great War with his colleague Winston Churchill, who 'called me into the Chamber to take a last look round. All was darkness except a ring of faint light all around under the Gallery. We could dimly see the Table but walls and roof were invisible. "Look at it," he said. "This little place is what makes the difference between us and Germany. It is in virtue of this that we shall muddle through to success and for lack of this Germany's brilliant efficiency leads her to final destruction. This little room is the shrine of the world's liberties."'[38] A generation later, in 1935, the diary entry of 'Chips' Channon, then a new Conservative MP, also recorded a glow, but with a troubling shadow: 'Most of the day at the Commons. Today for the first time I really liked it; boredom passed and a glow of pleasure filtered through me. But I wish I sometimes *understood* what I was voting for, and what against.'[39] Most MPs today would recognise both the glow and the shadow.

To say that there is ambivalence about the nature of Parliament, or inherent tensions in how it operates, is not to suggest that there is in any sense an equal struggle at work. It is difficult to see how there could be, in a constitutional system which fuses executive and legislature. When fused also with a strong party system, and majoritarian electoral system, this gives Parliament its essential character. The nature of the institution is necessarily a product of the kind of political and constitutional system within which it sits. It could hardly be otherwise. What this means is that those of us who have wanted to beef up Parliament's role in scrutiny and accountability have faced formidable obstacles. There have been some successes, but also notable failures. This is the theme of what follows.

Governing and Accounting

In some ways it is misleading even to refer to Parliament in a collective sense at all, as though it had an identity and purpose separate from the political forces which shape its character. It is above all the place where the contending parties meet and do battle, one side sustaining government and the other side sustaining opposition, with this battle itself now merely one site of engagement in a continuous election campaign to which it has to contribute. Doctrine may say that Parliament is sovereign; the reality is that sovereignty is conveniently and routinely exercised by the executive on its behalf and in its name. This has been described as 'the ultimate paradox of the British Parliamentary state.'[40] The legitimacy of executive action is secured partly by the fact of election, but also – and crucially – because it is endorsed by a Parliamentary process. This is why Samuel Beer once identified Parliament's essential role as the 'mobilisation of consent'.[41]

However, process matters. That was the point of the lament by the otherwise-forgotten Sir Kenneth Pickthorn MP to the Commons in February 1960 when he declared: 'Procedure is all the poor Briton has, now that any government which commands 51 per cent of the House of Commons can at any moment do anything they like.'[42]

Procedure can put the brakes on, and make life more difficult (and irritating) for governments than it would otherwise be. However, even here the fundamental fact is that, at least for the last century, the business of the Commons – what it does and when it does it – has been largely in the control of the executive, a fact enshrined in the rules of the House. In short, the business of the legislature is in the hands of the executive.

This is true of 'Parliamentary reform' too, that perennial topic, endlessly discussed and written about, which in the end depends upon executive action to advance it. Hence its uncertain progress and recurrent disappointments. As a Commons clerk has put it: 'A common misunderstanding is that the House has the ability to reform itself. Certainly the Procedure Committee or other committees can recommend change. Change can be implemented by a vote of the House itself. But in between these two steps are the hurdles that ensure only changes acceptable to the government of the day are put into effect.'[43] However, some comfort may be found from the evidence that in certain crucial respects – such as the independence of the Speaker, the extent of the power of the whips, the rights of individual Members – the House of Commons still does rather better in terms of vigour and autonomy than some comparable Parliaments elsewhere.[44] In New Zealand, for example, whips are able to cast votes on behalf of entire party groups.

At this point it is necessary to say something about the different ways in which the role of Parliament has been understood in the British political tradition. This gives context to any discussion on reform. In simplest terms, there has always been a 'governing' tradition and an 'accounting' tradition. The former emphasises the need for strong government; the latter for strong accountability. The 'governing' tradition has been dominant, on both left and right, and supported by a set of historically-rooted constitutional arrangements (as well as, in some accounts, by the predilection of the British people for strong government).[45] In democratic terms, the job of Parliament is to convert electoral mandates into executive action, while also sustaining a putative alternative government. The 'accounting' tradition has been much weaker, regularly embraced by opposition parties to castigate governments but no less regularly dissolving at the first sight of a red box and official car.

There is nothing disreputable about the governing tradition. It captures a key requirement of any effective government, and gives British government a particular capacity for action which is a valuable resource in tackling problems and facing challenges. It can claim a democratic pedigree, and a popular resonance. Here is Douglas Hurd, the former Conservative Cabinet minister, explaining in his measured and civilised Tory way why the job of Parliament is to sustain the executive and not to thwart it: 'If you went into the streets of Witney or Woodstock and asked people what they wanted of Parliament, they would not want more argument, more control, more political challenges and argy-bargy. They want better decisions of government – maybe fewer – but better. The instinct of the people is that they want the political class, whether in government or in Parliament (they do not really distinguish hugely between the two) to get on and do a good job in those areas with which they have to deal. They are not particularly interested in making life more difficult for government.'[46] In other words, government rather than accountability is what really matters.

It will be necessary to return to this kind of argument later, but for the moment it is enough to register its pervasive influence. When the Blair government came to office with a huge majority in 1997, its first message to its new Parliamentary party was that they should get out of Parliament as much as possible and see themselves above all as 'ambassadors' for the government. In pursuit of this end, Labour MPs were encouraged to be away from Westminster on regular 'constituency weeks' and some were removed from investigatory select committees so that they could instead perform campaign roles for the party. Those who, when at Westminster, voted against the party line would have their transgression reported to their local parties. This was the governing tradition with a vengeance, perfectly rational in governing terms, which put Parliament firmly in its place. The only accountability that mattered was to government and party.

Yet accountability of various kinds is built into the operation of Parliament, and should not be underestimated. Ministerial memoirs testify to the exposed ordeal of answering questions from the dispatch box (vividly so in the case of Alan Clark[47]). An appearance before a select committee can also be a daunting experience for a minister in difficulty, and can flush out uncomfortable information. (On one occasion a junior defence minister confessed to the Public Administration Select Committee that, in preparing for the committee hearing, he had realised that he could not defend the brief he had been given.) A minister who knowingly lies to the House will not long survive, a position fortified by the resolution adopted in 1996 in the wake of the Scott inquiry into arms sales to Iraq. The business of the Commons is a permanent whirlwind of questions, statements and debates, all requiring answers from ministers, across issues of every imaginable kind. Opposition parties now have substantial state funding to increase their effectiveness, while the combined impact of the Freedom of Information Act and Human Rights Act means there are fewer hiding places for governments.

When all this is said, though, the question of balance remains: between governing and accounting, and between executive and Parliament. Much of what passes for accountability feels like an elaborate game, in which the governing side always holds the aces. This is why the language of 'balance', and the need to redress it, has been the recurring *leitmotiv* of all discussion of Parliamentary reform. Introducing the proposals for a new system of select committees in 1979, Norman St John Stevas, as Leader of the House, said they were 'intended to redress the balance of power (as between Parliament and the executive) to enable the House of Commons to do more effectively the job it has been elected to do'[48]. Yet over twenty years later this was still the theme. The Hansard Society's Newton Commission declared that 'reform of the Commons must find ways of allowing MPs to balance their party role with their Parliamentary role.'[49] The Conservatives' Norton Commission similarly announced: 'We want to strengthen Parliament because we believe that the existing balance between government and Parliament is seriously out of kilter.'[50] The landmark report of 2000 from the Liaison Committee, representing the collective voice of the select committees and arguing for a strengthening of their role and independence, was simply called *Shifting the Balance*.[51]

Why then, if this has been the recurrent theme, has the balance been so difficult to shift? The agenda for a balance-shifting exercise has been endlessly rehearsed. The introduction of the new select committee system was supposed to achieve it. Why has a sovereign Parliament not asserted its rights – to control its own business, to elect its own committees – and confronted an over-mighty executive? The narratives of Parliamentary reform tend not to get inside this question, to the political dynamics of the institution, and content themselves with a politics-free account of how the heroic efforts of reformers are thwarted by the iron fist of executive power. Yet it is not really like that. The truth is that most Members of Parliament have been willing accomplices in their own subjugation. Unless this is properly understood, and the reasons for it, the search for a new balance is destined to remain elusive.

This repeats the mistake of thinking about Parliament in a collective sense at all, for in a crucial respect the institution is less than the sum of its parts. That is why its collective self can never, quite, get out; despite being often glimpsed and replete with possibilities. It is driven by the clash of party and the search for office (or, at least, re-election), and anything else has to insert itself into the few remaining cracks. There is nothing new about much of this, certainly no lost golden age of sturdy independence. The grip of party on Parliamentary behaviour has been an intrinsic feature of British politics for more than a century and, despite the conventional wisdom on the matter, has actually slackened somewhat rather than intensified in the very recent past and with a rate of rebellion higher in the 2001–05 Parliament than in any Parliament in the post-war period.[52]

Party is what matters, but this is not because of a slavish submission to the whips. Politicians are party animals by both instinct and interest. Party cohesion is not an imposition from without. Asked in a survey in the mid-1990s to rank the order in which they represented their constituents, the nation as a whole, and their party, MPs opted for constituents first (64 per cent), then the nation (22 per cent), with party trailing a poor third (8 per cent). This suggests a striking gap between what they think – or think they ought to think – and how they act. The same survey also asked how different aspects of the job were ranked, which found equally striking differences between a party being in government or opposition. Conservatives ranked scrutiny fourth when in government, but first when in opposition. In 1994, 38 per cent of Conservative MPs ranked scrutiny first or second; but this had jumped to 82 per cent in 1997. On the Labour side the trend went in the other direction.[53]

None of this is surprising, but it helps to explain why rectifying an imbalance between Parliament and executive (itself a somewhat misleading way to describe it when the executive sits in Parliament) remains a minority pursuit. Members of Parliament have other priorities. They want their party to prosper, and themselves to rise with it, and other parties not to prosper. They want to rise within their party, becoming ministers and shadow ministers. They are legislators whose main ambition is to join the executive. To do this they need to earn plaudits from their party managers, which they will not do if they cause difficulties for their own side by exhibiting an excess of independence. This presses most acutely on MPs on the government side, where vigorous scrutineering will win no prizes; in opposition there is a happier coincidence between scrutiny and bashing the government. Those MPs who do not conform to this general pattern find themselves described as 'mavericks', which confirms the truth of the broad picture.

Like the theme of rebalancing, and indeed part of it, has been the search for a career path for Parliamentarians which is not dependent on joining the executive. This was the stated purpose of the introduction in 2003 of a salary supplement to the chairs of select committees. By itself though, this is unlikely to shift the balance in any significant way. It may even increase further the power of party patronage, without changes to the way in which the chairs of select committees come into post. What kind of scrutiny committee is it that has its chair effectively appointed by those whom it is designed to scrutinise? The case for change on that front, and on others, is currently under review.[54] Further progress would involve reducing the number of ministers (and especially of the growing army of sub-ministerial PPSs), so diminishing the lure of the executive and strengthening the attractions of Parliament. The problem is that no government is likely to want to reduce the size of its payroll vote, and Parliament collectively does not have the political will to insist on it or to limit the possible job opportunities available to it. Yet it is worth recalling that it was once the rule that a Member of Parliament who joined the executive had to resign and fight another election.

There is a further development of recent years which has a direct bearing on the role of Members of Parliament, and in turn on the issue of accountability. This is the extent to which the focus of MPs is increasingly on their constituency, rather than on Parliament. Perhaps this is where the real job satisfaction is to be found now; or just the place where they can hope to bolster their own electoral prospects. Someone may be a very small fry at Westminster, but they are still a big fish in their constituency. There is a turning away from Parliament, a trend encouraged by the party machines. Often Parliamentary scrutiny (just think of PMQs) is merely an opportunity to generate a local press release. These days a Member of Parliament is likely to have a finger in every local pie, their traditional role transformed into that of community organiser with a Parliamentary outpost. There may (or may not) be gains in this for local communities, but for Parliament there is undoubtedly a loss. It certainly saps the continuing activity of scrutiny and accountability on which Parliament depends for its vitality.

This trend is evident on several fronts. For example, my own constituency was represented for twenty-five years after 1945 by the formidable Jennie Lee. Her periodic visits to the constituency were considerable events, recorded with gratitude by the local party.[55] Today a Member of Parliament who was not a permanent presence in their constituency would be seen as falling down on the job. The emphasis is on continuous local campaigning, supported by vastly increased allowances. The Commons chamber may be empty (except for the ritual confrontations), select committee attendance may be poor, but constituency activity is rampant. This is why Philip Cowley told a Commons committee inquiry into strengthening the role of the backbencher that 'there must be a strong suspicion that acquiring a pledge from the Liberal Democrats that they will never again campaign on the basis of potholes and drainpipes would probably do more to strengthen the role of the backbencher at Westminster than any other single proposal you will be able to produce'.[56]

There is a paradox here. Members of Parliament have more resources, in career terms they are more professional politicians, they are in some respects more independent-minded, the machinery of accountability has improved (above all with the post-1979 select committees); yet their engagement with Parliament has diminished. Of course this is not universally the case, and some MPs are the Parliamentary workhorses, but the trend is clear. Parliamentary activity increasingly just services a continuous election campaign, both nationally and in constituencies. In career terms, Parliament is not where the action is. It can be useful on the way up the ladder to office, and a compensation (as with select committees) for those who have either not managed to get on the ladder or have fallen off, but the real focus is elsewhere.

When the political dynamics of the institution are understood, it becomes clearer why the search for a new balance – between party and Parliament, and between executive and legislature – has proved so elusive. The best argument for reform has always been that strong government needs to be matched by stronger accountability. This was the theme of Bernard Crick's pivotal *The Reform of Parliament* in the 1960s, and the basis of his proposal for a strengthened committee system. Nor was it accountability for its own sake, but because better scrutiny would produce better government. As Crick put it: 'Parliamentary control of the executive – rightly conceived – is not the enemy of effective government, but its primary condition.'[57] This was the argument that the best batsman needed the best bowlers.

It is a good argument. It is also the answer to the kind of government-centric view advanced by Douglas Hurd earlier. A Parliament that is on its game in scrutiny terms is more likely to raise a government's game too. Thus the problem has not been with the argument, which has sustained the periodic reform initiatives, but with the conditions for its success. As government control intensified during the Thatcher years, despite the existence of a new committee system that was supposed to provide a new balance, Crick recanted his earlier institutional optimism.[58] It was clear that the institution could not be fundamentally reformed in isolation from the rest of the political system which gave it its character, and which deprived its members of the political will to do so. This is something to which it will be necessary to return.

Reform and Resistance

Both the Conservative government of Mrs Thatcher elected in 1979, and the Labour government of Mr Blair elected in 1997, arrived in office with commitments to major reforms of Parliament. In both cases the commitment was grounded in the argument that the executive had become too powerful, Parliament too weak, and that something ought to be done about it. The 1979 reforms, the product of an impressive Procedure Committee report instigated by the preceding Labour government and introduced when Mrs Thatcher was preoccupied on other fronts, produced the modern system of departmental select committee. In 1997 a new Modernisation Committee was established, chaired by the Leader of the House, to promote a continuing process of reform on a number of fronts.

Even after thirty years, it is difficult to make a definitive assessment of the impact of the select committee system. It has not fundamentally altered the character of Parliament, as some had hoped and expected (and others feared); but nor has it been without its effects. The fact that it is now impossible to imagine Parliament without a functioning system of select committees is perhaps the best indication of the success of the 1979 reforms. The select committee offers some kind of antidote to the organised adversarialism which dominates Westminster politics, in its emphasis on cross-party working and the production (if at all possible) of consensus reports. The committees have acquired more resources and support, and taken on key scrutiny tasks, now including some pre-appointment confirmation hearings. They have become a permanent part of the political environment within which government departments and their ministers have to operate, and can have a particular role when issues are contentious and divisive. For at least some of their members (and, in particular their chairs) the committees can provide a more satisfying and purposeful life than they would otherwise enjoy, even compared with life as a junior minister or whip.[59]

Whether this achieves the 'new balance' in the relationship between executive and Parliament anticipated by the 1978 Procedure Committee report is much more doubtful. Select committees vary considerably in their performance and influence, and in the commitment of members. In general they still exist in a kind of parallel universe to real Westminster life. Their reports do not have to be debated in the chamber, let alone voted on, and often sink without trace, unnoticed even by their Parliamentary colleagues. When they are debated, often only committee members turn up. They will generally attract media attention only if they are critical of government policy and performance. The cross-party working is not carried through into Parliamentary life generally, and committee reports can often receive only cursory responses from government. The committees are not equipped to undertake forensic fact-finding inquires.

It is therefore a mixed picture, but there is clearly much more to be done before the select committees can claim to play the role envisaged by their progenitors. This was recognised in the Liaison Committee's *Shifting the Balance* report: 'It is now twenty years since the setting up of the departmental select committees. Their establishment was a major step in making the executive accountable to Parliament, and so to the citizen and taxpayer. Over those two decades, the committees have done a great deal of valuable work; but their full potential has yet to be realised. In this report we have set out a programme of reform and modernisation which will do just that. There are some who see the House of Commons as a toothless adjunct of an all-powerful executive. We aim to disprove this.'[60] Part of this further reform programme involved a proposal to wrest control of select committee appointments from the whips. This received such a frosty response from the Leader of the House, Margaret Beckett, that the committee was prompted to produce a further report under the title *Independence or Control?*

Yet the Blair government was sponsoring its own programme of Parliamentary reform through the Modernisation Committee it had established. Since 1997 this has been the vehicle for an assortment of procedural changes.[61] These have included draft bills, programming of legislation, a second debating chamber in Westminster Hall, and changes to sitting hours and Parliamentary questions. It is a considerable list, which has had some important consequences. However, if tested for its balance-shifting achievement, the verdict has to be largely negative. There are various reasons for this. Unlike the Procedure Committee report of 1978 that produced the select committees, the Modernisation Committee had not begun its work with any serious analysis of what it wanted to achieve, or what the essential problem was that it had to tackle. There was therefore no clear yardstick against which to assess its progress, as there would have been if it had identified the balance between executive and legislature as the fundamental issue. Instead, it simply pursued assorted 'reforms'.

This was the problem with 'modernisation', that weasel word which often confuses more than it clarifies. Modernisation for what purpose? In relation to Parliamentary reform, it soon became clear that there was a confusion of purposes, which pointed in different directions. On one side, there were changes (for example, draft bills) which had the potential to strengthen Parliament's scrutiny role. On the other side, there were changes (for example, on programming and sitting hours) which were designed to enable government to process its business more efficiently and MPs to escape from Westminster more regularly. On balance, it is difficult to avoid the conclusion that modernisation-as-efficiency triumphed over modernisation-as-scrutiny.[62]

This can be seen in the case of draft bills, which were heralded as a way of improving the conspicuous deficiencies of the legislative process by expanding pre-legislative scrutiny. However, instead of becoming embedded as the legislative norm, the number of bills being produced in draft has actually dropped away (the high-water mark of twelve such

bills in the 2003–04 session has never been approached subsequently). On the positive side, another reform emerging
from the Modernisation Committee in 2006 saw the introduction of Public Bill Committees to consider government
legislation, with the ability to take preliminary evidence in
the style of select committees. This under-noticed development has considerable potential to improve the quality of
legislative scrutiny, but for this potential to be realised their
role would have to be significantly strengthened.[63] It is not
yet clear if this will happen, so contributing something to
balance-shifting, or will be another innovation – like draft
bills – that withers after promising much.

Perhaps the greatest moment of promise came when Robin
Cook was Leader of the House from 2001 to 2003 and
embarked on an ambitious set of reforms to make Parliament
more effective. However, he soon found himself at odds with
the Chief Whip and increasingly isolated. When he tried to
establish a new Committee of Nomination to weaken the
hold of the whips on select committee appointments, an
unofficial whipping operation on both sides of the House on
a supposedly free vote saw the proposal rejected by 209 votes
against to 195 for. This was a dismal moment for reformers
and balance-shifters, for on a fundamental issue of power and
control in Parliament – and on a free vote – it had not proved
possible for MPs to summon up the political will to stand
up for the rights of Parliament. A third of the House did not
even show up to vote. This episode, and this period, was a
sharp reminder of the political difficulties which confronted
serious reformers and balance-shifters, even if they were also
Leader of the House.[64]

There was one development in this period which deserves

particular mention here, as it owes much to Peter Hennessy. He had persuaded the Public Administration Select Committee that the omission of the Prime Minister from the scrutiny of select committees was a serious gap in the post-1979 reforms. PASC took up the cause, but the official response was that any such development would be constitutionally improper.[65] The Liaison Committee was then persuaded to take up the issue, with no more success. Then came the announcement by Tony Blair in 2002 that he would henceforth appear twice a year in front of the Liaison Committee. A constitutional impossibility had suddenly become a constitutional fixture. Whether it has yet contributed anything significant rather than symbolic to Parliamentary scrutiny of the executive is another matter.

At this point it is necessary to say something, briefly, about the House of Lords. If the Commons has difficulty with systematic scrutiny, which has to insert itself into the narrow gaps left by the party battle, then it is important that it takes place somewhere. This is the essential case in the British Parliamentary system for a second chamber, and for the House of Lords (or whatever it is one day called) to be a house of scrutiny. This it can more easily do because party presses less heavily, no party (particularly since the cull of the hereditaries) has an overall majority, and there is a non-aligned element whose support has to be won. Anyone seriously interested in strengthening scrutiny and account-ability has to be interested in the second chamber.

Even in its half-reformed state (indeed partly because of its half-reformed state) the House of Lords has acquired more legitimacy since 1997. In this sense there has been some shifting of balance in the system. This is probably more important than the endless argument about the precise future composition of a fully reformed second chamber. The primacy of the elected House of Commons means that the real question should be what kind of second chamber can best perform the scrutiny role that the system as a whole needs. A mixture of election and appointment has always seemed to me to be the approach most likely to secure this; and a second chamber that was a replica of the Commons the least likely.

However, these precise compositional arguments are less fundamental than the need to see the scrutiny task as a whole, involving both Commons and Lords. This is more fruitful than the approach which obsesses about whether the balance of power in any reform might shift between Commons and Lords. The real balance that needs to shift, involving both Commons and Lords, is that between executive and Parliament as a whole. As the Public Administration Select Committee argued in 2002 in response to a government White Paper on the Lords: 'Reform is not a zero-sum game in which advances for one chamber are inevitably threats to the other. This is where the White Paper is fundamentally misconceived, as was the Royal Commission, in its oft-repeated determination to ensure the pre-eminence of the House of Commons. No-one is casting any doubt on that pre-eminence. We believe that the real task is rather to increase the effectiveness of both chambers in holding the government to account for its actions and policies. The focus should be on the capacities of the institution as a whole.'[66] There is already evidence that, on a range of issues, Lords and Commons are becoming mutually reinforcing in relation to the executive; and this is a trend that should be encouraged.

A New Balance?

It is time to start pulling my theme together. The argument that strong government requires strong accountability is a sound one. It identifies the imbalance in the British system and sets out some ways in which it could be rectified. Over the years there has been a plethora of proposals from reformers to strengthen Parliament in relation to the executive. The Hansard Commission's recommendations were designed 'to place Parliament at the apex of a range of scrutiny mechanisms'.[67] There are schemes for strengthening select committees, and for the Commons to take control of its own business. In some plans a whole new committee structure is envisaged, in which specialist standing committees scrutinise the legislation in their own subject areas, or even merge with the departmental select committees in powerful multi-purpose committees. The difficulty has never been in describing what a more vigorous Parliament, taking its scrutiny and accountability role seriously, would look like; but in translating such proposals and ambitions into political reality. It has sometimes felt like making plans for an imagined Parliament.

In practice it has been a matter of securing such advances as become available (of which the select committees are certainly so far the most significant) and nailing them into the fabric of the system. However, in many respects the executive has tightened its grip, and significant reform to strengthen accountability – and so shift the balance – has proved elusive. This is plenty of accountability around (from the press to the judges, the regulators to the auditors) but Parliament sits more as appendage than apex of this system. In the wake of the Great Expenses Scandal that engulfed Parliament and incensed the public in 2009, reform was certainly in the air, but it was not clear that the public mood of anti-politics would translate into something more positive.

The impediments to serious balance-shifting between executive and Parliament lie not so much in the machinations of the former but in the character of the latter (and the political priorities of its Members). If Parliament is like it is, and Members of Parliament like they are, because of the kind of political and constitutional system which Britain has, this raises the question about the viability and limits of any significant balance-shifting project. Even political will is an expression of the personal and political priorities signalled by the system. Although matching strong government with strong accountability is the proper ambition of reformers, it is not clear how realistic this is in a system which gives control of the legislature to the executive and buttresses this with the routine disciplines of party.

The question is how far, in such a system, the balance can really be shifted. Are there intrinsic and inevitable limits to reform? This should be regarded as an open question, to be tested against the evidence, some of which has been reviewed here. Not to ask the question is to invite recurrent disappointment, which has often been the fate of Parliamentary reformers. Even if there are such limits, it is difficult to believe that they have yet been reached. Perhaps the expenses scandal will turn out to have provided an unexpected opportunity to nail down changes to select committees and control of Parliamentary business which would not have been achievable in more normal times. Perhaps there will be a public mood for rather more independence in their Parliamentary representatives; and perhaps the latter will find more job satisfaction by responding to that public mood. As party weakens in the electorate, its Parliamentary grip may also continue to slacken. Leading political figures, like Robin Cook in the past and the Speaker today, take up the cause of reform. Political events, such as a hung Parliament, might also play their part in altering the terms of trade between executive and legislature.

All of this is possible, and some of it may even happen. In that case the advantages of strong government, rooted in electoral mandates, would really start to be matched by the advantages of continuous and vigorous Parliamentary accountability. The constraints imposed by the fusion of executive and legislature would not have proved an insurmountable obstacle in the enterprise of balance-shifting. The advances secured on particular fronts – to select committee appointments here, to the scrutiny of legislation there – would begin to come together to change the way in which Parliament works. There might not have been a big bang, a great reform bill, but enough smaller bangs to make a real difference to the Parliamentary landscape.

There is, however, a different conclusion to be drawn from the evidence. On this view, if Parliament is like it is essentially because of the kind of political system within which it sits, then real change to the institution – and to its relationship with the executive – will only come if the nature of the political system itself changes. Without this any reforms will remain, at best, piecemeal and partial, and unable to effect a fundamental shift of balance. Reformers will be endlessly frustrated and disappointed if they do not recognise that only fundamental change to the political system itself will bring about what they want.

What kind of change? The main candidate is electoral reform. If a simple plurality system, untroubled by proportionality but usually effective in producing governing majorities, was replaced by a more proportional system, then it would be less likely that a single party would command both executive and legislature. There would have to be more negotiation and compromise, and more Parliamentary space within which scrutiny mechanisms could operate. The way in which politics was conducted would have to change, from tribal adversarialism to a more consensual and agreement-building approach. Party competition would have to sit alongside the need for party co-operation. The style of cross-party working that is currently only seen in the noises-off enclaves of the select committees would be generalised across the whole of Parliament. It would be easier, and more attractive, for Members of Parliament to develop a career path as Parliamentarians. Parliament itself might genuinely start to have a collective identity.

Whether some or all of this would actually happen, and whether it is really the experience of Parliaments in countries with proportional electoral systems (now including the devolved assemblies within Britain) is a matter for debate. However, it is at least a plausible scenario. On this view reform within Parliament, in terms of a real shift of balance between executive and legislature – and between party and Parliament – requires reform outside Parliament. There are other reasons why electoral reform might be desired, such as electoral justice and making all votes count, but the effect on Parliament is what is at issue here. Replacing an electoral system which produces governments with one which produces representatives who in turn have the task of producing governments would have major consequences for many aspects of British politics, including Parliament.

Some want to go even further, towards constitutional change of a more fundamental nature. If the fusion of executive and legislature, with government formed from the majority in Parliament, is what lies at the constitutional root of executive dominance and legislative enfeeblement, then digging out that root and replacing it with something more productive of Parliamentary vigour has obvious attractions. On this view formally separating powers, rather than allowing them to be fused, is the way forward. Until recently there were few advocates of such radical constitutional change.[68] Envious Parliamentary eyes might occasionally fix on the power and resources enjoyed by members of the United States Congress, and the congressional committees, but that was understood to be a wholly different constitutional world.

There are some signs that this may be changing. No less a figure than a former Cabinet secretary has recently proposed the separation of powers as the remedy for the ills of British government.[69] As Prime Minister, Gordon Brown has espoused a 'government of all the talents', making appointments from those outside Parliament and outside party; and a previous Prime Minister has proposed changes to Parliamentary conventions to enable this practice to become normal.[70] These could be seen as tentative steps towards a more embedded separation of powers. In local government, too, recent reform has been explicitly designed to separate out the executive function from the scrutiny function, most sharply so in the case of directly elected mayors. If such separation is seen as a route to a revitalised local government, then it might have a role in giving new vigour to

Parliament too. The danger, of course, is that it would not only strengthen accountability but make strong government much more difficult, as President Obama is currently discovering in his political struggle to reform the US health care system.

These are matters for institutional design, and for political culture. Effective government matters, but so too does effective accountability. Indeed, the latter can and should contribute to the former. That is why it is worth attending to the imbalance between governing and accounting, between executive and legislature, in the British Parliamentary system. The governing tradition, which has enjoyed such dominance, both recognises and welcomes such imbalance, rooted in both structure and culture. That is why reform and balance-shifting has proved so difficult. Those who have enjoyed the governing advantages of this system, or who hope they might, have naturally not wanted to change it; yet without such executive support Parliament has had no independent means of action (even if it wanted to act). The result is that strong government has not been matched by strong accountability, at least not in Parliament, despite the best efforts of those who have wanted it to be. The question is whether, and how, it could be.

There are, of course, other balances that need to be shifted too. Some might see the discussion here as an example of the internal preoccupations of a discredited political class, furniture-shifting on a sinking ship. What is really needed, it is argued, is a shift of power between the political class and the people.[71] There is clearly something in this (at least if the error of thinking there is a single 'people' is avoided), but that is the challenge of supplementing representative democracy with more participatory forms of political engagement. However, it is a matter of supplementing, not supplanting. Representative government is indispensable, and it is therefore essential that representative institutions are kept in good repair. In the case of Parliament, the vitality of representative democracy demands that there is some serious balance-shifting if Parliament is really to sit at the apex of accountability. As it properly should.

‡

It frequently requires a crisis or scandal to remove the entrenched roadblocks to reform (which is what the recent phone-hacking revelations have done in relation to the buried issues of media ownership and press accountability), and so it was with the scandal of MPs' expenses and allowances. This scandal did not drop from a clear blue sky, but had been silently waiting to explode for many years previously. The real scandal was that the matter was not attended to (but strenuously defended) by those who were its beneficiaries – and who would eventually become its victims. In a New Statesman *piece in 1996 that anticipated the Parliamentary expenses explosion that was to happen more than a decade later, I flagged up the issue and tied it to the wider Parliamentary reform agenda.*

Palace of Low-grade Corruptions
On my first day in the House of Commons back in 1992, I was given some useful advice from an old hand.

'Whatever else you do here,' he said, 'make sure you buy a Ford Sierra 2.3 Diesel.'

Initially puzzled, I soon discovered why this particular

vehicle (sadly no longer in production) was known in the trade as the MPs' car. It enabled you to claim the astronomical mileage rate for cars of 2300cc or above (currently 74.1 pence a mile) on a car that did astronomical mileage per gallon. When I mentioned this useful information during a Commons debate on MPs' pay, a senior colleague took me to one side afterwards and warned in solemn terms that I would probably never be forgiven.

But I've kept up my interest. Last year I tried to put down a Parliamentary question to find out how many MPs were claiming at each of the three mileage rates. I was approached by the 'usual channels' to withdraw the question before it appeared on the order paper, accompanied by suggestions that a small Parliamentary army was standing ready to persuade me. When I persevered, the answer that finally arrived (from Tony Newton, Leader of the House and Lord President of the Council) was vintage stuff, well worth waiting for:

6 Members claim all 3 rates (A), (B) and (C);
15 Members claim rates (A) and (B);
19 Members claim rates (A) and (C);
113 Members claim rates (B) and (C);
478 Members claim only one rate.

Clear enough? So how many MPs claim just the whopping A-rate, then? Here we have the Parliamentary answer as art form: there is nothing inaccurate about it, it is not even 'knowingly' misleading, but it has been carefully crafted so as to not tell you what you want to know.

I regrouped. This time I would simply ask how many MPs were claiming only the A-rate. Long months of silence. Then came a private 'Dear Tony' letter from the Lord President of the Council with this splendid opening sentence: 'I am sorry it was not possible prior to Prorogation to answer your written Parliamentary question on the rates of car allowance that Members claim.'

In other words, it would not be in Hansard. Just a private word behind the Parliamentary bike sheds instead. But he gave me the information: 317 Honourable Members claim the top rate for cars of 2300cc or above.

So at last we have it. Half the House of Commons is claiming 74.1 pence a mile. No wonder there was a lot of disgruntlement about the Senior Salaries Review Body's proposal for a lower standard rate.

But leave aside the particular issue of mileage rates. What really matters is that when the rest of the world is having to learn to live with the requirements of audit and performance indicators, the Westminster club will go to extraordinary lengths to avoid scrutiny of its own inner workings.

That makes it ripe for assorted low-grade corruptions. I shall spare the reader the sordid details. Far more serious is the corruption of the institution itself, which sooner or later infects those who work in it. On this the Senior Salaries Review Body displayed a charming innocence. It even came up with a 'generic job description' for MPs, whose purpose in life is to 'represent, defend and promote national interests and further the needs and interests of constituents wherever possible.' Not a greasy pole in sight.

It also thought it would serve some purpose or other to ask MPs how many hours they worked each week, which produced the surprising response that they toiled for more than seventy hours night and day with Stakhanovite industry to defend the national interest and further the needs of their constituents. A more illuminating enquiry might have been to identify not how long MPs said they worked but how usefully those long hours were spent.

This same survey revealed that 72 per cent of MPs spent an average of 8.5 hours a week on select or standing committees between 9 January and 3 April. When I asked the statistician in the Commons library to analyse actual attendances at select and standing committees during the three-year period 1992 to 1995, a different picture emerged.

I have in front of me a league table showing how every MP scores in terms of committee attendance over this period. It makes very interesting reading. Of course wild horses, let alone the sort of fee the *New Statesman* pays, could not drag the names out of me.

But what it reveals is that while forty MPs notched up more than 200 attendances each in this period, forty MPs did not get on the score-sheet at all. No fewer than 120 MPs, or 19 per cent of the House of Commons, managed ten or fewer committee appearances during this entire three-year period. Looking at some of the names, it is clear that a number of those who are loudest in their defence of Parliamentary sovereignty against the foreign Johnnies who would usurp it are the most conspicuous by their absence when it comes to practising it.

The fact is that lots of MPs work their socks off, while some think the Commons is just a cosy club. With no job description and no audit, every MP does a different job. The minimalists turn up to vote and do just enough to keep the constituency sweet; the maximalists regard it as a proper job and try to treat it like one. There are lots of staging posts in between. Nobody outside knows what MPs get up to and it is effortlessly simple to pass off incompetent sloth as frenetic endeavour on behalf of nation and constituency.

The arrival of local free-sheets, which generally bear as much resemblance to real newspapers as MFI stores to craft workshops, has provided an admirable vehicle for the verbatim recycling of self-promoting press releases. Of course MPs should be rewarded for doing all the things to which they devote their real energies – plotting, gossiping, greasing, climbing, waiting, wondering – because this keeps the political wheels turning and turn they must. But they should not be paid on the basis of a myth.

The myth is that Parliament, in some real collective sense, exists and defines what MPs do. It does not, on either count. Of course it exists as a place and as an idea. But the living reality is of Parliament as a continuous election campaign (to borrow Bernard Crick's phrase of a generation ago) conducted on the floor of the House and in every orifice and committee room, an unremitting struggle regulated not by the Speaker but by the coy world of the 'usual channels'. Never mind the knockabout futilities of question time: pop into a standing committee room on any day of the week and ask yourself if the game you see going on is the legislative 'scrutiny' described in the textbooks. The party battle, combined with the personal struggle for place and position and the bloated putrefactions of patronage, ensure that Parliament develops neither collective will nor career structures of its own.

Not only should this change (and I wish Labour had linked the pay issue to a clear reform agenda), but it may now have to. In voting for a serious professional salary, MPs were asking to be taken seriously. People will not take kindly to paying £43,000 a year to buffoons and hooligans. They may start to want to know what they are getting for their money. If they discover that Parliament really does not exist they may even want to reinvent it.

It is just possible that MPs have voted themselves a bigger package than they bargained for.

(*New Statesman*, 9 August 1996)

‡

The devastating effect of the 2009 scandal on the whole political class was evident, but one positive effect was to open up a reform opportunity for the Commons that had not existed previously and would probably not appear again once the crisis had subsided. Crucially, it was a moment when changes could be made that genuinely had the potential to shift the balance of power significantly between Parliament and the executive. That was the purpose of the Reform Committee I initiated and chaired, and in February 2010 I was able to introduce our Rebuilding the House *report in the Commons in this way.*

Rebuilding the House

I do not need to remind the House of the circumstances in which the Committee was established. It used to be said that political reform was a matter for constitutional anoraks, which overlooks the fact that anoraks are precisely what are needed in a storm. And Parliament has been battered by the most ferocious and damaging storm in its modern history. There is a massive enterprise of restoration and reconstruction to be undertaken. Let nobody think that once we have attended to the expenses issue, or had a general election, all will be well. As Mr Speaker said in a speech in Oxford just a couple of weeks ago: 'The challenge that faces the House of Commons is not simply about rescuing its reputation but is about restoring its relevance.'

Parliament's reputation will be restored *only* if its relevance is re-established. A window on our world has been opened by what has happened, and it will not be closed again. Fundamental questions are now being asked about what the House does and what its Members do. If anyone doubts this, they need only look at the consultation document on MPs' expenses issued by the new Independent Parliamentary Standards Authority: 'The time is right', it says, 'for a discussion on the proper role of a Member of Parliament, with a view to establishing a shared national understanding.' Be warned: this issue is not going to go away, nor should it.

Our terms of reference were deliberately more modest, although not I believe unconnected to this larger task. We were not invited to reform Parliament in a more general sense, or to pronounce on the role of a Member of Parliament, and I would be the first to recognise that there are important matters which we have not been able to deal with (even given a generous interpretation of the 'closely connected matters' in our terms of reference). But reform is a process, not an event; and we claim only to have made a start. The three matters we were directed to examine – appointments to select committees, the scheduling of business, and public initiation of proceedings – were long recognised as requiring attention. But they also all raised fundamental issues about the role of Parliament, to which we sought to apply consistent principles.

For example, in relation to select committees, we concluded that it could not be right for the House's scrutiny committees to continue to be chosen, directly or indirectly, by those they were charged with scrutinising. Hence our recommendation for election of the chairs by the whole House, and members by their parties. Not only would this remove some of the problems that have caused difficulty in the past; but would also give a positive boost to the profile and authority of the committees themselves. In case anyone is worried that our proposal is too radical, we remind the House that in the eighteenth century members were elected by secret ballot to select committees, with Members placing their preferred names in large glasses on the Table.

In relation to the business of the House, we concluded that it could not be right in a sovereign Parliament to have its business controlled so completely by the executive. As we say in our report, this both demonises governments and infantilises Members. Hence our recommendation for a backbench business committee to take responsibility for non-ministerial business; and for a House business committee to construct an agreed programme of business, ministerial and non-ministerial, to be put to the House for its approval. Not only would a backbench business committee reclaim for the House what had been lost and rightly belonged to it, but also provide the mechanism to enable the House to make imaginative innovations in the way it organises non-ministerial business. Similarly, a House business committee would want to ensure that all legislation received proper scrutiny, which we all know is not the case at present.

In relation to the public initiation of proceedings, we concluded that representative democracy could be strengthened if the public had a more active role in our proceedings. Hence our recommendation for an improved petitions system, and for further work on public initiatives. We also suggest a mechanism whereby Members can give their support to propositions which, if sufficiently endorsed, can trigger motions for debate and decision.

We make many other recommendations along the way – from the size of committees to the operation of opposition days, from sitting times to the Intelligence and Security Committee – but these three areas are the main focus of our attention. Some Hon. Members may want to dissent from some of our particular recommendations; but what would be disappointing – and troubling for a view of Parliament – would be if there was dissent from the principles which underpin these recommendations.

There is another principle I want to mention, which appears in bold throughout our report. This is the principle that an elected government should have the means to implement the programme on which it has been elected. That is fundamental to democratic politics. Nothing in our report cuts across that, contrary to what some may believe, which is why ministerial business is protected. But it does not follow that effective scrutiny is therefore unnecessary, or that the House should not control its own business. As Robin Cook never used to tire of saying, good scrutiny makes for good government. This is a particular challenge in a system of unseparated powers where the executive controls the legislature, and where the party battle dominates everything, but it makes it even more necessary to meet the challenge. That is what our report tries to do; and to set the balance in the right place between the executive and the legislature, between governing and scrutinising, between party and Parliament, and between democratic politics as the exercise of power and democratic politics as the control of the exercise of power. There has been imbalance in these respects in the past, as is now widely acknowledged, and any reforms have to get the balance right now.

This issue of balance occurs on every occasion that Parliamentary reform is contemplated or discussed. I have just been reading my way through the two-day debate in the House in February 1979 on the Procedure Committee report which proposed the select committees. The report was introduced by the Conservative MP Sir David Renton who commended it to the House with these words:

> For many years, governments of both main parties have enjoyed dominion over the House of Commons. That is not merely because they have had a majority, large or tenuous, but more because of their power, which has grown over the last 100 years or so, of controlling business, including controlling, in effect, the amendment of Standing Orders. The recommendations in the report would help to restore the balance between the government and the rest of the House in ways that would be advantageous to both. They would also be advantageous to the people who sent us here. (*Official Report*, 19 February 1979, vol. 963, c. 55.)

I could use identical words today in presenting our report. Then almost the only voice of resistance to the Procedure Committee's recommendations came from the then Leader of the House, Michael Foot, who feared for the vitality of the chamber. Now we fear for the vitality of the whole House.

But the most interesting contribution came from Enoch Powell, and I offer it as reassurance to those who think that we are seeking to redress the balance too far. Enoch Powell reminded Hon. Members: 'The House comprises parties and, for most of the purposes of the House, its partisan character overrides its corporate character.' He went on to say:

> It is therefore courting disappointment to take the report and say 'Here are proposals which, if we enact them, will redress the balance of power between government and House of Commons and will put us, the backbenchers, in the envied positions of power and influence now occupied by those upon the Treasury Bench.' If that is the notion on which we approach the proposals, we are in for a disappointment, but that does not justify our not addressing ourselves on a lower plane of expectation to the major recommendations of the Committee.
>
> (*Official Report*, 20 February 1979, vol. 963, c. 336.)

There seems to me to be much political wisdom in those words, and I call them in aid of our own proposals if it enables some to support them on this 'lower plane of expectation'.

I am sorry to have detained the House with a reminder of a similar moment in the past; but I hope it is helpful in the present. I note, in passing, that a decade earlier, in 1965, reform-minded Labour MPs had tabled a Commons motion calling for comprehensive modernisation of the House: among their demands was 'hostel accommodation' for Members. It has taken half a century, and an expenses scandal, to revive that one.

It has not been entirely straightforward to get to this point with our report, but I believe that we are now nearly there. It has been cheering to see the enthusiastic support for our proposals both from within the House and from outside. It is clear that people have not given up on their Parliament, even if they have recently despaired of some of its Members. Even in this pre-election period, when party disagreement is obligatory, seemingly on everything, it is significant that all the party leaders have given their support to this reform initiative. I pay particular tribute to the role of the Leader of the House, and to the shadow Leader of the House, and to the constructive tension between them in a good cause.

I say that we are 'nearly there' for two reasons. First, because it is essential that the House has an opportunity to vote on *all* the proposals in our report, not just those which meet with the approval of the front benches. That is why I would have liked the House to be given an opportunity to vote on the draft resolution proposed by the Committee, which could have been done on an amendable motion. But this is not a moment to be churlish. We still have to nail down one or two matters, but we *are* nearly there. Second, though – and this is the crucial point – this package of reforms is not for the front benches to accept or reject, but for Members to decide on. They have to decide what kind of House they want, and what they think their own role in it is. When Robin Cook asked that question in 2002, Members opted, narrowly, depressingly, for the status quo. After what has happened recently, I hope that enough Members will now conclude that the status quo is no longer an option.

Let me conclude by saying this. There was no Parliamentary golden age. When there was supposed to be – in the middle of the nineteenth century – Gladstone was already writing about 'The Declining Efficiency of Parliament'. Nor was there a golden age when politicians were loved. It was in the 1960s that Henry Fairlie wrote that: 'Today, more than ever, the politician appears to be held in contempt.' Members of Parliament work harder now; they are more professional; and are much better supported in their work. When all this is properly said, though, we know that the House stands at a critical moment in its history. Something has gone wrong, beyond the expenses issue, and we have an obligation to put it right. Our constituencies are cultivated as never before, but the vitality of the House is diminished as never before. More is expected of us than just cheering or jeering. Members of this House have a number of roles; but the fundamental task of *Parliament* is to hold power to account. Our proposals are designed to strengthen Parliament in that fundamental role. We call our report 'Rebuilding the House' because that is what is required – and because this is the moment to do it.

(House of Commons debates, 22 February 2010)

‡

One of my refrains at the time was that procedural reform by itself was not enough and that it would have to be matched by a culture change among MPs themselves in order to exploit the new opportunities becoming available to them. There are some positive signs that this may indeed be happening (especially on the select committee front, as with the phone-hacking hearings), but it is early days and coalition politics presents its own challenges for Parliament. Too often discussion of Parliament misses out the real issues regarding politicians themselves – what they actually do and what they see as important – yet this is indispensable to any understanding of the institution. For example, fatal cracks in the coalition are far more likely to occur because of thwarted ministerial ambitions than because of policy disagreements. As Hugh Dalton once said: 'Jealousy is the foundation of public life. Green eyes glare from every thicket at every passer-by in the political jungle.' The question of what MPs are for is one I was invited to address in 2010 at the University of Liverpool, in a lecture in memory of that redoubtable independent MP Eleanor Rathbone.

What are MPs for?

It is the highest and most legitimate pride of an Englishman to have the letters of MP written after his name. Anthony Trollope, *Can You Forgive Her?* (vol. 2, 1865, pp. 44–5).

This lecture honours the memory of Eleanor Rathbone, who sat in the House of Commons as an independent member representing the Combined Universities from 1929 until her death in 1946. On her death, the *Manchester Guardian* said: 'No Parliamentary career has been more useful and fruitful.' On all the issues she cared about – from the rights of women to the needs of children, from the governance of India to the plight of refugees – she was a formidable and relentless campaigner. Her memory deserves to be honoured, and her example followed.

I think Eleanor Rathbone would have been puzzled by the question in the title of this lecture, or at least by the need to ask it. For her the answer was self-evident. Being a member of the House of Commons enabled causes to be pursued, and good to be done, from a platform that had to be heard. As an independent member she could roam freely, making alliances where she could find them, to advance the causes she cared

about. She was a progressive without a party, and a remarkably effective one. When university seats were abolished, the
last residual independent element in the House of Commons
went too. I sometimes think it would be useful to find a
way to restore such an element, as a leavening ingredient, if
only I could feel confident that it would produce an Eleanor
Rathbone rather than an Esther Rantzen.

Today, though, we do need to ask the question about
what Members of Parliament are for, not least because they
are asking it themselves and others are asking it of them.
This inevitably raises questions about what Parliament is for
too. The immediate context for the question is the Great
Expenses Scandal of 2009, which has rocked the Commons
to its foundations and left its members demoralised and
disoriented. Some did not survive this political earthquake;
others are desperately trying to put their political lives back
together. Yet this is only the immediate context that has
pushed the question of purpose to the fore, in an urgent
way that demands an answer; but it was already on the table,
awaiting its moment.[72]

Listen to what one long-serving Conservative MP said in
the Commons recently: 'As the years have gone by, I have
wondered more and more what the real duties of a Member
of Parliament are. Today, they seem to be to attend to emails
every five seconds and to respond on diverse subjects to
constituents on matters about which I know very little. Our
real duty, which is to scrutinise legislation – to look at it line
by line – seems no longer to be important or the part of our
lives that it should be ... We all need to ask ourselves what is
the role of a Member of Parliament now and what it will be
over the next ten years.'[73] A columnist in the *Sunday Times*

declares that 'we no longer have any clear idea of what an MP is for'.[74] More significantly, the new body charged with determining MPs' expenses (and, in future, pay) has said that, once it has sorted out the expenses system, it intends to turn its attention to the wider matter of what MPs are for: 'The time is right for a discussion on the proper role of a Member of Parliament, with a view to establishing a shared national understanding.'[75]

It is difficult to think of any other occupation where the nature of the job is so elusive. Even as a university lecturer, with all its flexibility and autonomy, I still had a framework of teaching to do and books to write, and some kind of formal appraisal system. I thought it would be difficult to find any other job with a similar degree of freedom. I was wrong. As a Member of Parliament, I found a job without any job description at all, no means of knowing what I should be doing, and with no means of assessing how well I was doing it. The result is that all Members of Parliament do the job differently, having tried to work out their own job descriptions. There are certain core elements – such as dealing with constituents, voting in divisions, sitting on committees – but how these are done, and what else is done, are matters of considerable variety.

Members of Parliament regularly tell researchers (and pay-review bodies) how busy they are, routinely reporting a seventy-plus-hour week, but the exact nature of this busyness is much less clear. As Chris Mullin observes, 'There is a good deal of pointless activity in politics' and it is easy to 'confuse busyness with effectiveness'.[76] Hamsters are also very busy, but to no great productive effect. Some MPs are clearly much more assiduous than others, but the purpose of the assiduousness may be uncertain. MPs from different periods have expressed this nicely. John Morley described the life of an MP as 'business without work and idleness without rest'; while Nigel Nicolson wrote: 'There is no place where a man can occupy himself more intensively or usefully, and no place where he can hold down his job by doing so little.'[77] Even today a glance at the Register of Members' Interests is enough to demonstrate that a significant number of MPs still manage to find ample time for other activities.

From time to time there are attempts to pin down exactly what it is that MPs are supposed to be doing. A list of functions was produced by the House of Commons Modernisation Committee in 2007, and has since been drawn on by the Committee on Standards in Public Life and others.[78] The suggested functions are:

- supporting their party in votes in Parliament (furnishing and maintaining the government and opposition);
- representing and furthering the interests of their constituency;
- representing individual constituents and taking up their problems and grievances;
- scrutinising and holding the government to account and monitoring, stimulating and challenging the executive;
- initiating, reviewing and amending legislation;
- contributing to the development of policy, whether in the chamber, committees or party structures and promoting public understanding of party politics.

Now the trouble with a list like this (almost certainly drafted by a Commons clerk) is not that it is wrong, but that it does not really describe what MPs actually do. It is altogether too high-minded and unpolitical. For example, absent altogether from the list is an activity that could be called 'campaigning to get re-elected', yet this drives almost everything that MPs do. Their activities feed into a continuous election campaign. MPs are politicians, and what they do is politics. Vast amounts of time are spent gossiping, organising, positioning, persuading, campaigning and plotting; not activities which usually appear in lists of the duties or functions of MPs but which are central to everything they do. It is not surprising that pay-review bodies are forced to make tortured (and futile) attempts to translate 'doing politics' into spurious comparabilities with other occupations.[79]

What MPs have in common is that they are members of a professional political class, paid for out of public funds to sustain the national and local political battle. Other people take part in politics; but for MPs it is their job. It is a job, moreover, which is performed in a particular political and constitutional setting. This is one in which nearly all MPs are elected because they are members of a political party; and in which the majority party in Parliament controls the executive. From this two consequences follow for the role of MPs. First, it means that party allegiance and loyalty is strong; and second, that MPs are legislators whose successful career path in politics usually involves joining the executive (so much so that MPs who move from the back benches to the front bench of their parties are described as having acquired a 'job', as though they did not already have one). As one veteran MP recently put it: 'Most of this place is stuffed with people looking for ministerial office.'[80]

When he gave evidence a few months ago to the committee

I chair, John Major recalled how unnervingly effective it was when Tam Dalyell, that formidably iconoclastic former MP, would respond to a minister's answer with one single and simple word: 'Why?' This made me suggest that a useful distinction in thinking about MPs is between the 'when' people and the 'why' people. The 'when' people are interested in when they are going to get a job, or a better one; the 'why' people in why policies are adopted or actions taken. It is the distinction between those who think that politics is about the exercise of power and those who think it is about the control of the exercise of power. I can think of Parliamentary colleagues who fit easily and neatly into one or other of these categories. It also invites questions about the balance between the 'when' people and the 'why' people in our political system, and what this means for the nature of Parliament.

Yet of course this distinction, while useful, is in other respects incomplete and misleading. We need both 'when' and 'why' people; and at different times individual politicians will sit in these different categories. Politics is about *both* exercising power *and* controlling it. Eleanor Rathbone was both a 'when' and a 'why' person; and her 'when' was not about getting a job but achieving the purposes and causes she believed in. In an article in 1856 (entitled 'The Declining Efficiency of Parliament'), Gladstone gave one of the best descriptions I know about the nobility of wanting to exercise power, of being a 'when' person with a purpose: 'He must be a very bad minister indeed, who does not do ten times the good to the country when he is in office, that he could do when he is out of it; because he has helps and opportunities which multiply twentyfold, as by a system of wheels and pulleys, his power for doing it.'[81] It should also never be forgotten that an indispensable purpose of MPs – what they are for – in our system of unseparated powers is to provide the rather shallow pool of people from whom governments have to be chosen. Without a steady supply of MPs willing and able (at least in a basic sense) to serve as ministers, our system of Parliamentary government would not function. Goats may provide useful reinforcements, but the sheep are the Parliamentary foot-soldiers from whom the officers emerge.

I want to suggest a different way of categorising MPs, which does not merely list the various functions and duties they are said to have but tries to get closer to the differing ways in which they see their role and what they actually do with themselves. This categorisation builds on the three key relationships that MPs have: with their party, with the executive, and with their constituencies. These are sometimes expressed in terms of a partisan function (the party relationship), a scrutiny function (the executive relationship) and a constituency function (the relationship with constituents). If we put all these together, we get a range of possible roles which I will categorise under six headings and label (in no particular order) as: Lickspittles, Loyalists, Localists, Legislators, Loners and Loose Cannons. I shall say something about each (while carefully mentioning no names).

First, the Lickspittles. These are those MPs who will stoop to any level, or suffer any humiliation, in order to curry favour with their political masters. There are, alas, such MPs. They can be spotted when they ask Parliamentary Questions, probably supplied by the minister's lackeys, asking the minister to describe the most recent of his many magnificent achievements or something similar. Fortunately such questions tend to elicit a silent or audible groan from nearly everybody else. Slavish adherence to the party line in all circumstances is of course a requisite for an authentic Lickspittle.

Second, the Loyalists. Most MPs are loyalists. They are party animals, and their loyalty is generally willing rather than enforced. They want their party to do well and opposing parties to do badly, and know that their own fate depends on this. Some MPs are more tribal than others, but the sense of political tribe is strong and widely shared. Loyalists take the view that they have been elected as party representatives to serve the party, and that is what they will do. Some super-Loyalists may come close to being Lickspittles; but others are critical-Loyalists whose loyalty is routine but not unconditional. Loyalists are what the parties count on to keep the parliamentary wheels turning. And the wheels usually do keep turning, despite the increased 'dissidence' (in terms of votes) that has become a well-documented feature of Parliamentary behaviour in recent years.

Third, the Localists. These are MPs who make the constituency focus the main centre of their activities. All MPs have a constituency focus of course, but the Localists regard their Westminster role as subsidiary to, and servicing, their constituency role; rather than the constituency role supplementing and servicing their Parliamentary role. These are MPs who perhaps find more job satisfaction doing constituency work, or believe it will enhance their own electoral prospects, while the party leaderships are happy to encourage this continuous local campaigning. In recent years MPs have also voted themselves a new allowance (now abolished as part of the expenses clean-up) to fund self-promoting communications with their constituents. There is no doubt that there has been a significant shift towards the constituency role on the part of many MPs in recent times, and away from the Westminster role; and supported by much increased resources. Indeed, for some the Westminster role (a Parliamentary Question, or intervention in debate) may be designed primarily for constituency consumption: the Question is really a local press release in disguise.

The story is told of yesteryear, when two MPs – Tory knights of the shire both – were loading their bags on to a train at Euston to travel to their constituencies. One lamented the effort involved, to which the other responded: 'Yes indeed, and what makes it worse is having to do this every year.' My own constituency was represented for twenty-five years after 1945 by the redoubtable Jennie Lee, who 'even by the standards of 1945 ... was not an assiduous constituency MP' and by the 1960s was visiting the constituency only every six to eight weeks, at one period not visiting for nine months.[82] Something has clearly changed. It is not just that the constituency focus is now much stronger, but the nature of that role has changed too. No longer is it just a matter of dealing with constituents' problems or attending local functions, but of relentless local campaigning combined with a ceaseless civic activism. Some MPs (and others) regret this trend; the Localists embrace it.

Fourth, the Legislators. In key respects these are the reverse of the Localists. They see Westminster as their primary focus, and their role in the legislature as their central activity. For them what matters about Parliament is that it passes laws, which must be properly examined. They are also the scrutineers, who take seriously the task of holding the executive to account, interrogating ministers and exploring the purpose and impact of policies. It might be said that these

MPs are the Parliamentary workhorses, and in many respects they are. However, much Parliamentary committee-sitting, especially looking at legislation, is enforced labour rather than voluntary service, so it would be misleading to regard all the workhorses as Legislators. Their natural territory is the select committee system, which provides a Parliamentary space where the party battle is less intense and an ethos of continuing scrutiny prevails.

Fifth, the Loners. These are MPs with a strong streak of independence, either because of temperament or because they are attached to causes which do not fit easily into the routine antagonisms of party. They may see Parliament primarily as a platform for pursuing their own activities, promoting their own causes, or expressing their own views. Some may not feel very clubbable or sufficiently tribal. They tend to be liked by the media (and by constituents) because of their willingness to express independent opinions, but regarded with suspicion by party colleagues and despair by party managers. They may find themselves described as 'mavericks', because of their unfortunate tendency to want to think for themselves when there is a system in place to think for them. Loners provide the House of Commons with the nearest approximation to a team of independents; except that, by definition, Loners do not play as a team.

Sixth, the Loose Cannons. This is something of a catch-all category, covering an assortment of MPs. Just as some Loyalists might be confused with Lickspittles, so some Loners could be confused with Loose Cannons. But they are essentially different: Loners are the independent-minded; the Loose Cannons include the weird and the unhinged. These are people who are capable of saying, and doing, almost anything. They sound off all over the place, always happy to provide an outrageous quote, demanding this or denouncing that. However, a further category of Loose Cannons are really Fixed Cannons, but ones which are as likely to shoot friends as enemies. These are the ideological warriors, not Loners because they are often highly organised, but likely to fire off in unpredictable directions. They are often described as the 'usual suspects' in terms of their deviant Parliamentary behaviour.

Now of course these six categories are just ideal-types, a useful device for making the point about there being no single approach to the job of being an MP. In practice the categories are mixed up and overlapping. Although it is possible to think of MPs who get very close to the pure types identified here, most are hybrids of some kind. That is because they are trying to find their own answer to the question of what MPs are for. Academic researchers regularly survey MPs and ask them to rank how important they regard different aspects of their job. In particular they want to know in what order MPs place their partisan role, their scrutiny role and their constituency role. I always read these survey results with a sense of unreality, as though MPs are trying to give what they regard as the right answers instead of describing what they actually do.

Take the constituency function, always given top ranking. What does it mean when MPs say (as they like to do) that their main job is to represent their constituents? Most MPs clearly do not represent their constituents in any literal sense, as a majority of voters will have voted for somebody else. Moreover, constituents have widely different views and interests and it is obviously not possible to represent them all. All it can really mean is that MPs devote most of their time to dealing with constituency cases and issues, and that this is what they think they ought to do (or say they do). However, they may be doing this because that is what they think best serves their own electoral interest, which should therefore be ranked as the primary consideration. But of course it would not be, because it would not feel like the right answer.

Similar difficulties arise with the partisan and scrutiny functions. Few MPs would want to say that their main job was doing what they were told by their party leaders, yet it is clearly their main Parliamentary job as far as the party machines are concerned and one which they are routinely prepared to perform. They might (and do) say that their constituency function is more important than anything else, but in practice it is clearly the partisan function. As for the scrutiny function, this is something of a poor relation, having to insert itself where it can into the party battle. There is not much political incentive to scrutinise your own side too closely or vigorously; while the kind of scrutiny that comes from political opponents is unremittingly partisan. The conclusion from all this is that not much enlightenment comes from asking MPs what they are for. They deceive researchers; but also deceive themselves.

Churchill, characteristically, saw these matters rather more directly. Shortly before resigning as Prime Minister in 1955, he identified the duties of a Member of Parliament:

The first duty of a Member of Parliament is to do what he thinks in his faithful and disinterested judgement is right and necessary for the honour and safety of Great Britain.

His second duty is to his constituents of whom he is the representative but not the delegate. Burke's famous declaration on this subject is well known. It is only in the third place that his duty to the party organisation or programme takes rank. All these three loyalties should be observed, but there is no doubt of the order in which they stand under any healthy manifestation of democracy.[83]

Here Churchill is really describing himself, of course, not describing what actually happens. In practice, Members of Parliament soon acquire an enviable capacity for deciding, in their faithful and disinterested judgement, that the national interest is identified with the political interests of their own party.

Like everybody else, MPs respond to the incentive and reward structures within which they work. There is an obvious incentive for them to cultivate their constituencies and service their constituents (especially in marginal seats), which therefore receives a high priority. There is also an incentive to climb the political career ladder, which means getting a job in government or the party's front bench, producing the sort of compliant behaviour which is designed to make this more rather than less likely. Even the monitoring of MPs now through websites like theyworkforyou.com contributes to the incentives structure, as some MPs feel the need to get good ratings, with local political opponents ready to pounce if they do not; so Parliamentary Questions are asked, and votes clocked up, simply to 'get the numbers up'. This is a reminder that with MPs appearance should never be confused with reality.

It is only by understanding what structures the activities of

MPs that it is possible to understand what makes Parliament operate in the way it does. As with MPs, it is not enough to produce a list of functions without getting underneath the skin of the institution to see how it actually works. At its heart is the party battle, between government and opposition, and this structures almost everything else. It can be misleading even to refer to Parliament in a collective sense at all, as Enoch Powell once told the House of Commons: 'The House is not just a corporation, and simply to talk about the House *vis-à-vis* the government is a totally inadequate description. The House comprises parties and, for most of the purposes of the House, its partisan character overrides its corporate character.'[84] Without any separation of powers, one party controls the legislature and forms the executive; while another party wants to. The central activity for MPs is therefore supporting or opposing, cheering or jeering. The only effective opposition to a government is likely to come from its own side, not from the routine opposition of the other side, intra-party not inter-party. On the Iraq War, for example, the opposition came from a majority of Labour MPs not on the payroll vote.

There is always a tension between supporting and scrutinising, and this is obviously felt most acutely in the governing party. As a Labour MP elected in 1992, for me Parliamentary life was inevitably much more fun before 1997 than afterwards. As the young Winston Churchill put it in 1906: 'Even in a period of political activity there is small scope for the supporter of a government. The whips do not want speeches, but votes ... The earnest party man becomes a silent drudge, tramping through the lobbies to record his vote and wondering why he came to Westminster at all.'[85] These days such a person is likely to be wondering when he is going to be given a job, or turning his attention to frenetic constituency activity, or perhaps settling for one of the other available roles.

So far I have tried to describe, rather than prescribe. Unless there is a realistic understanding of what MPs do – and how Parliament operates – now, it is difficult to make suggestions for change. There was no golden age either, despite periodic lamentations about the 'decline' of Parliament. In all sorts of ways MPs work harder than they once did, are more professional, and Parliament is much better organised to support them than it used to be. Nor is it clear what people want MPs to do (apart from sorting out problems and not fiddling their expenses). They may say they want MPs to be more independent, but at the same time they take a dim view of parties that are divided. When all this is said, though, there are now some questions which need to be asked – and answered – about the role of MPs, and of Parliament; and it is to three of these that I now turn.

First, it used to be said (and I used to say it) that MPs should not be turned into social workers, trying to sort out all the problems that constituents bring to them. This trend has certainly increased in recent years, with MPs becoming a sort of all-purpose local ombudsman. The tradition of 'going to your MP' with a problem is strong and getting stronger; and it is not difficult to see why. MPs can demand, and get, responses from bureaucracies in ways that the individual citizen cannot, right up to ministers if necessary. It clearly makes sense for citizens to use a service that is both free and, often, effective. For many MPs too this role is attractive: there is both job satisfaction and political benefit in trying to resolve the problems brought to them by constituents and in pursuing local issues. It also helps to ground MPs in the experience of their constituents.

The question is whether this role has now gone too far, at the expense of other activities. As Philip Cowley has said: 'There must now be a real concern that MPs are so focused on the parochial they have no time for the national, let alone the international, picture.'[86] Just the other day a Liberal Democrat MP used a primetime Question to the Prime Minister to ask about the Number 41 bus route in Birmingham. By usurping the role of local councillors, and local government, it could be argued that MPs are themselves contributing to the political centralisation that they frequently deplore. Nor should it be the case that MPs are dealing personally with all the cases that are brought to them. That may once have been necessary, but they are now provided with the resources to employ staff to do the routine casework for them.

There is a related issue. Perhaps because of the distrust of politics and politicians, perhaps for other reasons, there seems to be a growing requirement for MPs themselves (and those who want to be MPs) to be more genuinely local. This is seen, perhaps, as a badge of authenticity and commitment. If an MP is not already local, he or she rapidly sets about becoming so. Living in the constituency, even if another life is lived elsewhere, is normal now when it was abnormal once (and this has played its part in the allowances issues around second homes). This may seem to be a beneficial development; but if it serves to narrow further the pool of people who become MPs – or narrow their focus – it may turn out not to be so beneficial. People may want more local MPs, but not at the expense of effective government or a vigorous Parliament. What is clear is that this whole issue of the increasingly local focus has to form part of any serious consideration of what MPs are for.

The second question concerns the role of MPs in the House of Commons, and indeed the role of the Commons itself. This question lies at the heart of the recent report of the Select Committee on Reform of the House of Commons, which I chaired.[87] Our recommendations – for example, on electing the chairs and members of select committees, and on giving the Commons more control of its own business – were predicated on an enlarged and strengthened role for Members in the way that the Commons works. This is controversial territory. One critic of our proposals, a government whip, said that they threatened to 'depoliticise' Parliament. What was meant by this was that they failed to recognise that what happened in Parliament was above all a continuous battle between parties, and that nothing should be done to undermine or complicate that battle.

This is a plausible argument, and does describe accurately how the Commons essentially operates. It is a place where the rival political armies meet and do battle, each side marshalled by the party managers. The majority party, which controls the government, has the decisive say on how the battle is conducted. This is put too simply, but not excessively so. The twin rationale for these arrangements is that, first, the party battle structures the political choices for the electorate and, second, that a winning party has a mandate for its programme that entitles it to control the Commons and get its business done. These are powerful arguments. The question is whether they are pushed too far, in a way that diminishes the role of MPs and restricts the effectiveness of Parliamentary scrutiny in relation to a dominant executive.

These arguments are engaged whenever there is periodic discussion about the need to 'reform' Parliament. They were engaged thirty years ago when the proposal was made to set up a departmental select committee system; and they are engaged again now. It does not seem necessary, or sensible, to some of us that the chairs and members of select committees should be chosen by the whips or ministers, the scrutineers selected by the scrutinised. Nor does it seem sensible or necessary for the executive to control all the business of the legislature. The argument is always about the proper balance between governing and scrutinising, between party and Parliament, between executive and legislature, and between exercising power and controlling the exercise of power.

It is also about how MPs see their role, and what they think they are for. As I suggested earlier, there is no agreement on this and they choose a variety of different roles. There was a dismal moment in 2002 when Robin Cook, as Leader of the House, offered MPs a modest opportunity to acquire a little more independence from the whips, but a majority of MPs voted to decline the offer in favour of the status quo. It is difficult to believe that the balance is yet right in these matters. I do not understand why general support for a party programme, even one endorsed by the electorate, means that support for every clause of every bill has to be enforced by three-line whips; or why cross-party co-operation should not be encouraged; or why a defeat for a government on a clause of a bill should be seen as a political disaster rather than a triumph for scrutiny. In his first State of the Union speech recently, President Obama said he thought people were frustrated by a kind of politics in which 'every day is election day'. If he is right (and I think he is), then we should start doing something about it.

This brings us, thirdly, to the question of who MPs are, and who we would like them to be, as this impacts on what they are for. This is often discussed now in terms of the 'professionalisation' of politics. In other walks of life becoming more professional would be regarded as a positive development, but with MPs it is much more ambiguous as it suggests a form of separation and careerism. Nor is being a politician a member of a profession in the normal sense of having approved qualifications or regulated practice standards. That is also why it is difficult to determine an appropriate level of pay, for an occupation in which there are no formal qualifications and an over-supply of applicants. Even apart from such complications, reliable data on the professionalising trend is elusive, although its features can be identified. They have been well described by the former Cabinet Secretary, Lord Turnbull: 'There is a growing trend for people to come into politics more or less straight from university. They lick envelopes in Central Office, become a Special Adviser, and on and on it goes, and by the time they are in their mid-thirties they are Cabinet Ministers, barely touching the sides of real life.'[88]

Does this matter? Surely it is entirely natural that people who are engaged by politics might want to pursue it as a career; and the fact that it is increasingly regarded as a full-time occupation is an indication of the seriousness of the pursuit. Yet when all this is properly said, it seems to me that it does matter, for a number of reasons. At a basic level, there is something impertinent about someone who has not 'touched the sides of life' claiming the right to represent people who have, or of people who have never run anything in their lives claiming the right to run the country. If this is what the professionalising trend means, and if it is becoming increasingly dominant (as seems to be the case), then it does raise questions about the nature of politics and those who engage in it.

Above all, it has implications for how politics is conducted. If it is a career, rather than a vocation, then the career ladder becomes ever more important. The executive swells to accommodate all those who want to get a foot on the ladder (hence the explosion of Parliamentary Private Secretaries (PPSs)), the effective payroll vote expands and the vitality of Parliament diminishes. In other words, the ranks of the 'when' people are strengthened and the 'why' people weakened, and it becomes even harder to develop an alternative Parliamentary career structure. It also means that political life tends to be conducted in an internal bubble of its own, what Shils called 'that exclusive preoccupation with political events to the point where every human activity becomes evaluated not in terms of its intrinsic value but in terms of its political significance'.[89] Anyone who has lived inside that bubble for any period of time will have no difficultly in recognising this description.

If this is what the rise of the career politician means, it clearly impacts on how such MPs see their role. At the very least it suggest that, if there are gains in what has happened, there may also be losses. This was the conclusion of Anthony King, who first analysed the rise of the career politician, and said: 'It is hard to escape the conclusion that the demise of the non-career politician has led to a certain loss of experience, moderation, detachment, balance, ballast even, in the British political system.'[90] If this is so, it is worth discussing how the balance could be righted, how the political mix could be made richer, and how different career paths could be nourished. This has implications for political recruitment, and for the balance between the executive and Parliament. It also returns us to the question of what we think MPs are for.

If all these issues are put together, then it is clear that the question of the role of MPs – what they do, and what they are for – prompted by the expenses scandal has much to chew on. The *Guardian* journalist (and MP's daughter) Jackie Ashley wrote recently that 'there is another issue … and this is, in its own way, just as much of a scandal as expenses fiddling: what MPs do all day to earn their salaries.'[91] There are likely to be new attempts to describe the various duties and roles of Members of Parliament; and even newer attempts to measure their performance of these duties and roles. A window on their world has now been opened, and it is unlikely ever to be closed again. The question of what MPs are for has ceased to be a matter of interesting academic discussion and has become a matter of urgent political necessity.

It is also being asked at a time when politics itself is in considerable difficulty. There is a disengagement from party, and voting is on course to become a minority activity. Distrust of politicians has reached toxic proportions. It is not too much to say that there is a kind of civic crisis. A vision of a political future opens up in which a political class ceases to have organic connection to the wider society but floats over it, its accountability enforced not by an active democracy but by an assortment of external regulators. Already there is discernible movement in this direction.

These issues are too large to be pursued here, except in so far as they involve the role both of politics and of politicians. Until we remember what politics is for, and why it is necessary, we shall not get very far in understanding what politicians are for. This is where Eleanor Rathbone can still help us. For her, politics was the place where a society took collective decisions about the direction it wanted to travel, a place where freedoms could be enlarged, evils confronted, and justice done. She also practised politics in a way that contributed to an informed civic conversation, combining passion and principle with the art of the possible. She gave politics a good name.

Her masterly biographer, Susan Pedersen, provides this conclusion on her life: 'In dark times, Eleanor Rathbone kept faith with politics. For fifty years, Rathbone held to the belief that purposive collective action in a democratic state could improve human life, could prevent the world from foundering on the shoals of untrammelled selfishness, mutual hatred or apathy ... And yet, for all her consistency, Rathbone was never sentimental or unrealistic: she knew that the achievements won through democratic politics were always partial and tainted by compromise ... But for all that (she would have said), what might be the alternative? Unless we cede to the market, to bureaucrats or to strongmen the task of determining our common fate, we have no other means through which to work for the redemption of our world.'[92] And that, finally, is the answer to the question of what MPs are for.

(The Political Quarterly, July–September, 2010)

‡

Too often MPs have been content to grumble about their treatment at the hands of the executive, without having the collective political will to do anything about it. Thus, select committees are formally empowered to 'send for persons and papers', but in practice they have allowed themselves to be deprived of the ability to undertake the kind of forensic fact-finding inquiries that would really get to the bottom of matters, then complained about their own impotence. I found it frustrating and demeaning that on major issues a formally sovereign Parliament was content to demand that governments should set up inquiries without taking the initiative itself. Nowhere was this more evident than on Iraq, where an inquiry was clearly needed – the Blair government refused to set one up and MPs could only bleat about its absence. I took up the issue in a piece for The Guardian.

Inquiry and Iraq

Compare and contrast. Here is Mrs Thatcher in the House of Commons on 8 July 1982, announcing the nature of the Falklands War inquiry: 'The overriding considerations are that it should be independent, that it should command confidence, that its members should have access to all relevant papers and persons and that it should complete its work speedily.' Now here is Tony Blair, in the Commons yesterday: 'I have answered the allegations.'

There is a further contrast. The 1982 inquiry had wide terms of reference to 'review the way in which the responsibilities of government in relation to the Falkland Islands and their dependencies were discharged in the period leading up to the Argentine invasion'. The Iraq inquiry to be conducted by the Intelligence and Security Committee will have a narrow focus on the intelligence issue. It will not, in other words, attempt to answer the real question, which is why we went to war when we did.

The difficulty in getting a clear answer to that question in the period before the war has continued since, except that the fog has grown even denser, with assorted allegations swirling around, now including the extraordinarily serious charge by a leading Cabinet minister that there are 'rogue elements' in the security services. Not since the 1970s, when plots by generals to take over the country were regularly rumoured, have we had such excitements.

What does all this tell us about Tony Blair? He clearly does believe that he has answered all the allegations. He is irked, even affronted, that they should be made at all. 'Absurd' is one of his favourite words. He does not believe that vultures should be fed, or they will keep coming back for more. More than any previous Prime Minister, his style of governing is intensely personal. He routinely speaks of 'my' rather than 'our'. When things get rough, he makes issues into matters of personal trust and integrity.

This was Mr Blair's war. While many of the rest of us were anguishing about it, he was single-minded and resolute throughout. His narrative remained clear and honest. No serious link with Al-Qaeda or terrorism was claimed. Although the liberation of the Iraqi people from tyranny would be a happy by-product of war, it would not be its cause or justification. It all came down to weapons of mass destruction and the failure to disarm. Even when UN cover could not be obtained, this was why war was nevertheless necessary.

If there were difficulties with this argument before the war (Was Iraq really a threat to anybody? Why abort the inspection process?), they are as nothing compared with the post-war difficulties of explaining why the basis for the alleged threat has not been established. No wonder those who saw Iraq as the George W. Bush re-election war, or the war for US strategic interests in the region, feel vindicated.

Perversely, as one of those who did not support the

government, I take a rather different view. The only war I would have supported would have been one to remove a totalitarian monster. But this was expressly not the war we were being offered. Wars are a serious business and it is not surprising if people want to know on what basis they are being engaged in.

This is why a full inquiry is needed. Here the Prime Minister will have to overcome his instincts. It is not an affront to personal integrity to try to establish in a democracy what happened. Notice how Mr Blair often refers in a very personal way to his responsibility for what happens 'on my watch'. This betrays a rather old-fashioned sense of public duty, a felt obligation to do some good while he is at the nation's helm. If he has an ideology, this is probably it.

He sometimes seems to have an almost Gladstonian sense of the need to account to history (and to himself, and perhaps to his God) for what he has been doing. It is also why one day, at a moment of his own choosing, he will stop doing it.

These are attractive qualities, at least to me. They are part of the sense in which he is not an ordinary party politician, certainly not the sort of politician who sits in a party bunker and only sees the world through the narrow slit of light that enters. In this respect, by the way, he is quite unlike Mrs Thatcher.

But these are also qualities which carry their own dangers and disabilities. One of them is an irritation with the need to account to anybody else, and a restlessness in the face of procedural constraints. Yet this is what democracy requires. It would not be a sign of weakness, or an abdication of personal responsibility, to have 'absurd' allegations properly inquired into. It would instead be a bold declaration of democratic strength.

(The Guardian, 5 June 2003)

‡

If we want more effective scrutiny of government, then it is necessary to think about Parliament as a whole. This raises the perennially unsettled question of the role and composition of the House of Lords, left in its semi-reformed state after the removal of the hereditary peers and with further reform proving elusive. Public opinion seems to favour an elected second chamber, but one that exhibits a sturdy independence from party control, which is an unhelpfully contradictory combination of attributes. It has always seemed to me that if scrutiny is the essential function of the Lords, and if the Commons has undisputed primacy, then it is possible to construct a second chamber (minus the silly titles) that is neither a rival nor replica of the Commons. I plied this line with boring consistency, as in this piece from 1999, during one of the periodic (and abortive) bouts of Lords reform.

Reforming the Lords (Again)

'Who lies i' the second chamber?'
Macbeth

'If we had an ideal House of Commons ... it is certain we should not need a higher chamber.'
Walter Bagehot

The Royal Commission on Reform of the House of Lords is currently taking evidence and its report is promised for the end of the year. It is rare to have an opportunity to review and reconstruct a central institution of the political system, especially where reform has proved so elusive in the past.

Yet this also imposes a considerable responsibility: to find an approach that both commands wide support now and proves durable in the future. This means engaging with fundamentals. There will be a temptation for the Commission (and perhaps pressures on it) to find its way around issues rather than resolving them. It is important that the Commission does not succumb to fudge, either in its general approach or in its particular recommendations. Only clarity of analysis, and boldness of prescription, will ensure that this is not another abortive episode of Lords reform.

The starting point has to be an understanding of the central problem of the political system to which a reformed second chamber would provide a significant part of the answer. Unless the problem is properly identified, an appropriate response is unlikely to be constructed. This precedes questions about powers, functions and composition. It is also why examination of second chambers elsewhere may not prove especially useful, for they answer (or should do) to the particular needs of different political systems – for example, to represent states in federal systems or to reconcile divided and fragmented societies. Our situation, and our need, are quite different.

Those who identify the central problem wrongly (for example, by suggesting that post-devolution integration of the United Kingdom, or the need to represent under-represented groups, is the key issue) will also be mistaken in their proposed remedies. A second chamber will only be effective if it is a response to a need that has been correctly identified. It can certainly perform several functions, and respond to a plurality of needs, but its central role must be clear.

There can be no serious doubt that the distinctive feature of the British political system to which a second chamber should provide a remedy is unchecked executive power. A generation ago this was famously described as 'elective dictatorship'. It is a commonplace among serious observers that the concentration of executive power available to a party government with a secure majority in Britain is unparalleled in comparable democracies. This is an observation, not a judgement. It reflects the way in which our political system has developed. It is said to reflect a predilection for 'strong' government. One aspect of this, among many others, is the fact that we really have a unicameral system, with two chambers.

The system is poorly constitutionalised, lacking the familiar apparatus of checks and balances to be found elsewhere. Some of these are currently being developed. Devolution checks centralisation and promotes pluralism. The Human Rights Act offers protection for citizens. Freedom of information checks a traditional secrecy. Unregulated areas of the constitution (for example, party funding) are being legislated for. These are important developments, part of a constitutionalising trend, but they do not go to the heart of executive power. This is where a reformed second chamber is crucial.

Strong government has to be matched by strong accountability. At the moment this is not the case, with the result that the political system is unbalanced. The consequences, not least in terms of poor legislation and inadequate scrutiny, are well documented. It is the task of a reformed second chamber to achieve the rebalancing that is required. The watchword of reform should be accountability. It is this that identifies the central problem of the British political system and points towards the appropriate solution. In Britain an effective second chamber should be seen as a house of accountability.

This inevitably requires some reference to the House of Commons, for the relationship between the two houses determines the character of Parliament as a whole. The Commons has many virtues, but accountability and scrutiny of a serious kind are not among them. It was once described, accurately, as the scene of a permanent election campaign. Its partisan character routinely trumps its collegiate character. Its politics are rough and raw. It lives on immediacy. Party dominates all; and its career structure does not reward a concern for accountability. There is no indication so far that the 'modernisation' of the Commons will alter this picture in any significant way. It is because the Commons is like this that a reformed second chamber is so essential – and why reform has to be crafted in such a way that it is genuinely able to fill the accountability gap.

If this is seen as the task, then the potentially troublesome questions about the relationship between the Commons and a reformed second chamber become easier to answer. The Commons is the primary chamber, always able in the last resort to get its way. It is the directing, initiating and governing chamber. It is rooted in an electoral system which (even in the event of the Jenkins reforms being implemented at some future date) has a bias towards the production of majority party governments that have a final political accountability to the electorate. None of this will, or should, change. What should change is the ability and credibility of the second chamber in relation to the continuous activity of accountability. A second chamber is required that is neither a rival to nor a replica of the primary chamber. Its role is to be genuinely complementary. It is precisely because the Commons is like it is that the second chamber has to be enabled to become what it needs to be in order for Parliament as a whole to perform its functions more effectively.

The particular functions of the House of Lords – in revising, amending, checking, scrutinising and inquiring – are well established. They can and should be developed further, drawing upon the existing strengths of the Lords and involving areas where Parliamentary scrutiny is currently weak.

Obvious candidates are pre-legislative scrutiny (why is legislation wanted and is it likely to work?), post-legislative scrutiny (how well is the law working?), secondary legislation, Next Steps executive agencies and quangos, and cross-cutting thematic inquiries on complex issues (which the departmental select committees in the Commons are not well equipped to undertake). European scrutiny, already well established, provides a further area. A reformed second chamber, charged with accountability, will have ample scope to develop its functions and activities.

There is a particular role for a second chamber in constitutional matters. A feature of our system is the failure to make any distinction between 'ordinary' and 'constitutional' legislation (except in terms of certain procedural conventions).

This is an accountability gap that a second chamber should properly fill. It is already recognised in terms of powers in relation to any proposal to extend the life of a Parliament; and in terms of functions in the work of the Delegated Powers and Deregulation Committee. This constitutional role should now be made explicit and its implications explored for other areas of activity. It should be the place where standing scrutiny of our constitutional arrangements takes place. The Commission should pay particular attention to the ways in which the role of the second chamber in constitutional matters can be extended and strengthened.

This raises the matter of powers. The existing powers of the second chamber are generally satisfactory, except in constitutional matters. The exemption from the Parliament Act provisions in relation to any proposal to extend the life of a Parliament should be extended to other matters of fundamental constitutional importance (for example, any attempt to remove the rights of opposition). On such matters only a referendum should break a deadlock. Beyond this, in a reformed second chamber the self-imposed constraints on powers (as with the Salisbury Convention) will no longer be necessary or appropriate. In a reformed second chamber, more confident in the use of its existing powers, new arrangements will be needed to resolve disagreements between the two houses and prevent gridlock. Such arrangements will enshrine the final primacy of the Commons, but also safeguard the rights of the second chamber to be heard. This is another matter to which the Commission will need to give particular attention.

None of this can be done satisfactorily until and unless the matter of composition is resolved. Without an underlying legitimacy (capable of providing an answer to the question 'Who are these people?'), a reformed second chamber will not fulfil its potential. Unless it has to be taken seriously, it will not be taken seriously. This is the problem with the mixture of inheritance and patronage in the present arrangements. If the central task of a second chamber in Britain is to provide a check on the power of a strong executive, matching strong government with strong accountability, this can only be done effectively if its legitimacy is clearly established.

How this is achieved is not as straightforward as it might seem. It is necessary to balance different (and sometimes competing) considerations. There is a strong case for direct election, as this is the accepted basis of legitimacy in a democracy and would create a chamber that could not be ignored. The case for this approach is well made in the paper *Reforming the Lords* published by the Institute for Public Policy Research in 1993. If elections were held on a regional basis (with party lists) this would also strengthen the post-devolution role of the second chamber in representing the different parts of the United Kingdom. Yet there are also drawbacks with a wholly elected second chamber. Election is not the only route to legitimacy in a democracy. Judges are not elected; nor are jurors or magistrates. If a party list system of election produced a second chamber made in the image of party, more closely resembling the House of Commons, this would erode the element of independence which should instead be strengthened if accountability is to be enhanced. It is not clear how a party nominee on a closed list system is different in substance from a direct appointee, even if the cloak of legitimacy is somewhat stronger.

These considerations are different from the usual ones about an elected second chamber being a rival to the primary chamber. This would only be the case if its powers were extended, or if it could claim a superior electoral basis to the Commons (for example, by being more proportional, or elected more recently).

These are not necessary or intrinsic difficulties; though it is clearly important to create a robust chamber that is not also a rival one. Considerations of this kind have led some to propose an indirectly elected chamber (as with Bryce in 1918), as a third way between the Scylla of pure nomination and the Charybdis of pure election. This also has attractions, if an electoral college of a suitable kind could be identified (it is doubtful if Bryce's proposal for regional groupings of MPs would be acceptable) and if suitable and representative people could be found who would not be found through the usual channels of party and election. The same applies to the idea of 'functional' representation, based upon constituencies of interests and occupations.

Yet such schemes suffer from considerable difficulties. Some are practical, making it difficult to see how they would actually work. Others are more fundamental and turn on the question of legitimacy again. An indirectly elected body would simply not have the clout that an effective second chamber needs. This is even more true of a nominated body, whatever devices were put in place to avoid crude patronage and to secure a spread of representation. This is no doubt why the Conservative Party's Home Report (1978) concluded that 'moral authority can only come from the direct election of its members'; and why Tony Blair, in his John Smith Memorial Lecture in 1996, said (inaccurately): 'We have always favoured an elected second chamber.'

Faced with this range of considerations, the sensible course is to have the best of both worlds. This means a mixed chamber. There should be enough election to ensure legitimacy and clout; enough appointment to ensure expertise and independence. Legitimacy (and clout) demand that a majority of members are directly elected. This will happen through the party system, on a regional list basis, and give the chamber its underlying political direction and organisation.

Yet this needs to be balanced by a strong non-partisan element, comprised of people with the kind of experience and skills that such a chamber of accountability requires (at a time when the Commons is increasingly dominated by political professionals) and who would be excluded if party and election were the only gatekeepers to public office and public service. This should be the task of an independent Appointments Commission, cultivating applications from a wide range of sources. There is room for argument about the exact balance, as long as the elected element predominates. Beyond this, the denser the mixture the better. This would further emphasise its difference from the Commons and strengthen its identity. There is no reason why some elements of the non-directly-elected part of the chamber should not come from sources other than nomination. For example, there could be an element elected indirectly (perhaps on a regional basis) if a workable model could be devised, and even a small element of statistical representation (lot). There is more than one way in which people can be represented, and more than one route through which suitable candidates for public office can be found. Within a predominantly elected framework, the Commission should be as imaginative as possible in mixing the mix.

Difference from the Commons, and the avoidance of conflict while maintaining independence, can also be secured by further devices. These include fixed (non-renewable) membership of the second chamber for nine years, with a rolling (three-yearly) cycle of election. The term of membership might even be extended to twelve years (as Bryce proposed). Such a rolling membership would ensure continuity, safeguard independence, prevent party control and avoid rivalry with the Commons.

Other matters are secondary to this general approach,

but should not be dodged if reform is to be durable and comprehensive. A few of them can be mentioned briefly here. If accountability is to be the watchword of the new chamber, those factors which impede its effective operation in the Commons should be attended to. Party is one, but patronage is another. Considerations of office-holding are central to the life of the Commons.

There is a case for removing such considerations altogether from the new second chamber, by removing office-holding. Ministers from the Commons (whose numbers have grown faster than their workload over the years) could attend upon the second chamber. There are arguments of collegiality against such a proposal, but it is something the Commission might nevertheless wish to consider.

Whatever else is done, the link between membership of the second chamber and the honours system must be broken. It is the source of much confusion and ineffectiveness. If existing nomenclature was to be retained in the interest of historical continuity, it would be a characteristically British solution to have a House of Lords without lords (with its members plain 'ML'). There is obvious need to attend to the position of the bishops and the law lords. It is not possible to have an inclusive chamber while maintaining the privileged position of the bishops: they should join an enlarged category of religious and spiritual representation. The judicial function of the House of Lords should be organised separately: legal expertise in the new chamber can be ensured by other means. Finally, the present position of the Lord Chancellor is clearly anomalous: even in a system which likes anomalies, reform of the second chamber is the moment to reform this role too.

The approach to the reform of the House of Lords sketched here should command wide support and so prove durable. As the failure to achieve consensus has prevented reform in the past, this is a significant consideration. The emphasis on accountability defines a clear mission for a new second chamber. It would fill a critical gap in our constitutional arrangements, by linking strong government with strong accountability, and make for better governance. It would build upon, and extend, the current role of the Lords. The combination of election and appointment (with the possibility of other additions) ensures the legitimacy required to make a second chamber robust enough to do its job with the expertise and experience required for that job to be performed effectively. If this is not to be another moment in the long history of abortive Lords reform, it has to be a moment for realistic radicalism.

(The Political Quarterly, July–September, 1999)

‡

One underlying problem with the Lords – the source of all the scandals about peerages doled out to party donors and political friends – was that it confused honours with service in a second chamber. Many people craved the former, but had no commitment to the latter. That was one indispensable reform that was needed; but this was also an opportunity to make some radical reforms to the honours system itself, not least in the matter of titles. The committee I chaired came up with a comprehensive reform package and, as in this newspaper article in 2000, I tried (with a notable lack of success) to sell it.

A Matter of Honour

It's gong time again. The Queen (otherwise known as the Prime Minister) is about to dish out her Birthday Honours. There will be lots of Little Honours for 'ordinary' people who have done good works and served their communities. Then there will be the Big Honours – the ones that come with a fancy title – for the politicians, soldiers, diplomats, civil servants, tycoons and assorted celebs whose time for a gong has arrived.

It is time to stop all this silly nonsense. Don't get me wrong. I am very much in favour of a proper honours system. We need a way to pay tribute to the selfless public service that keeps our society going, honouring the quiet dedication of people who deserve to be honoured. What we don't need are titles. These come with all their associated baggage of class, pomp, vanity, deference, snobbery and patronage. They play to our worst instincts, when the honours system should play to our best. One corrupts and demeans the other.

Never underestimate the lure of the gong in Britain. It keeps the wheels of patronage turning. This serves the interests of those who give as well as those who receive. It helps to keep people in line and the money rolling in. I remember the elderly Conservative MP, desperate to get that self-inflating 'Sir' in front of his name ('Of course I don't want it for myself, but my wife, you know...'), explaining how painful it was when honours lists came and went without him. He had done everything asked of him by his party, abased and humiliated himself on command over a political lifetime, but still he was made to wait. It's pathetic of course, but it also shows why honours matter. They are an instrument of power.

So far the system has only been tinkered with. John Major tweaked it a bit, and Tony Blair has done the same. What it really needs is radical reform. That is what the Labour government in New Zealand is doing right now. It is getting rid of the honours with titles it inherited from Britain in favour of its home-grown democratic honours like the Order of New Zealand. In doing this it is following the lead already taken by Australia, Canada and other Commonwealth countries who have ditched this hangover from the British class system. These countries want an honours system that is modern and inclusive – and we should want the same.

We could start with the House of Lords. The recent report of the Royal Commission on Lords reform proposed that membership of the Lords (or whatever the reformed second chamber will be called) should no longer be linked to the honours system. About time, too. Linking peerage-as-honour with membership of the second chamber of Parliament has been a confusing nonsense. That's why we get 'working' peers who in practice prefer the titles to the work. We don't yet know if the government is going to accept this proposal from the Royal Commission. It should, and soon.

But it should also go further. It could immediately stop giving peerages to those who are being appointed to sit in the 'interim' second chamber. That would be in the spirit of what the Royal Commission proposed. It would also have stopped Ashcroft in his tracks, as it was clearly the title rather than the slog of the second chamber that was the prize he was after. Yet even this would only be a start. Without a House of Peers there ceases to be any point in having a peerage, except as a piece of historical flummery.

This is the moment to consign it to history, along with the social vanities and deferential hierarchies that have disfigured Britain's class-ridden past. Tony Blair should announce that he will recommend no more peerages to the Queen. Then watch the feathers and ermine fly.

Having done that, he should go on to announce a fundamental reform of the whole honours system, with new honours with new names for new kinds of public and community service, and an end to all those titled honours that devalue and deface what a democratic honours system should be all about. Little Lord Fauntleroy has had a good run for his money but the game is up. Some people will find it harder to book tables in restaurants, or jump queues, or have their vanities fed. The image of Olde England may take a knock. But this is a small price to pay for cleaning out the democratic stables of their inherited clutter.

Democracy is not just about institutions and procedures. It is also about social attitudes, how we think and feel. Honours have a place in a democracy, but titles do not. They just get in the way. It's time for them to go. Tony Blair believes in being modern and inclusive. He wants to unblock the arteries of an old society and sweep away privilege. Reforming the honours system is one way to do this. So, off with their titles!

(Daily Express, 15 June 2000)

‡

We did manage to get more transparency into the system, but even changing the word 'Empire' was judged too radical. In this, as in other areas, it seemed to me that it was sensible to introduce reforms in a considered way rather, as was more usual, in conditions of scandal and crisis. This was my line in relation to the Monarchy too, which was in deep trouble following the death of Diana and which, despite the recent boost of a popular royal marriage and the deep respect for an exemplary and enduring monarch, cannot forever avoid a serious reform process of its own. In this article in 2001, prompted by one of the periodic embarrassments of a minor royal, I described what this would involve.

Monarchy for Grown-ups

The Monarchy matters. That is why it deserves serious attention. It matters because a head of state is an important part of the constitutional architecture, a symbolic representation of a public interest above politics and party. That is why being a servant of the crown sounds a more daunting obligation than being a mere employee of the state.

Of course, if we were starting from scratch, we would not have a hereditary Monarchy to perform the role of head of state, not least because you simply do not know what you are going to get – from the mad to the bad. Authority and respect is all. We could easily do it differently. There would be a loss of symbolic continuity but a more reliable outcome. Parliament could elect a head of state for a fixed term – much as it now elects a Speaker. This is a standing option.

But we are not starting from scratch. We have a constitutional Monarchy, and a monarch who is a rock of public duty and propriety. Unless it was discovered that the Queen was embezzling the Civil List to keep a toyboy in Tooting, the Monarchy will continue. The question is how it will continue. By making this question inescapable, silly Sophie may have performed her greatest public service.

Two kinds of people provide no help in finding an answer to it. Firstly, there are those who want to maintain a 'Keep Off' sign around the Monarchy. These are the Monarchy's worst friends, for they fail to see the blindingly obvious fact that future survival depends upon present actions. Secondly, there are the radical chic republicans who fail to understand that we already have a 'crowned republic' (H. G. Wells, after Tennyson) and that the democratic offensiveness of the Monarchy ended when its political power was removed.

Today's question is not whether a Monarchy is desirable or not but whether it is possible or hot. The real threat to it comes not from the disciples of Tom Paine but from the followers of Max Clifford. The cause of death will be tabloid overdose. It will be a lingering death, an endless royal variety show of embarrassing acts and declining audiences. This is simply too awful to contemplate.

So what is to be done? The first task is to recognise that the fairytale is over; we now need a Monarchy for grown-ups. The old support, of deference and magic, has gone for good. From now on, the only justification for a constitutional Monarchy will have to be a rational one. This almost certainly means rescuing the Monarchy from the Royal Family, as the latter is now proving to be seriously damaging to the former. This is a public interest, not a private concern. A core Monarchy requires a royal cull.

It also has to be a Monarchy that genuinely stands above party. The historical evidence shows the extent to which the Monarchy has always been an organised conspiracy against progressives of all kinds. Sophie's recitation of routine golf-club prejudices merely put on public record the traditionally private world view of an institution. For this to be so fatally disables the Monarchy as a public institution. So does all the flummery, stuffiness and double-barrelled tweediness. This is not an age in which the peasants will only have their hands shaken by someone wearing gloves.

A democratic Monarchy may be a contradiction in terms; and it is the hardest trick to learn, but it is also the precondition for survival in an age that has stopped touching its cap. That is why the Scandinavian monarchs got on their bikes a long time ago and are still pedalling away merrily.

Nor can we have a Monarchy that institutionalises discrimination against certain religious faiths or privileges one faith – or discriminates against women in the succession. It is extraordinary, but it is an indication of an entrenched unwillingness to get to grips with what needs to be done. The residual prerogative powers also need to be properly constitutionalised. None of these are insuperable tasks, but the failure to engage with them in quiet times makes it more urgent to attend to them when the times become turbulent.

The difficulty has never been in identifying a reform agenda, but in finding a way to drive it forward. It is clear now that it cannot be left to the Monarchy itself, despite the current desperate attempts to shore up the creaking defences. The moment for internal reform has come and gone. It is time to recognise that the Monarchy is a public institution, not the private property of the Royal Family. Those of us who still want a constitutional Monarchy to work have an obligation to try to reform it. This is now a challenge for

Parliament, which would be unwise to duck it. When a public institution is in trouble, there is a public duty to do something about it. It is not enough to wait and hope for a handsome young prince to come along and rescue it.

(The Independent, 12 April 2001)

‡

The Monarchy has been an integral part of the symbolic glue that holds the country together. But what is 'the country' now that we are (for the moment) still a union state but no longer a unitary one? With the traditional building blocks of Britishness weakening, will the glue hold for long? As Scotland contemplates secession, is the end of Britain in sight? Such questions prompt a new politics of identity – familiar elsewhere but not here – as we are required to decide who we are and what this means for how we are governed. If Britain is to survive, it will be because enough people decide that they want it to and enough imaginative statecraft is deployed to this end. This seems to me to be a particular challenge for the English, the dominant partners in the union, who now have to decide who they are and how they want to be governed, as I argued in this piece on the English Question in 2000.

England, Whose England?

'Much of the existing machinery in England was created for the purpose of dealing with conditions widely different from those of today, and for exercising powers far narrower in scope than those which are now imposed upon it by legislation, or which the community demands that it should acquire.' That was how the Fabian Society saw the English

Question in 1905, launching its New Heptarchy series of pamphlets on English regionalism (or 'Municipalisation by Provinces' as it described it in Fabianese). A century later, the question is with us again.

This time, though, it is asked with more urgency and in circumstances that are more pressing. Where does England fit into the reconfiguration of Britain? What should be the English response to what is happening elsewhere in Britain? Does England need political reform of its own – and, if so, of what kind? What does it now mean to be English? Questions about identity jostle with questions about governance. The English Question turns out to be a cluster of related questions, but the need for some convincing answers becomes daily more evident and urgent. The English propensity for muddling along is an exhausted option.

It all used to be so much simpler, even if the simplicity came at a price. In his best-selling chronicle of journeying around Britain, the American writer Bill Bryson came upon the grave of Asquith in an Oxfordshire churchyard and found it odd that the Prime Minister of Britain, at the high point of empire, should be described on the headstone as having been the Prime Minister of England. It is a revealing mis-description, but one which remained unexplored for most of the twentieth century. This was the British century, in which nice distinctions could be easily forgotten – not least by the English.

The British have long been distinguished by having no clear idea about who they are, where they are, or what they are. Most of them have routinely described England as Britain. Only business people – and *Eurovision* presenters – talk about a place called the United Kingdom (or, horror of horrors, UK plc). It is all a terrible muddle. Yet, with the savage exception of Ireland, it has also long been a largely serene and undisturbed muddle. On this front, as on others, muddling through has been the British trademark. Untroubled by who they were, with an underlying unity that seemed to transcend their evident divisions, the British offered the world a model of stable representative government.

Yet it is now clearer than perhaps it once was that 'Britain' was a historically contingent experience. From the deliberate forging of Britons in the eighteenth century to the cementing of Britishness in the twentieth century, it is the story of a historical construct. War, empire and Monarchy provided much of the historical and symbolic glue. New institutions – such as the BBC in the 1920s and the NHS in the 1940s – also played their part. So too did the Labour Party, for a politics of class integrated as well as divided. The twentieth century was emphatically the British century, with the mid-century of Blitz and Beveridge as the high tide of Britishness. The Festival of Britain in 1951 was just that, in the way that the Millennium Dome is clearly not. The twentieth century ends, and the twenty-first begins, with the idea of Britain in deep trouble. There is a growing recognition, even among the formerly untroubled, that things are not as they once were. Muddling through no longer seems adequate, or even available.

What has changed? The traditional support systems of Britishness have all weakened. The collective endeavour and sacrifice of total war is a fast-fading memory. The lived experience of empire is even further distant. Polls show that most people do not think the Monarchy will still exist in fifty years' time. These are momentous changes, with cumulative consequences for our ideas of Britishness. When others are added in (the impact of post-war immigration, the fading of class politics), along with the general effect of globalising trends and supra-national European institutions, it is not difficult to see why a traditional version of Britishness is no longer sustainable. Space has opened up for a new politics of identity, culture and territory. An old doctrine of sovereignty is no longer capable of holding the line against those who wish to distribute power differently. With governments and Parliaments in Edinburgh, Cardiff and (we still hope) Belfast, it is no longer possible (even for the English) to miss the fact of a multinational kingdom.

Does all this mean that Britain is finished? It would be foolish to deny the possibility. Breaking up is not so very hard to do. The right of the people of Northern Ireland to leave the union if and when a majority so wishes is part of the new constitutional settlement there. No similar right has been formally conceded in the case of Scotland, but the political reality is that independence is available to Scotland if and when this becomes the majority will of the Scottish people. The recent poll which showed most people in Britain expecting Scotland to leave the union within the next ten to twenty years is merely a realistically relaxed view of constitutional possibilities.

There is clearly no desire in England to detain anybody against their will. Those who predicted that devolution was the slippery slope to disintegration might well claim that their prediction is on course.

Yet this conveniently ignores the fact that devolution, certainly in the case of Scotland, had become a political imperative, irrespective of arguments about its desirability. A century ago

Gladstone mocked those 'disunionists' whose blind opposition to Home Rule made it more likely that the union would be destroyed entirely; and such disunionists are still in evidence today. The sheer political unintelligence which Conservatives have brought to bear on constitutional matters in recent times has provided a depressing commentary on the party's larger difficulties. Now there is an unholy alliance between separatists in Scotland and right-wing nationalists in England in gleeful support of the proposition that Britain is being abolished. The former embrace a Europe of the regions which is squeezing power out of the old national states; the latter denounce the same process and want to lift the siege on England from above and below. The politics of resentment, which has long fed nationalism in Scotland and Wales, has now made its unlovely appearance in England. Devolution manages both to restrain a politics of this kind and to provoke it.

The abolitionists of Britain may be right. Perhaps there is a functionalist logic about the hollowing out of the traditional nation-state as powers shift upwards to Europe and downwards to smaller units. Similarly, perhaps England will decide that it would like finally to rid itself of what it may come to regard as its troublesome and subsidy-draining peripheries. Yet there is nothing inevitable about any of this. The only certain fact is that one version of Britain does not work any more. This is the top-down, centralised and unitary version, with its old supporting props of Britishness, English myopia, obsession with sovereignty, and general failure to understand its own nature. The abolition of that version of Britain is both inevitable and desirable. Yet this does not mean that another version is not capable of being created. Indeed, the process of devolution carries with it the explicit belief that it can be.

There are some positive grounds for this belief. It is not the case that devolving power is the route to disintegration, as examples from Spain and elsewhere show. Refusing to devolve can be disintegrating; and resolving to devolve can be integrating. Nor has power-sharing at the European level been accompanied by an erosion of national states. It can even be argued that the EU has embodied and strengthened the idea of the nation-state. Furthermore, there are much more positive conclusions to be derived by England from the process of devolution than a rancorous resentment or grumpy abandonment of the idea of Britain, not least an exploration of how devolution might usefully be applied to itself.

The fundamental issue, though, is less one of constitutional architecture, important though that is, than of basic identity. In simplest terms, a new version of Britain will be developed if sufficient inhabitants of this island believe the enterprise is worthwhile. Those ethnic minority voices which say they could never feel 'English' (too excluding) but can feel 'British' (more inclusive) provide at least one important reason for thinking that it may be worthwhile. This kind of Britain will be loose and untidy, with power organised at different levels, a home to experiment and diversity. It will be a union state, but not a unitary state. A part will no longer confuse itself with the whole. Its inhabitants will be easy with the idea of overlapping identities and multiple loyalties. A mixed-up and mongrel people, they will have the capacity to show the world that identity is not the same as territory and that democracy can be vigorously pluralistic. There is no guarantee that this is the version of Britain that will win through; but nor is it an unworthy or unrealistic aspiration.

But where does this leave England and the English? The

short answer is that a new kind of Britain will only work if the English – as the overwhelmingly dominant partner – commit themselves to making it work. It is time for England to engage, for we really are Chesterton's 'people of England, that never have spoken yet'. The English have been the silent and uninvited guests at the devolutionary feast. Scotland has a Parliament, Wales an Assembly, while England only gets some regional quangos. When Rover collapsed, who was there to speak (and act) for the West Midlands? A striking feature of the devolution legislation has been its total neglect of the union (and English) dimension.

Scottish over-representation at Westminster is to be reduced, but Scotland retains a Secretary of State as well as acquiring a Parliament while England has neither; the West Lothian question (why should Scottish MPs vote on English matters when English MPs can't vote on Scottish matters?) remains unanswered; and the public spending formula continues to be over-generous to Scotland. Once a government at Westminster is dependent on Scottish votes to secure English measures, such matters will cease to be merely anomalies and will become the stuff of constitutional crisis. That is why it is sensible to attend to them now. Whatever the devolution settlement was, it was clearly not a settlement. And it leaves the English Question unresolved.

This is the question of where England fits into the new union that is now being created – and what kind of England will make its distinctive contribution to this union. If it's a surly English nationalism, then the new union state will be in trouble from the start. The chances of creating what Gladstone a century ago called 'a partnership of four nations' will be bleak. Instead, it will soon become a bad-tempered failure. But if England puts its inevitable dominance (with 85 per cent of the UK population and 529 out of 659 MPs at Westminster) to imaginative use in the service of the new union, then the prospects are transformed.

The English never really got the hang of the old union. They thought that Britain was just England by another name. Bagehot's famous book of the 1860s was called *The English Constitution*. Britain has been a contrivance; England an identity. But what kind of identity? It's difficult not to be confessional at this point. I know that I am irredeemably English. There is nothing I can do about it. In Orwell's words, suet puddings and red pillar boxes have entered my soul. But I am also aware that I like one kind of Englishness as much as I dislike another kind. My England is about quiet patriotism and undemonstrative decency. It's the sort that says, 'Still, mustn't grumble', trades in gentle irony, knows that it takes all sorts, believes in fair play, distrusts fundamentalists and tries to make things work. This is the kind of Englishness that makes living in England so agreeable.

There is another kind, though, that is altogether less appealing. This is the Englishness that always believes somebody (usually foreign) is diddling them. It's smug, stuffy, arrogant, class-ridden and excluding. Its language is that of the 'home counties' and the 'provinces'. It says England when it means Britain. It can't see beyond the end of its xenophobic nose. It's the kind of Englishness that makes minorities feel they might be British but never English. It's top-down and centralising, intolerant of diversity and wants to put people in their place. It is the kind of Englishness which means, in the first year of the twenty-first century, that there are still more Old Etonians in the House of Commons than members of ethnic minorities.

Why does this matter now? Because devolution has given this kind of unlovely Englishness a new lease of life. English nationalism joins hands with the separatists in wanting the new union to fail. Its difficulties are celebrated; its release of civic energy ignored. The Europhobes of the right add Scotland and Wales to the list of those who are diddling us. Unable and unwilling to understand the real meaning of devolution, which is an attack on the curse of centralism, they defend the old centre against the upstart peripheries. Their demand for the chimera of an English Parliament is really the refusal of a certain kind of (southern) Englishness to recognise the democratic claims of what Orwell called 'the England that is only just beneath the surface'.

It is this other England that now has to speak. When it does, it will attend sensibly to the need to represent England in the new union. This will mean procedural changes at Westminster to ensure that England speaks (and votes) for England. It means fair and transparent funding rules. It will certainly mean radical decentralisation within England. From now on devolution stops being an argument about somewhere else and starts being an argument about England. But there need be no uniformity or pressing of issues to their logical extremes. The evolving union is messy, lopsided and asymmetrical – and all the better for it. Living with anomalies and preferring common sense to logical abstractions is supposed to be what the political genius of the English is all about. In the words of Burke, the Irish father of English conservatism, 'it is in the nature of all greatness not to be exact'.

The inhabitants of England are a wonderfully mongrel people. London is the most vibrantly cosmopolitan city in Europe. To respond to the remaking of Britain, and to a decentralising moment, with a mean-spirited nationalism would be a victory for the worst kind of Englishness over the best kind. It would also be a missed opportunity of historic proportions. For devolution gives us the chance to lift the curse of centralism in England too. A new British union state – pluralistic, inclusive, multinational – that could be an example to the world is in the making. It would be a place of easily overlapping identities and decentralised governance. The question for the English is whether they will make it happen, and what part they will play in it.

So far the running has been made by those on the right, who have seen the renegotiation of Britain as an opportunity to play the nationalist card in England. This will not bring us the Balkans, but it will make life on our small island much more unpleasant. It is not enough for the rest of us to treat this prospect with contempt or disdain, for that is to let necessary arguments go by default. Identity politics may make liberals uncomfortable, but the version of Englishness peddled by the right has to be countered and resisted. There is a different version of England whose voice now needs to be heard.

Nowhere is this more evident than on the question of how England should be governed. The operation of central government at a regional and local level is a mess. Local government has lost functions to local quangos, been stripped of its financial independence, experienced a botched attempt to revise its boundaries, and now faces an internal reorganisation forced from the centre. What is missing is a vision (and a strategy) for a serious local democracy. The NHS is to be modernised, but in a sternly centralist way and with no suggestion that new mechanisms of local and regional democratic accountability might form part of the modernising agenda. Public services groan under the weight of centrally imposed performance targets, reflecting a belief that the man in Whitehall (or, more precisely, in the Treasury) can and should control everything that moves.

We now have to decide if we really want England to be governed like this. We also have to decide if we are prepared to continue with the habits of mind that make it like this. 'British contempt for provincialism is total', writes Simon Jenkins in *The Times* (17 January 1998): 'Ask most readers of this article to name a principal street in Manchester, Birmingham, Newcastle or Liverpool and they will look blank. Ask when they last visited Leeds, York, Bristol or Plymouth and most will say never, with a shudder. Crests would fall at failing such a test about Florence, Nice, Barcelona, or New York... To fashionable London, provincial England is a cultural swamp.' The civic patriotism that distinguished our great Victorian cities (such as Joseph Chamberlain's Birmingham) has been grievously eroded, along with the powers that they possessed and the functions that they performed. We have paid a heavy price for this civic atrophy. Elsewhere – in France, Germany, Italy, Spain – there are cities that look and feel like great regional capitals, because that is what they are. Elected mayors are no substitute for political and economic clout.

What distinguishes the right-wing response in England to devolution is a total failure to recognise, let alone accept, that England might need devolution and decentralisation too. There is metropolitan contempt for the idea that the English regions might require democratic expression of their interests. Proposals for an English Parliament are deliberately intended as a centralist alternative to the devolution of power within England itself. Yet the left has had its own blind spots too, not least in a centralising tendency to believe that an attachment to class equality trumped any concern with geographical inequality or the territorial distribution of power. It is curious that a Labour movement formed out of interests far away from the metropolitan centre should not have pressed harder on the politics of territory. For territory, power and wealth sit together in England. Internal regional differences are certainly important and should be recognised; but regional inequality remains a basic feature of English life. Those who want to remedy it need an effective means of expression.

There are different views on how this might be done, just as there are different views on all the other matters touched on here. What is crucial is that we make a serious start in thinking about them. In the 1970s we had a Royal Commission on the Constitution. In fact, it was nothing of the kind; merely a response to the devolutionary and separatist pressures in Scotland and Wales. Now we do need a Commission on the Constitution, of a proper kind, with the future governance of England at its centre. The English Question is now on the table and will not go away.

(In *The English Question*, Fabian Society, 2000)

‡

This is just one of the many issues on which we need an intelligent civic conversation. It is difficult to have this with a rotten (and, as we now know, corrupt) tabloid culture that prefers to play in the sewer and with politicians who are too often content to engage in their own games with the media. Journalists and politicians should have a complementary role in holding power to account; however, that requires both sides to raise their game dramatically. There should never be a cosy relationship, but there should be an honest one. We now have an inquiry that is looking at the relationship between politicians and the media, which was something I wrote about in an article in 1998.

Inside the Whale: The Media from Parliament

Here's what it's like these days. I returned to our tiny *Guardian* office in Westminster to find three – count them, three – Liberal Democrat spin doctors clustered around.

They were like ants at a picnic. You'd leave one at the door, and find another waiting by your computer screen. As soon as you'd dealt with him, another would turn up over your shoulder.

'Did you like Paddy's intervention?' asked one. 'Wasn't he funny?'

'Jackie Ballard was terrific, wasn't she,' said another. 'She was so poised!'

'Look, here's a copy of what Blair actually said last year', said a third, and there was a photocopy of Hansard, proving beyond doubt that, as Leader of the Opposition, Mr Blair has described as mere 'sticking plaster' a sum of money larger than his own government proposes to spend on the NHS.

I suppose we ought to be flattered. Maybe we should be like those old theatre critics who used to drop phrases into their reviews hoping they'd appear on the posters ('I laughed till my prostate ached!' – Monty Maltravers, *Daily Beast*). This would provide publicity for them as well as for the show, implying that theirs was the good opinion which everybody craved.

Ms Ballard could seek re-election in Taunton with similar quotes: 'Terrific … poised – *The Guardian*'; 'Ms Ballard is as welcome in Parliament as an Airwick in an abattoir – *Daily Telegraph*'.

Don't misunderstand me. All those three spin doctors are intelligent, thoughtful, well-informed young persons. It's a pleasure to do business with them. Their party should pay them huge sums of money.

But you have to wonder about the state of British politics, in which there is such an obsessional concern about these tiny soundbites from the smallest of the three main parties.

It's an aged cliché that nobody now has an attention span. But we do. The actual remark made in the House might last for only ten seconds. But the debate over each single word is pursued for hours.

This is Simon Hoggart, of course (*The Guardian*, 6 November 1997). And this *is* what it's like these days. Walking along the media route between the Commons and Millbank one evening recently, I heard a couple of earnest young spinners discussing their day's work. 'I just wish', said one, 'that we had gone the extra mile.' 'Yes', replied the other, 'I think we might have got GMTV.'

But who is getting whom? And for what? More important still, what if anything can be done about it?

It is not possible to talk about any of this unless we have a reasonably clear idea what the political role of the media should be. The technology may be changing at a bewildering pace, but this makes it even more important to hang on to a firm sense of the civic role of the media in a democratic polity. If that sounds rather serious, then so it should. We need something against which to measure what is happening both to politicians and to the media, and consider what might be done about it. To suggest that something might need to be done is not to succumb to a form of golden-ageism. There is much to celebrate – the extension of choice, the explosion of information sources, the end of deference in broadcasting, the opinion pages of the broadsheets – but there is also much to be concerned about. This presents a challenge both for politicians and the media.

Back to the civic role. The media should be the place where a mass democracy communicates with itself. This involves a whole range of activities: informing, discussing, arguing, questioning, reflecting, investigating, exposing...

Without a media that performs this role, the nation is deprived of its collective street corner, market square and noticeboard. If deprived in this way, the quality of its democracy will suffer. This is recognised in what we traditionally say about the importance of a free press, the quasi-constitutional status that is bestowed upon the fourth estate, and the public service obligations imposed upon broadcasters. Either we still believe in what we say about all of this or we do not.

Of course there are difficulties, tensions, and contradictions. The public service requirements placed upon broadcasters (or some of them) are not matched by similar requirements (except weak and voluntary ones) placed upon the press. In the name of a free press, tabloid editors have been able to dispense with any notion of civic responsibility. Faced with the prospect of a balancing test between privacy and information of the kind contained in the provisions of the European Convention on Human Rights, most of the press have simply gone into denunciation mode. Yet a democratic society requires a press that is free and responsible. The fact that there are inevitable tensions here does not mean that a civic interest cannot be identified. The same applies to issues of ownership, quality and access across the media.

If we believe in the civic role of the media, there are disturbing developments around. Some come from politicians, others from the media themselves. Let's start with the politicians. They like to be thought well of and want to control the message and the messengers as far as possible. There is nothing new or even disreputable about this: it comes with the job. What is new, though, is the systematic and professional way in which it is now undertaken. The wearisome gibes about spinners and soundbites do capture the modern enterprise of news management that is central to contemporary politics. The practitioners of these black arts are increasingly the key figures in the political world. As communication flows are deliberately centralised, their authority as the source of information and opinion is further enhanced. Their task is to ensure that there is a coherent and consistent message and that everyone stays 'on message' in their dealings with the media. Labour honed these skills in opposition and has carried them into government. Political communication in Britain will never be the same again.

In party terms it represents a huge achievement. Anyone who remembers the shambles of the old Labour Party will scarcely complain about the fact that it has become the sleekest machine in town. Nor is this the only way in which today's politicians have seen the new opportunities for news management. Of course Peter Riddell is right to point to the various ways in which Parliament is losing its central place in political debate, but for politicians there have been compensating gains. The televising of Parliament has brought major new opportunities for self-presentation. Not only is this true for the party leaders in the gladiatorial encounters at Question Time, where phrases in search of headlines are routinely exchanged, but for the foot-soldiers too. A single intervention in prime time is worth more than a string of worthy speeches in the long hours that follow.

Even just being there is enough, if carefully positioned. Politicians know that they can be beamed effortlessly into the living rooms of their constituents. A seat on the row just behind the front benches is the most prized spot, always remembering to nod vigorously in agreement with even the most banal statements. Then there is the clustering around questioners and speakers, with more nodding and general harrumphing, in full camera shot. The minority parties take this 'doughnuting' particularly seriously, often rushing members into the Chamber to fill a camera angle in order to give the appearance of massed strength, especially important when the clip is shown in Scotland, Wales or Northern Ireland. This is a reminder of the often neglected role of the local media. The fact that Scotland has its own national media system, whereas in Wales it is much weaker, was extremely important in the referendum campaigns.

When backbench politicians perform in Parliament, their real eye is frequently on their local media. This means both regional television and local newspapers. The regional television companies all have their Westminster presence and all have their space to fill, both in their news bulletins and their other slots (usually a weekly political programme in the case of the BBC regions). An intervention in the House of Commons is invariably a press release for the local media in the making ('MP challenges Minister on West Wittering hospital crisis'), while adjournment debates – not debates, of course, just a lonely exchange between a Member and a minister usually when everyone else has left – are a reliable way of raising local issues and attracting the attention of the local media. Press releases are far more effective than speeches in engaging local media interest and thereby conveying an impression of frenetic Parliamentary activity on behalf of constituents. The growth of local free newspapers, paid for by advertising and delivered to every door, has been a major development as far as politicians are concerned. These free sheets routinely reproduce press releases verbatim, presenting an opportunity to politicians that they have not been slow to exploit.

So there is a paradox. The decline in the importance of Parliament, reflected in the waning media attention, has gone hand in hand with an expansion of the opportunities available to politicians to use their membership of the House of Commons for media purposes. A particularly nice example of this paradox is the way in which MPs are able to acquire video stills of themselves on their feet in the Commons Chamber for use in their campaign literature. In this sense, at least, the green benches still retain their importance. It plays to a mythology. So, in a different way, does the fact that some newspapers carry an annual report of the number of times that MPs have voted during a session. It is an absurd statistic, yet produces a culture among MPs in which they speak of 'keeping their voting record up' so that they will not fare badly in the newspaper league tables. Those Labour MPs currently enjoying their regular 'constituency weeks' may find that this is an unwelcome and unintended consequence of their authorised absence.

We may lament the way in which Parliament is treated by the media, but it is scarcely irrational or inexplicable. The decline in serious reporting of Parliamentary debates, and its substitution with the lampooning of gallery sketch-writers, accurately reflects the changing character of Parliament itself. At a party to mark the first anniversary of the 1992 intake of Labour MPs, John Smith remarked that it was important to remember that the Commons was really an 'intimate theatre'. It is not surprising therefore that it attracts theatre reviewers rather than serious analysts. The only real remedy is for Parliament to make itself a more significant institution. There is a regular fuss from MPs about ministers making statements in studios or press conferences rather than in Parliament, but this is a desperate clutching at past form rather than an engagement with present substance.

For argument, debate and investigation has gone elsewhere. For a minister with something to hide, the Commons Chamber is much less intimidating than the *Today* programme or *Newsnight*. Parliament becomes an echo chamber for issues and arguments generated in the media. The Nolan Committee was invented because the Commons could not deal with matters of Parliamentary conduct that the media had exposed; and the Scott inquiry was initiated after the Commons had failed to make progress with an inquiry of its own. Ministers now resign, not because of the traditional canons of ministerial responsibility to Parliament, but because the media have successfully claimed their scalp. It is difficult to blame the media for neglecting or trivialising Parliament, when Parliament has allowed itself to become neglected and trivialised. Even the 'great Parliamentary moments' are not what they once were, largely confined to dramatic resignation statements (Norman Lamont, Geoffrey Howe) that are conventionally delivered to the Commons first.

Who Wants to Change?

The media will only have to start taking Parliament seriously when Parliament starts taking itself seriously. It is not difficult to come up with a list of reforms that would help to bring this about – they all involve making it less easy for the Commons to be rolled over routinely by the executive steamroller – but it is difficult to see how these are to be achieved without wider political reforms. What is being suggested here, though, and what is much less noticed, is the way in which politicians are complicit in what is happening – despite protestations about their desire for reform – because of the way in which the present arrangements enable them to make use of the media for their own political purposes. They are now equipped with daily press releases on which they are required only to fill in their name. They are supplied with more money to run their offices, which they can use to run a permanent election campaign in their local media or buy the computers on which they can target subsets of voters. It may not be very edifying, nor have much to do with the glories of Parliamentary democracy, but it does help to explain why there are compensations for politicians in the way they are treated by the media. It may also help to explain why the 'incumbency' advantage of sitting politicians seems to be increasing; and why the decline in public regard for politicians in general looks rather different when people are asked about their own Members of Parliament.

So much for the politicians. They have increasingly become professional media managers, in different ways and at different levels, and it is entirely sensible from their point of view that this should be the case. The problem arises only in relation to the effects on the civic role of the media. It can compress and stifle debate, reducing political communication to the crudest kind of propaganda. The ability of the media to counteract this tendency is reduced by the extent to which journalists also become complicit in the process. As political communication flows are centralised, with a small number of key gatekeepers, not only is access to other sources restricted, but a relationship of dependency can develop. When set alongside some of the other trends in the media of the kind there is certainly cause for concern.

This goes beyond the sheer awfulness of the tabloids at their worst. Their abandonment of public issues in favour of private titillations has a corrosive effect on civic life. What *The Sun* would have done with Gladstone's nocturnal activities (and erotic diaries) is too appalling to contemplate. We are fast reaching a point when nobody who cares about preserving a private life will want to go anywhere near politics. This may turn out to be the durable contribution of the tabloids to our democracy; either this or a political reaction of a kind that damages the legitimate freedoms of the press. It is not just what is being done, but the loss of what might be done instead. If the tabloids set about popularising the real public issues, or devoting their investigative resources to all those matters that need investigating, then their civic role would be transformed. Some chance. It is far more likely that politicians will want to appease the tabloid agenda.

It may be that debasement, trivialisation and irresponsibility is the price that we have to pay for a free press. In an important sense this must be so. Yet this does not mean that it is either impossible or undesirable to put a public interest framework of some kind around the press, above all in relation to the balance between privacy and intrusion. Either this will happen through effective self-regulation by the Press Complaints Commission, or through judges using the balancing provisions of the European Convention on Human Rights, or through a new privacy law passed by Parliament. There is room for argument about the respective merits and demerits of these different approaches. Where there is no room for argument is on the need for a satisfactory public interest framework. The same applies to the need to ensure that the diversity of the press, fundamental to a democracy, is sustained against monopolistic tendencies. If market power is used unfairly to drive out competitors and diminish diversity (the charge made against the predatory pricing tactics of the Murdoch empire), then there is a clear public interest in making sure that this does not happen.

More Technologies, Less Argument?

Similar considerations apply to the new broadcasting technologies, where it is the task of the state to ensure that the terms of access are not controlled by those who own the technology. But some of the current trends in broadcasting raise other issues too. It is not necessary to believe that a general dumbing down is in full swing to think that the democratic role of the media is weakened by some of the prevailing tendencies in broadcasting. The fear of joined-up argument among broadcasters marches hand in hand with the soundbite syndrome among politicians. The effect is to create an episodic jumble of talking heads. The sterile adversarialism of British politics is too often simply reinforced by the broadcast media. Where is the space within which ideas can be discussed and arguments developed? It is no doubt easier to treat the issue of European monetary union in terms of party splits rather than as a challenge in explanation (just to take a leading example), but it represents a bias against understanding with a vengeance.

If politicians have to do politics differently, then so too do the broadcasters. Indeed, the broadcasters have a crucial role to play in bringing this about. If their escape from an old deference was a precondition for this, the conversion of politics into light entertainment represents an opposite danger. At present it remains only a danger, but a real one. When some of the current trends are logged – the decline of documentaries on the ITV network, the recurrent desire to shift *News at Ten* to a less pivotal place in the schedules, the BBC plan to disengage from some of its Parliamentary programmes – it is difficult not to feel that a retreat is in progress. Developments of this kind are far more serious for the quality of our democracy than the complaints by politicians that some broadcasters now just want to beat them up on air. It is the job of the broadcasters to give politicians a hard time; but it is also the job of public service broadcasting to ensure that arguments and voices are heard. There are inevitable and wholly welcome tensions here.

But who speaks for the public interest in all of this? In

crucial areas nobody does. There is a deficiency here that requires attention and remedy. This is well illustrated by the example of election broadcasting. We know that broadcasting, above all television, provides the main route through which voters learn about election issues and shape their electoral judgments. This is not because voters like watching election television, but because they like watching television and therefore get elections. So it matters hugely, which is why it receives such obsessive political attention. Yet the arrangements under which election broadcasting take place are a curious mix of formal rules and informal agreements between parties and broadcasters. It is difficult to claim that what results is what the public needs. There are much better models available (of the kind to be found long ago in Jay Blumler's little book *The Challenge of Election Broadcasting*), in which the right of politicians to make their case is linked to a duty to have that case critically examined. The parties may not like this, but the public interest would be better served by it.

Similar considerations apply to the ritual exchanges on the eve of general elections between the party leaders, and between the parties and the broadcasters, on the question of whether there should be televised debates between the leaders. We have to endure the wearisome on–off stories about who is running scared of whom. Yet there is surely a clear public interest in matching Prime Ministers, current and putative, against each other in televised debate under rules designed to allow arguments to be tested and judgments made. There is currently no mechanism through which this public interest can be asserted. Our uncodified make-it-up-as-we-go-along kind of constitutional arrangements are here reflected in the lack of rules and machinery for the conduct of election broadcasting.

The remedy is an independent commission with responsibility for all aspects of electoral conduct, including broadcasting. This should be seen as an integral part of the political reform programme that the Blair government is implementing, sitting alongside those other areas (such as party funding) where independent rules are slowly replacing informal practices. A commission of this kind could take the whole of party political broadcasting under its wing, as this is really part of a permanent election campaign and there are soon to be many more elections and referenda. The broadcasters have recently proposed an end to party political broadcasts outside elections. The politicians (or at least some of them) have responded by asserting their right to communicate directly with the electorate. There are good rival claims involved here. The broadcasters are right to want to banish items of crude propaganda that viewers dislike. The politicians are right to assert the importance of unmediated political communication. But where both are wrong is in thinking that such matters should be settled either by unilateral declaration or by brokered deal. It is possible to find a model that meets the different objectives, but this requires a public interest framework of a kind that an independent commission would provide.

The larger and longer question, extending far beyond specific issues such as election broadcasting, is whether a public interest framework of any kind will be achievable in the new media age that lies immediately ahead. In particular, can the civic role of the media be sustained and developed, or is it doomed to wither and die? The answer is entirely unclear. It is possible to be either chirpily optimistic or gloomily pessimistic about the prospects. One kind of future looks replete with democratic opportunities; another kind represents a form of civic death. What is at stake is the ability of the media to continue to perform the functions in a democratic society that have traditionally been assigned to them. It is clear that a period of media history is coming to an end. Whatever the particular criticisms that can be made of it, in Britain it has been a period in which the media – above all, in the form of public service broadcasting – have played a notable civic role and made a significant democratic contribution. What is not clear is how, or even whether, this will be possible in the future.

On the pessimistic view, the deterioration that is already apparent is set to intensify dramatically. The fragmented multichannel future represents the end of a common arena in which issues of shared concern are discussed and public figures interrogated. A general conversation is replaced by disconnected babble. The continuing dialogue that is essential to democratic politics is crowded out by the media ghettos of particular interests. Broadcasting becomes a choice between undifferentiated pap or narrow sectionalism, while newspapers continue to shift remorselessly away from hard news and analysis to softer 'lifestyle' and gossip. The implications for political life of such developments are very serious. An environment is created in which the media enable citizens to escape from the domain of public life altogether, while politicians further hone their skills of media manipulation to send messages of slick simplicity at moments of political choice. In such a future the idea of an informed democracy becomes a bad joke.

More Technologies, More Democracy?

The optimistic prospect looks radically different from this. Digital broadcasting brings with it a huge expansion of choice and diversity. Alongside government on-line, electronic democracy and the rich resources of the internet, the new media age opens up exciting civic possibilities. A pluralist democracy is sustained by a vigorously plural media system. In place of an era in which political broadcasting has been strictly rationed and controlled, there arrives a period in which the whole range of positions can be represented and all views expressed. Dedicated channels, partisan and specialist, enable both majorities and minorities to be heard. Arguments and opinions can be explored fully. Local radio and television will provide major new opportunities for local issues to be discussed. In all these ways the prospect is of a political culture that is energised and a democracy that is enriched. As the political system itself is changed, with power decentralised and new sites for democracy opened up, a media system that matches this change becomes a crucial source of new civic energy.

These are compelling alternative futures. It is useful to set them out, if only to bring into sharp relief what is at stake. Of course matters are unlikely to be as clear-cut as this in practice. Elements of each will no doubt come together to shape a new mixed economy in the media. But it should not be a question merely of waiting to see what happens. Public policy in a democracy has a responsibility to ensure that the framework exists in which the civic role of the media can be sustained and developed. At a time when there are both threats and opportunities on a dramatic scale, it has never been more important to get this framework right.

(In J. Seaton (ed), *Politics and the Media*, [1998])

‡

Politicians like to be popular, of course, which is why the media are so important to them. As Matthew Parris puts it, 'politicians run on publicity like horses run on oats'. They want to be popular with their party leaders, because that is the path to advancement, but this may sometimes clash with the need to be popular with their constituents. This can produce some wondrous contortions. Just the other day I heard a Tory MP from the Midland shires explaining that, while he was very much in favour of the new high-speed rail line, he had concluded that the proposed route, which just happened to pass through his constituency (where it was upsetting his voters) was in the wrong place. There are many politicians (not all, fortunately) who will go to extraordinary lengths to avoid saying anything that they think may be unpopular with any of the people who elect them. A typical mailing to constituents might say something as politically courageous as: 'I am campaigning for tougher sentences for muggers and murderers. Let me know if you are backing my campaign.'

The only time I really hit trouble with my local party members was when I was a dissident on the hunting ban. I loathed the idea of killing animals for sport, but thought there were layers of hypocrisy around the issue that had put politicians in hock to a pressure group and represented an intolerant kind of politics. I was foolish enough, in party terms, to spell this out in a piece in The Guardian.

Hypocrisy and Hunting

How on Earth did we get into this mess? It is difficult for many of us to get very worked up about foxhunting, but it is easy to get worked up about the idiocy that has brought us to where we are now.

It was obvious from the start that it would end badly. The loss of proportion is staggering. Whatever progressive politics is about, or worth taking on opposing interests for, it is not about views on alternative methods of pest control. Talk of invoking the Parliament Act is like declaring a state of emergency because of a patch of fog on the M4.

I dislike the idea of blood sports. Some of the people who engage in them seem especially unlovely. Unseating the 'toffocracy' is appealing. The trouble comes when we start converting personal prejudices into State action. Not only do we stir up all sorts of unnecessary trouble, we also wander into a bog of hypocrisies, inconsistencies and contradictions.

Many of my colleagues have a passion for the issue that is in inverse proportion to its significance. Others have allowed themselves to be imprisoned by pressure groups. Some (including Tony Blair and most of the Cabinet, I suspect) would just like it to go away. It is the last stand of a kind of gesture politics that Labour has taken much trouble to banish on other fronts. The alarm bells first rang for me a few years ago when a packed meeting of Labour MPs howled down the suggestion of an independent inquiry on the issue. The government did set up an inquiry, but it need not have bothered. Minds were already made up.

A similar fate awaited the elaborate hearings conducted by poor Alun Michael. The compromise bill he constructed was dead even before it reached the Commons. It was a triumph for deaf absolutism.

Hunting is cruel, but so are the alternatives. That was the Burns Report finding. A sensible fox, asked to state a preference between being hunted, shot, snared or gassed, would tick the 'None of the above' box. A further finding was that, particularly in upland areas, hunting with dogs is an effective way of controlling fox populations. Yet the House of Commons now seriously proposes to criminalise a farmer in the fells who takes out a pack of hounds to hunt the fox that killed his chickens. As Oscar Wilde might have said, this is the unpersuadable in pursuit of the unpoliceable.

The fact is that we routinely do unspeakable things to animals; hunting is scarcely up there with our ordinary cruelties. I have just watched a local council pest control officer on television explaining how he kills rats by giving them a poison that stops their blood clotting until they eventually die. I have yet to hear such practices denounced from the Commons benches. If sport is the issue, then why not ban all killing of animals, birds and fish for pleasure? Exchanging substance for symbolism is the worst form of hypocrisy.

Nor can it be a matter of political and moral sensibility. Robin Cook opposes a ban, Ann Widdecombe supports one. Hitler famously loved animals, but hated Jews. We should at least try to stick to the merits of the issue and avoid the rival moral frenzies. Instead, we have allowed the fundamentalists (on both sides) to take over, with predictable consequences.

When this happens, reason and compromise are the first casualties, and we end up with our own homely version of civil war.

It is being waged in the name of democracy. A majority in the elected House has voted emphatically and repeatedly in favour of a total ban. For some, that is the end of the argument. But this is crude majoritarianism, not liberal democracy.

That was previously our complaint against the governing style of Margaret Thatcher – pushing half-baked measures through the Commons, refusing all compromise, simply because she had the majority to do so. A mature liberal democracy should always try to find as much common ground as possible, especially on measures that arouse rival passions and where agreement is necessary to make them work.

There is no difficulty in constructing a sensible compromise. We could strengthen the laws that outlaw unnecessary animal cruelty, and force hunting to justify itself in relation to them. The Lords would approve it, the hunters would have to put up with it, most people would find it satisfactory, and a small advance for civilisation would have been made.

An outbreak of sanity is now needed. It would be a final madness for my Parliamentary colleagues to prefer to die in the ditch for an unenforceable ban than to secure an achievable, if partial, victory. Having had a good run, it is time for this issue to go to ground.

(*The Guardian*, 12 October 2004)

‡

Politicians are also required to be optimists, the carriers of hope – except when they are describing the ruinations perpetrated by their political opponents. This is why the clash with reality can prove so perennially painful. There were times when I felt almost too gloomy to be a politician; when I was too acutely aware of the gap between the confident words I was saying and the intractable nature of the issue; and when the limitations of politics was the one fact that dared not speak its name. I was worried, in particular, that we were becoming an increasingly uncivil society, despite all the advances, and that this was a profound cultural problem that defied the routine political responses on both left and right. In the wake of the urban rioting and looting of August 2011, there was much anguished hand-wringing to this effect. Yet this was only the most extreme mani-festation of a growing incivility that had been slowly creeping across the land. After one constituency advice surgery a decade ago, which had thrown up more than its usual share of seemingly insoluble human misery, I went home and wrote a piece – really for myself, I think, and published here for the first time – about how I felt.

Notes after a Surgery

The petition came from the residents of Hardie Green, one of several streets in my constituency that bear the name of Labour movement heroes. It might have come from Attlee Crescent or William Morris Court, or from a street on the Bevan Lee estate. These street names, bristling with the progressive civic pride that put them there, make the con-temporary lament of their residents especially poignant.

From the frail signatures on this petition it was evident that many of the residents were very elderly. Some have lived there for half a century. They describe how the trees they have loved have been broken down, how their windows are stoned, how they are afraid to go out. Routine stuff, of course, from streets and estates across the land. This petition is followed by a deputation from another street that wants its children's play area removed, because the yobs and druggies have made it unfit for any parent or child to go near it.

So it goes on, as the rising tide of incivility makes life ever more unpleasant for ever more people. Some mark the con-trast between easy-going, family-friendly evenings spent on holiday in towns across Europe with the sea of violence and vomit they have to endure in their own town and city centres.

From Alicante to Zakynthos, there are cries for protection from the behaviour of booze-sodden Brits. A fifth of our schools, according to the chief inspector, now have problems in maintaining basic order. Hospital staff are exposed to drink-fuelled violence on a regular basis. Children's football leagues are having to expel teams because of the foul-mouthed obscenities from parents on the touchline. The neighbours from hell are increasingly to be found next door.

It is not necessary to believe that there was once a golden age of civility to know that something has gone badly wrong in the last generation or so. Perhaps those of us who grew up in the 1950s have a warped perspective on these things. Even now I have vivid recall of the day I had to cycle the ten miles to my father's place of work with the sandwiches he had forgotten and suddenly realising that I did not know how I should properly describe him when I handed them over to the man on the gate. I finally settled on 'Frank', thinking that was how he would be referred to at work, even though I had never used his first name before and it feeling quite wrong, only to have a strip torn off me for not asking for 'Mr Wright'. Now even teachers seem to want to be on familiar terms with their pupils.

The unprecedented enrichment of our society, along with the stripping away of the old constraints and embrace of new freedoms, bringing welcome relief from stuffiness and deference, has gone hand in hand with a collapse of civility. The ties that bind have come apart at the seams, in fractured communities and broken families. There is more criminality of course, but there is also a general coarsening of our culture. Crudity of language combines with offensiveness of behaviour on a scale that eventually forces politicians to take notice. That is why the politics of behaviour has recently shot up the political agenda.

The trouble is that there is no easy policy fix for behaviour and culture, nor even a reliable frame of ideological reference. The left sometimes tries to squeeze the issue into a narrative about 'Thatcher's children', the release of a rampant individualism that trampled over social and moral solidarities. The right prefers to focus on the corrosive legacy for traditional authority of 1960s-style liberalism. All we really know is that something has changed and that, while so much has got better, we have a crisis of incivility on our hands (and in our streets).

This raises some uncomfortable questions, not least for progressives. Their world is one of freedoms gained, not of disciplines lost. This can make it difficult to engage with critical issues. Take the family, that traditional school of citizenship, which has undergone a revolution over the last generation. A child born in 1958 had a 90 per cent chance of still living with both natural parents at age sixteen. For a child born in the mid-1980s that figure has collapsed to 65 per cent. Ours is an age of disposable relationships and transferable children. One in six babies is born into a house without a father; and for Black Caribbean babies it is almost half. This is how we choose to live now. Doubtless it is a kind of emancipation, but our children may experience it rather differently.

Or take the media. In the face of those who worried, Whitehouse-like, about the coarseness and violence of modern media culture, the progressive case for freedom could always call in aid the evidence of the protective blanket provided by family, school and community that enabled image to be distinguished from reality. This blanket is now seriously holed. It is no longer possible to be so sanguine about the effects of media portrayals of violence. As other sources of language and behaviour weaken, for increasing numbers of people the media define how life is to be lived. There is a corrosive coarsening at work, even if it describes itself as freedom, and this should worry liberals as much as anybody else.

This matters, if we care about a civilised society. It would be bad enough if it was simply a case of becoming unmannered, as some polite commentary seems to think; but it is altogether more serious if it is part of a wider and deeper rejection of the civic.

The political response involves both control and support. On this side, ASBOs; on that side, Sure Start. The trouble is that the State is always going to be a poor substitute for other sources of civic virtue. Launching the 'respect' agenda, Tony Blair spoke of the 'deep-seated causes' of children growing up without proper discipline, and said: 'I can start a debate on this and I can legislate, but what I can't do, I can't raise someone's children for them.' We do need a debate about the crisis of incivility. But the residents of Hardie Green also need protection from its consequences, now.

‡

None of this means that we should give up on politics, despite the fact that its limitations – especially in relation to culture – are acknowledged and it often promises more than it can realistically deliver. Politics remains the place where our continuing civic conversation takes place, and where we seek to negotiate our common problems and advance our contending views of what constitutes a decent society (and world).

There is plenty of work for politics to do in digging us out of the mess we are in, even if the failure of politics and politicians has helped to get us into the mess. Our fraying social fabric is in desperate need of repair, requiring action on many fronts to ensure that security and life chances are enhanced so that every-body feels they have a stake in their society. The cost of not doing this is now evident for all to see. As the debt crisis spreads from banks to states, rocking the foundations of the world economy and enforcing a politics of austerity that snuffs out all alterna-tives, the need for a new global financial architecture demands political leadership with courage and ability of a kind that has not so far been forthcoming.

Events of recent years have ensured that the financial class, political class and journalistic class have all suffered severe reputational damage. This encourages a further flight from the civic, a loss of faith in institutions and a retreat into a personal world over which it is still possible to feel some sort of trust and control. All this is compounded by a sense that the forces which are reshaping the world are beyond political control – on issues like climate change, for example, politics has proved unequal to the challenge. It is going to be a long way back (or forward), but it is only through politics that this will ever be possible, so we had better start discussing how to do it.

Nor does all this mean that we should give up on politicians. It is easy – too easy – to make fun of them, not least because they so often invite it themselves. But the simple fact, in all times and in all places, is that politicians are indispensable if we want demo-cratic politics to work. In that fundamental sense, they need to be taken seriously, which means examining what they do and how they do it. If people do not like the politicians we have, they should set about getting better ones. Ditto with the political system itself. When I was invited to give a public lecture at Birkbeck College in the spring of 2011, I decided to offer a defence of politicians. It seems the appropriate note on which to end this book.

In Defence of Politicians

> A drunkard or a gambler may be weaned from his ways, but not a politician.
> Anthony Trollope, *Phineas Redux* (1874), p.110.

Let me start, as one always should, with *The Archers*.

Not with the recent shoddy sensationalism of poor Nigel Pargetter plunging to his doom from the roof of his ancestral pile, but with a more typical scene from the everyday story of country folk. A peregrine falcon has taken up residence in the Ambridge churchyard and the village do-gooding busybody Linda Snell immediately hatches a project to erect a nesting box for it in the churchyard. This is opposed by the shooters and farmers; and a meeting is held in the church hall to thrash the issue out. It is Linda Snell versus Brian Aldridge, the agro-capitalist, property developer and general cad-about-the-countryside.

Warned that Brian may sway the meeting, Linda says: 'Well, he *is* quite the politician.'

It is that word 'politician', heavy with all its unflattering associations, that I want to talk about. To say 'politician' is to say scheming, dissembling, evading, spinning, deceiving, misleading and much more in the same vein. As someone who was a professional politician for nearly two decades – that is, I was paid to do politics for a living – I always went to considerable circumlocutory lengths to avoid describing myself as one. With the Parliamentary expenses scandal, of course, it all got a good deal worse. To the familiar inventory of infamy was now added cheating, fiddling and defrauding. Only the disgraced bankers were more unloved, but even then the politicians could be blamed for not sorting them out properly.

I shall spare you all those depressing opinion surveys and league tables showing just how mistrusted and unloved politicians are; but I shall not spare you a few pickings from the rich harvest of jokes made at politicians' expense. I particularly like the line from Henry Kissinger: 'It's 90 per cent of politicians who give the other 10 per cent a bad name.' It was once said of Harold Wilson that: 'You can always tell when he's lying – his lips move', but it could equally have been said of any other leading politician. Then there is Bernard Shaw: 'He knows nothing and thinks he knows everything – that points to a political career.' And Adlai Stevenson: 'A politician is a person who approaches every problem with an open mouth'. (It was Stevenson who famously said to Richard Nixon: 'If you stop telling lies about me, I'll stop telling the truth about you.') Just one more. A group of professional people are debating which is the oldest profession. Each one makes a claim for their own profession. The doctor invokes Adam's rib. The lawyer mentions the justice of Solomon. The accountant refers to thirty pieces of silver. The architect comes in with the creation experience. So it goes on, until the politician plays the trump card: 'My profession is clearly the oldest, because in the beginning there was chaos.' There is a strong temptation, which must be strenuously resisted, to harvest ever more from this abundant storehouse of mockery and denigration.

There is no point in trying to mount a defence of politicians against these kind of charges. It is much better simply to enter a guilty plea, then offer some mitigating considerations to be taken into account. For the truth is that politicians are required to engage in forms of behaviour that those of more fastidious sensibility (that is, most people) would find troubling, distasteful or, at the very least, embarrassing. They frequently say things that they know are not true, or at best half-true, or that they would like to be true. They have an enviable capacity for persuading themselves, when they are even aware of it, that this is entirely justified for the higher purpose of advancing their own position, or that of their party. They routinely express confidence in leaders in whom they have no confidence and in policies about which they have grave doubts. In case it is thought I am talking about other people, let me make clear that I have done all these things. They also insist on the absolute rightness of their own position (am I alone in wanting to scream every time that David Cameron says he is doing something 'because it is the right thing to do'?) and the total error of their opponents. They forget that tediously predictable point-scoring ensures that people just stop listening. They say the same thing, in the same leaden language, over and over again until the last drop of freshness and meaning has long evaporated. They can be awesomely shameless, not least in self-promotion, and tend to think that appearances are what matters.

Even this does not exhaust the charge sheet. Politicians profess certainties where uncertainty is more appropriate. One of the joys of no longer being a professional politician is that I do not have to pretend to certainties I do not feel, or to knowledge I do not have, or to views I do not hold, and can happily sit on as many fences as I like. Expectations are deliberately inflated by uplifting promises ('Things can only get better') that are frequently converted into disappointment and disillusion when the collision with reality arrives, as it inevitably does. The real charge against Tony Blair on Iraq is not that he lied, but that he believed too much. There was a kind of messianic certainty when there should have been cautionary doubt. Similarly, the real charge against the Liberal Democrats on university tuition fees is not that they lied to the electorate, but that they distributed political promises with the reckless irresponsibility of people who did not think that they would ever be called upon to exercise responsibility.

Politicians do these things not because they are bad people (in my experience, many of them are rather good people), but because this is what politicians do, just as footballers have tantrums and dispute refereeing decisions and academics scatter references around their writing like confetti to show how clever they are. It goes with the territory. Some politicians struggle against these tendencies more than others, a few (like Vince Cable and Ken Clarke) with a measure of success, but they are still all in the same game. One of the many unusual attributes of Barack Obama was the way in which, even before he was elected, he was already seeking to tutor his exuberant supporters in the nature of politics (involving, as it was once said, campaigning in poetry and governing in prose) and preparing them for the inevitable disappointments ahead.

So it would be foolish to try to mount a defence of politicians on the basis that they are other than they are. Politicians engage in politics; this is how politics operates. We should certainly try to make it work better, more honestly and intelligently, but it would be naïve to expect it to change its essential nature. After all, it has been like this for a very long time, in one way or another. The language of spin may be recent, but it was Machiavelli who advised the wise prince to be 'skilful in simulating and dissembling'. Those attached to exact meanings or scrupulous discourse would be unwise to contemplate a political career. In his book on *Political Hypocrisy*, the political theorist David Runciman shows how hypocrisy has been seen as intrinsic to politics (and the discussion of politics) from Hobbes onwards. His conclusion is therefore not that politicians should be damned as hypocrites, which in some sense they necessarily are, but that we should concentrate our condemnatory attention on only the most egregious kinds of hypocrisy.

This may not be very inspiring, but it is better than the lazy and routine denigrations of politicians and all their works. A few years ago Jeremy Paxman (the outstanding modern practitioner of Mencken's doctrine that the proper relationship of journalist to politician is that of dog to lamp-post) wrote a mildly amusing book about politicians, called *Political Animal.* At the launch party for the book, at the Savoy Hotel, Paxman made a little speech in which he said that, notwithstanding his book, he actually believed that most politicians were a pretty decent lot who tried to do their best. But that's the point. There is no book in that, of course. It is easier (and more lucrative) just to poke fun, especially when there is so much to poke fun at.

People become professional politicians for all sorts of reasons, good and bad. They may be inspired by a desire for human betterment and a belief in public service; or they may be self-serving egomaniacs who want to feel important and boss other people around. There are many other categories in between. This has always been the case, and doubtless always will be. Each generation also tends to think that contemporary politicians are pygmies compared with the giants of yesteryear. This is a charge much heard about the current crop. Yet there was no golden age, when politicians were garlanded with bouquets of respect and approbation. The only sure way to win plaudits as a politician is to be a dead one.

What *has* changed is the amount of scrutiny and accountability that politicians are subjected to. They used to inhabit a secret garden; and now live in a goldfish bowl. On the whole this is a positive development, as power (and those who exercise it) should always be held to close account. But we should at least acknowledge the change that has happened. Today Churchill would no doubt be pilloried as a hopeless drunk. As for Gladstone, with his nocturnal perambulations to save the souls of prostitutes, just think what the tabloids would have made of that: 'Now Glad says he was only trying to save them!' David Cameron may want to cover up his Bullingdon Club past, and all the rich-boy hooliganism associated with it, but it is no longer possible.

So politicians are required to engage in forms of behaviour that most other people would regard as demeaning, silly or morally objectionable. They are also exposed to a kind of public accountability – involving everything from derision to eviction – that most groups of people manage to avoid. In addition to all that, they are paid much less than top earners in the public sector, or than other professional groups like lawyers and doctors, and vastly less than the higher reaches of the corporate world. You might ask why on Earth anybody would want to take on such a job. But that is not the question I want to explore here. My question is rather why we might *want* people to take on the job. For that is the only secure ground upon which any defence of politicians has to be mounted.

The answer to the question can be summed up in just six words: because somebody has to do it. That may not sound very heroic or noble, but it is nevertheless fundamental. Somebody has to take responsibility for brokering the disagreements, reconciling the competing interests and negotiating the policy dilemmas that are the stuff of democratic politics (and for being held to account for the way they do it). This is not required when we stay at the level of face-to-face democracy of the Ambridge parish meeting, concerned only with whether or not a nesting box is to be placed in the churchyard, but it is clearly required once democracy has to operate at the level of the wider community (and of the global order beyond that).

That is where we need politicians. The dream of a world without politicians is really a nightmare. As we watched the popular uprising against tyranny and corruption in Egypt – so moving and so magnificent – I was struck by the voice which said: 'Now we need our politicians.' The people had made the revolution; but they now needed politicians who would take on the responsibility of making democracy work. This idea that political life is a responsibility goes right back to the Athenian conception of what it means to be a citizen, of governing and being governed in turn. It means stepping up to the civic plate, not shrinking away into the irresponsibility of a merely private life. In his *The Fable of the Bees* in 1733 this was Mandeville's swipe at the high-minded Whiggery of Locke and Shaftsbury, which did not deign to get its civic hands dirty: 'Virtue consists in Action, and whoever is possest of this Social Love and Kind Affection to his Species, and by his Birth or Quality can claim any post in the Publick Management, ought not to sit still when he can be serviceable, but exert himself to the utmost for the good of his Fellow Subjects.'

It is much more comfortable not to take on this responsibility, and the accountability that goes with it. As a politician, I was supposed to have a coherent position on every issue under the sun and to be able to defend such positions on demand. As a non-politician, I can hold as many contradictory positions as I like and nobody (apart from my wife) can pin me down on any of them. I can also, without any guilt, take to my bed before *Newsnight*. Newspaper columnists and internet bloggers can sound off about any issue they like without ever having to be informed, accountable or consistent. The *Daily Mail* was not required to declare itself unfit for publication because of its dalliance with fascism in the 1930s. Everybody, apart from politicians, can happily hold a hundred different opinions before bedtime.

I throw in a gratuitously disobliging reference to what Orwell called the 'mechanical snigger' of the Bloomsbury intellectual. As an academic as well as a politician I recognise this all too well. It is that Olympian disdain for those who grapple with the affairs of the world rather than of the mind, coupled with an implicit assumption of superiority in being able to understand and deal with such matters compared with the pathetic endeavours of politicians, although the precaution is invariably taken of never putting this to the test (with Keynes as a notable Bloomsbury exception). Too many social scientists in particular seem prone to write in a superior tone, in impenetrable self-referential language, about matters on which they rarely have anything very practical or useful to say.

Governing complex societies is tough stuff. Democratic

politics is a noisy bundle of competing demands and interests. Policy choices often involve unwelcome trade-offs and sometimes the adoption of least-worst options (in John Major's words, 'Sometimes in politics the choice is between bad and awful'). But somebody has to do it; and that is the responsibility taken on by politicians. It is also why the transition from opposition politician to governing one is so sharp (there are, of course, different kinds of politician doing different kinds of job). In opposition it is possible to pretend that none of this is true, a pretence that the electorate is encouraged to believe, but the reality of office soon provides a brutal political education for all concerned. Hence the rapid talk of betrayals and u-turns (or as it was nicely said in relation to the recent climbdown on selling the forests, a yew-turn). Unpopularity duly ensues; and the whole cycle soon starts up again. Politicians change, but the problems remain the same. Even the best government is, at bottom, only a government.

The lesson from all this is not that it is not worth bothering with politics, or that there are not big issues and choices at stake, or that politicians are 'all the same' (the charge that every politician has to get used to having thrown at them on the doorsteps of the land). Even if it does not always seem like it, politics is the collective means for deciding what sort of society (and world) we want to live in; and politicians frame our political choices.

It is simply to acknowledge that democratic politics is necessarily difficult; and that those who engage in it as politicians take responsibility for negotiating its difficulty. Politics is not like shopping, because you often do not get what you want. It can offer inspiration, but also often delivers disappointment. The point is to know all this, yet still to engage in it. That is the challenge for all of us; but it is a particular challenge for politicians.

As individuals and groups, we naturally press our own demands and interests. Spend money on us, we say; protect us from cuts; adopt our policies. This is the routine fare of democratic politics, and rightly so. As a Member of Parliament, every day brought a new stack of representations from the whole galaxy of groups and organisations pressing their own case and cause, with none of them having the responsibility of taking account of the implications for others. So too with the democratic tradition of protest and demonstration, now again in robust health in relation to a range of issues. This is a fundamental right (and one which I have certainly exercised); but it is still easier to shout 'No!' than to take responsibility for the consequences of the naysaying. That is what we expect politicians to do, even though we might not say so (or thank them for it).

When the last Labour government set up a system of online petitions, the most massive petition by far was in opposition to a proposal for road pricing. This showed that motorists did not want to pay to drive, but it did not solve the problem of congestion. Consider some other examples. There is understandable anger about the proposed level of university tuition fees, but behind this there is the issue of how the move from an elite to mass higher education system is to be paid for, what the balance is between the public good of higher education and the private benefit for the participants and how this balance might be reflected in how the system is financed. Where the public interest lies will be disputed, but somebody has to try to define (and defend) it. Somebody has to do the same in relation to the proper balance between liberty and security in the face of the threat from terrorism. Or how we pay for pensions, and provide care for the elderly, when demographic change forces difficult policy choices. Or how we have an energy policy that keeps the lights on without warming the planet. Or how the deficit is to be reduced. The examples can be multiplied endlessly but the central point remains the same: somebody has to do it (and to be held to democratic account for taking this responsibility).

This point is so obvious and elementary that you might think it would be more widely and readily acknowledged. Politicians are often ludicrous, frequently devious, and sometimes make catastrophic mistakes; but they nevertheless do something that somebody has to do. In that sense they make democratic politics work, as that voice from Egypt recognised. What we really need to worry about is the growing army of anti-politicians, which wears a number of different uniforms but is unified in its contempt for politicians and all their works. These forces are on the march. Some are disguised as friends of democracy. They are to be found on both left and right. If we care about democratic politics, they need to be resisted.

Let me identify some of them. Making fun of politicians is always enjoyable, and exposing their hypocrisies indispensable (which is why I need my daily dose of Simon Hoggart); but if we *only* have a culture of mockery then that brings its own attendant dangers. There was a survey recently of the Google links to 'politicians' by people in different countries. In Germany, for example, people also wanted to know about the employment history of politicians; but in Britain what the survey showed was that 'we are more interested in taking the mickey out of our elected representatives and will be searching for jokes about them' (*The Times*, 25 February 2011). Perhaps this just confirms that we have a better sense of humour than the Germans. Or it may suggest that we have a different problem of our own. I remember an edition of the *News Quiz* in the week of Obama's election, when one panel member – Paul Merton, I think – cut in to say (to loud studio applause): 'I know we are supposed just to mock politicians, but I don't feel like doing that now.' Perhaps this cultural lop-sidedness explains why, amid all the satire and lampoonery, there has not been a British *West Wing* which tries to get politics (and politicians) in the round.

This only matters if it feeds a wider culture of contempt and denigration. This is the charge made against much of the news media. It has been put most sharply by the journalist John Lloyd in his book *What the Media are Doing to Our Politics*, in which he argues that many of the leading voices in both the broadcast and the print media 'see politicians as a debased class'. Tabloid rant and cultural sneer combine to produce a distorted view of politics and politicians, in which it is only the stupidity or bad faith of politicians that prevents all problems being easily solved. The effect is to corrode trust, nourish cynicism and promote either disengagement or a dangerous kind of anti-politics that feeds the peddlers of various kinds of extremism.

There is enough force in this argument to take it seriously. It is also an abdication of the civic role of the media, which is to provide citizens with the information and understanding needed to make democratic choices. That certainly means holding politicians to continuous and robust account; but that is not the same as a culture of systematic denigration. Nor, sadly, has the political blogosphere provided the civic antidote to the failings of the mainstream media that some anticipated. Too often it is the place where the normal courtesies of argument are dispensed with, the person rather than the ball is played (usually very unpleasantly) and vitriol is the default mode of expression. This is not quite the expanded civic conversation that was promised.

Central to tabloid rant is a lazy and dishonest populism that sets people against politicians. Yet a similar populism sometimes infects the arguments of political reformers too (some detected it in the *Power Report* of a few years ago, for example), when the suggestion seems to be that only the political class stands in the way of the vibrant expression of popular sovereignty. It is populism, too, that fuels demands for the direct democracy of referenda in place of the muddy compromises of representative politics, conveniently forgetting that a decision rarely sits in isolation but usually has consequences for everything else. A vote against a tax, for example, does not answer the question about how desired services are to be paid for. Nor can a referendum (even one on a European treaty) distinguish between elements of a proposition that are liked and those that are disliked. This is not an argument against all referenda, but it is an argument for making them as narrowly defined and self-contained as possible. Above all, though, it is an argument against believing that direct democracy somehow dispenses with the need for politicians.

There are two further categories of people I want to defend politicians against, one from the right and the other from the left. The first are those who want to get politicians out of the way so that markets can prevail. This is usually described as replacing the heavy hand of the State with the freedom that markets bring. The trouble with this line of argument is not with markets themselves, which can certainly offer choice, competition, innovation and dynamism, but with thinking that they can substitute for politics and politicians in areas in which it has been decided that market values and choices should not prevail. It is that prior decision which is really at issue. It is a basic constituent of public accountability that elected people will be expected to take responsibility for services that it has been democratically decided to run on a non-market basis. Just as getting the State out of the way can often mean a loss of practical freedom for people rather than its enlargement, so getting politicians out of the way can bring with it the loss of a public accountability that was previously taken for granted.

There is an even larger point here too. If politicians are powerless in the face of forces over which they seem unable (or unwilling) to exercise any effective control – whether media moguls or bankers – then the credibility of democracy itself is threatened. Why should people bother with politics or politicians if democracy cannot deliver what it promises? This has been highlighted in the starkest possible way by the financial crisis, with bankers effectively telling the politicians that – despite the catastrophe and misery that they have themselves brought about – they are untouchable. In the 1930s it used to be said that either democracy will control finance or finance will control democracy; and that remains the case today. The credibility of democracy depends upon the ability of politicians to tame irresponsible private power.

The second category of person I want to defend politicians from are those whose doctrine of radical transparency carries with it a contempt for politicians of all kinds and in every place. If this doctrine needs a name, it might be called Assangeism. Let me not be misunderstood. I am very much against secrecy and in favour of transparency (in fact, as a politician I had a hand both in getting strong freedom of information legislation and in protecting whistleblowers), but recognise that there is always a balance to be struck in particular cases between a public interest in disclosure and a public interest in confidentiality. That is why independent mechanisms have been established to enable judgements to be made about where the balance of public interest lies, often to the discomfort of politicians.

It seems to me pretty obvious that there is value in having a protected space in which frank political discussion can take place in confidence. Without such a space it is unlikely that the peace process in Northern Ireland would have been possible, just to take one obvious example. The proponents of radical transparency have no time for such nice considerations, even if people get hurt along the way. On their view politicians are always engaged in a conspiracy to conceal their dirty tricks and the only public interest is in exposing them. Transparency is their ideology: and politicians are their enemy. As we have seen, there is a ready market for this sort of approach. This has nothing to do with the merits of particular disclosures. It may be that this is how the world is now, that technology has ripped apart the old order for good or ill; but this does not mean that the anti-politician ideology that accompanies it should be embraced too.

My final defence of politicians is against themselves. They do make it much harder to defend them than it really ought to be, for the sort of reasons I discussed earlier.

After all, it is through politics and politicians that some of the things we value most have been achieved: from free health care to national parks, and from public service broadcasting to clean air. This list could be much extended; but the point is that these things did not happen by chance but because democratic politics produced politicians with the courage and imagination prepared to make them happen (often at very difficult times). It is easier to see all this in retrospect of course, but it is still the best reminder of what politicians are for. Unless or until we are content to be ruled by a tyranny, either of the State or market kind, we shall continue to need the services of democratic politicians.

Notice that I have not sought to defend politicians, as I might well have done, by listing all the various activities they engage in. This would include pursuing issues on behalf of individual constituents and the areas they represent, a permanent and core activity. It would also include all the question-asking and inquiry-holding activity that, if done conscientiously and energetically, should put politicians and Parliament at the apex of accountability. These are important functions, but I have deliberately sought to place the defence of politicians on a broader and more general foundation.

The trouble with mounting any kind of defence of politicians, apart from the fact that it is so deeply unfashionable and counter-intuitive, is the danger that it brings of being misunderstood. I therefore want, briefly and finally, to make it clear what I am not saying. There are two respects in particular where this is necessary.

In the first place, to defend politicians is not to defend all or actual politicians, or how they behave; nor to suggest that the political structures within which they operate are satisfactory or incapable of improvement. None of this follows from my defence of politicians as people engaged in a necessary democratic activity. Some politicians are contemptible, many are irritating and some are hopeless; but so are other people. Some aspects of the political system certainly need reform; but reform of some kind is always required. Defending politicians on the grounds that I have done here in no way prevents the most searching and stringent criticism of what politicians do, how they behave, and the structures within which they operate.

This point can be made more positively. It is because politicians are so necessary that there ought to be much more attention paid to who they are, what they are like and where they come from. The question of what kind of politicians we want, and how we can get them, should be far more central than it currently is. So too should the need for the best people (in every sense), not just those who think they are the best people, to feel that entering public life and taking on its responsibilities is, at least for a period of life, something that it is important and valuable to do. We all have an interest in encouraging and promoting this. My argument is that this is unlikely to be fostered by a culture of contempt and denigration, which is not the same as a culture of scrutiny and accountability.

There is a second respect in which the defence of politicians should not be misunderstood. To defend politicians is not to suggest that politics is, or should be, the preserve of professional politicians. Nothing could be further from the truth. Politicians are necessary, but they are not a sufficient condition for a well-functioning polity. This requires a vibrant culture of citizenship, which provides the connecting rod to the politicians and sets the framework within which they operate. The best antidote to the development of a separate political class is a body of engaged, informed and critical citizens, nourishing a dense network of organisations and institutions. A culture of anti-politics does not help with this; while 'big society' rhetoric has little or nothing to say about political citizenship.

I end where I started, in Ambridge. Somebody has to decide whether there should be a nesting box in the churchyard. That is what politics does. Somebody also has to decide whether the plans for a new market will be approved (conman Matt Crawford claims to have fixed the planning committee). That is what politicians do. Mock them and watch them, certainly. Take comfort that it is them and not you that have to do it. But at least recognise that somebody has to do it. And that they are called politicians.

Notes

1 D. Marquand, *The Progressive Dilemma* (1992).

2 D. Sassoon, 'European Social Democracy and New Labour: Unity in Diversity?', in A. Gamble and T. Wright (eds), *The New Social Democracy* (1999).

3 A. Blair, 'Let Us Face the Future – the 1945 anniversary lecture', Fabian pamphlet 571 (lecture given by Tony Blair to mark the fiftieth anniversary of the election of the 1945 Labour government, 5 July 1995, London).

4 L. T. Hobhouse, *Liberalism* (1911).

5 L. T. Hobhouse, *op. cit.*, pp. 172–3.

6 G. D. H. Cole, *Great Britain in the Post-War World* (1942).

7 G. D. H. Cole, *Workers' Control: A Dialogue* (1923).

8 A. B. Ulam, *Philosophical Foundations of English Socialism* (1951), p.95; Margaret Cole, 'Guild Socialism and the Labour Research Department', in A. Briggs and J. Saville (eds), *Essays in Labour History*, II (1971), p. 261.

9 *The Syndicalist*, February 1914, quoted in B. Russell, *Roads to Freedom*, (1918) p. 91.

10 S. G. Hobson, *Pilgrim to the Left* (1938), p. 190. S. G. Hobson and A. R. Orage, in the *New Age*, were the real parents of the modern Guild idea, which Cole turned into a movement, elaborating the idea in the process.

11 E. Barker, *Political Thought in England, 1848–1914* (1915), p. 249; H. J. Laski, *The Problem of Sovereignty* (1917), p. 117.

12 H. Belloc, *The Servile State* (1912), p. 101.

13 R. MacDonald, *Syndicalism* (1912), p. 5.

14 A letter to the *Leeds Weekly Citizen* (6 August 1915) asserted that 'the free-born Briton has, for the past few years, been undergoing a Prussianisation that bids fair to leave its prototype in the rear', and, at the 1917 Annual Conference of the National Guilds League, Cole confessed to his 'intense hostility to the State ... I feel at the moment that the State is more dangerous than the employer' (Cole Collection, Nuffield College, Oxford).

15 G. D. H. Cole, *The World of Labour* (1913), p. 10.

16 G. C. Field, *Guild Socialism: A Critical Examination* (1920), p. 46.

17 Cole frequently stressed the particularity of the English and the need to 'make our own revolutionary conceptions' (*The World of Labour*, p. 202).

18 G. D. H. Cole, *The World of Labour* (1913) pp. 416, 419.

19 S. G. Hobson, *National Guilds* (1914), pp. 53, 58.

20 G. D. H. Cole, *Self Government in Industry* (1917), p. 35.

21 S. G. Hobson, *op. cit.*, p. 217.

22 Report of the 1917 Annual Conference, National Guilds League (Cole Collection, Nuffield College, Oxford).

23 G. D. H. Cole, 'The New Statesmanship', *The University Socialist* (1913), p. 108–10.

24 G. D. H. Cole, *Guild Socialism Restated*, 1920, p. 12.

25 G. D. H. Cole, *Social Theory* (1920), p. 108.

26 G. D. H. Cole, *Guild Socialism Restated* (1920), p. 50; *Labour in the Commonwealth* (1918), p. 86.

27 S. G. Hobson, *National Guilds and the State* (1920), pp. 126, 133.

28 There is a strikingly modern note in Cole's demand for democracy in the classroom: 'Until a large measure of student self-government is developed, democracy in the school will not be realised and the power of education as a liberating influence will not have been properly developed', *Guild Socialism Restated* (1920), p. 112.

29 G. D. H. Cole, *Labour in the Commonwealth* (1918), p. 143.

30 S. G. Hobson, *National Guilds* (1914), p. 107.

31 G. D. H. Cole, *Guild Socialism Restated* (1920), pp.187, 191.

32 M. I. Cole (ed), *Beatrice Webb's Diaries, 1912–1924*, p. 36.

33 'The interest of the ordinary man would lapse altogether, and the final result would be the not very exciting spectacle of a handful of busybodies manning all the "functional" committees.' M. Cole, *loc. cit.*, p. 274.

34 G. D. H. Cole, 'Recent Developments in the British Labour Movement', *The American Economic Review*, 1918, vol. 8, no. 3, pp. 485–504.

35 G. D. H. Cole, *The World of Labour* (1913) p. 2.

36 G. D. H. Cole, 'The Meaning of Guild Socialism', *Theosophist*, 1921.

37 P. Hennessy, 'The Annual History of Parliament Lecture: An End to the Poverty of Aspirations? Parliament Since 1979', *Parliamentary History* (2005), vol. 24, pt.2, pp. 216–25.

38 Quoted in Hennessy, *ibid.*

39 R. Rhodes James (ed), *Chips: The Diaries of Sir Henry Channon* (1967), entry for 10 December 1935, p. 61.

40 D. Judge, *The Parliamentary State* (1993), p. 207.

41 S. Beer, 'The British Legislature and the Problem of Mobilizing Consent', in E. Frank (ed), *Lawmakers in a Changing World* (1966), pp. 30–48.

42 House of Commons Debates, 8 February 1960, vol. 617, col. 70.

43 A. Kennon, *The Commons: Reform or Modernisation* (The Constitution Unit, 2000).

44 M. Russell and A. Paun, *The House Rules? International Lessons for Enhancing the Autonomy of the House of Commons* (The Constitution Unit, 2007)

45 The tradition is discussed in A. Wright, 'The Constitution', in L. Tivey and A. Wright (eds), *Party Ideology in Britain* (1989), pp. 184–205.

46 D. Hurd, 'The Present Usefulness of the House of Commons', *Journal of Legislative Studies,* 1997, vol. 3, no. 3, pp. 1–9.

47 A. Clark, *Diaries* (1993), entry for 5 July 1983, p. 23.

48 House of Commons Debates, 25 June 1979, vol. 969, col. 36.

49 Hansard Society, *The Challenge for Parliament: Making Government Accountable* (2001), p. 19.

50 *Strengthening Parliament*, Report of the Commission to Strengthen Parliament, Conservative Party (July 2000), p. 7.

51 Liaison Committee, *Shifting the Balance: Select Committees and the Executive*, HC 300, 1999–2000.

52 P. Cowley, *The Rebels: How Blair mislaid his majority* (2005).

53 These figures are taken from M. Rush and P. Giddings, Memorandum to Select Committee on Modernisation of the House of Commons, *Revitalising the Chamber: The Role of the Back Bench Member*, HC 337, 2006/07.

54 In the wake of the expenses scandal, in July 2009 a new select committee on the Reform of the Commons was established.

55 'Local party members were suitably grateful when Jennie opened a Christmas fayre, or occasionally graced a General Management Committee': P. Hollis, *Jennie Lee* (1997), p. 138. In 1949 Jennie Lee attended the party AGM and the local Labour newspaper observed that 'the fact that she had travelled especially from London in order to be present, demonstrates her keen enthusiasm' (quoted in Hollis).

56 P. Cowley, Memorandum to Select Committee on Modernisation of the House of Commons, *Revitalising the Chamber: The Role of the Back Bench Member*, HC 337, 2006/07.

57 B. Crick, *The Reform of Parliament* (1970 edn), p. 259.

58 B. Crick, 'Beyond Parliamentary Reform', *The Political Quarterly* (1989) vol. 60, no. 4, pp. 396–9.

59 The diary of Chris Mullin MP, *A View from the Foothills* (2009) has this as one of its themes.

60 Liaison Committee, *op. cit.*

61 The story is told in A. Kelso, *Parliamentary Reform at Westminster* (2009).

62 This was the verdict in A. Wright, 'Prospects for Parliamentary Reform at Westminster', *Parliamentary Affairs* (2004), vol. 57, no. 4, pp. 867–76.

63 On this, see J. Levy, *Strengthening Parliament's Powers of Scrutiny?: An Assessment of the Introduction of Public Bill Committees* (The Constitution Unit, 2009).

64 An insider account of this episode, and period, is G. Power, 'The Politics of Parliamentary Reform: Lessons from the House of Commons 2001–2005', *Parliamentary Affairs* (2007), vol. 60, no. 3, pp. 492–509.

65 The exchanges were published in Public Administration Select Committee, *The Ministerial Code: Improving the Rule Book*, HC 235, 2000–01, Appendix 4.

66 Public Administration Select Committee, *The Second Chamber: Continuing the Reform*, HC 494, 2001/02, para. 36.

67 *The Challenge for Parliament, op. cit.*, p. vii.

68 One was the Labour MP Graham Allen in his *The Last Prime Minister: Being Honest About the UK Presidency* (2003).

69 A. Turnbull, 'Why we need separation of powers', *Financial Times*, 3 June 2009, p. 13.

70 J. Major and D. Hurd, 'Bring outside talent to the dispatch box', *The Times*, 13 June 2009, p. 22.

71 A recent example of this argument is the concluding chapter of V. Bogdanor, *The New British Constitution* (2009).

72 See, for example, A. Bevins, 'The question is: What are MPs for?', *The Independent*, 1 March 1989. When sleaze made its appearance in the 1990s, an article in the *Financial Times* declared: 'Amid all the rancour, the real question may have yet to be addressed… Why has no one ever thought of defining what an MP should do?', 6 November 1995.

73 Humphrey Malins MP, House of Commons, 3 November 2009.

74 M. Martin, 'Busy-bee MPs have lost their real purpose, so let's cull some', *Sunday Times*, 8 November 2009.

75 *MPs' Expenses: A Consultation*, Independent Parliamentary Standards Authority, January 2010, p. 15.

76 C. Mullin, 'Welcome. Are you a lickspittle or a loner?', *The Times*, 19 January 2010. The terms used in the Mullin article first sparked the idea for the typology used here.

77 Quoted in M. Rush, *The Role of the Member of Parliament since 1868* (2001), pp. 114–15.

78 Select Committee on Modernisation of the House of Commons, *Revitalising the Chamber: The Role of the Back Bench Member*, HC 337, 2007, p. 9.

79 An example is the job evaluation model applied to MPs by Pricewaterhouse Coopers for the Review Body on Senior Salaries: *Review of Parliamentary Pay, Pensions and Allowances 2007*, January 2008, Cm 7270-I.

80 Edward Leigh MP, House of Commons, 26 January 2010.

81 W. E. Gladstone, 'The Declining Efficiency of Parliament', The *Quarterly Review*, vol. XCIX, June and September 1856, pp. 521–70.

82 P. Hollis, *op. cit.*, pp.138, 373.

83 Speech on 26 March 1955. This extract was published in *Parliamentary Affairs*, vol. 8, 1954/55, p. 302.

84 House of Commons, 20 February 1979.

85 Quoted in M. Rush, *op. cit.*, p. 188.

86 Memorandum to Select Committee on Modernisation of the House of Commons, *Revitalising the Chamber: The Role of the Back Bench Member*, HC 337, 2007.

87 Select Committee on Reform of the House of Commons, *Rebuilding the House*, HC 1117, 2009.

88 Public Administration Select Committee, *Goats and Tsars: Ministerial and other appointments from outside Parliament*, HC 330, 2010, p. 11.

89 Quoted in A. King, 'The Rise of the Career Politician in Britain – and its Consequences', *British Journal of Political Science* (1981), vol. 11, no. 3, pp. 249–85. See also P. Riddell, *Honest Opportunism: The rise of the career politician* (1993).

90 A. King, *op. cit.*, p. 285.

91 'What a job's worth', *Public Finance*, 6–12 November 2009, p. 5. Similarly, Graham Brady MP suggested that the electorate might have a 'deeper unease' after the expenses scandal: 'Could it be that they are starting to wonder what their MPs are actually for?', *The House Magazine*, 9 November 2009, p. 38.

92 S. Pederson, *Eleanor Rathbone and the Politics of Conscience* (2004), pp. 377–8.

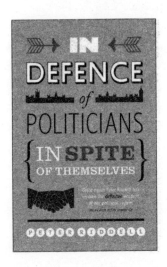

Also available from Biteback

HOW TO BE AN MP

Paul Flynn

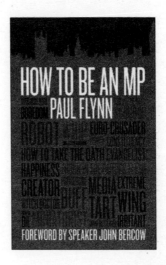

Not for everyone the title of Prime Minister, Foreign
Secretary or other such hallowed callings; the vast
majority of the House of Commons is made up of
backbenchers – the power behind the constitutionally
elected throne. Here is a guide for anyone and everyone
fascinated by the quirks and foibles of Westminster
Palace, covering all species of backbencher and
providing every hardworking MP and political
enthusiast with the know-how to survive life
in Parliament.

272pp paperback, £12.99

**Available from all good bookshops or order from
www.bitebackpublishing.com**